Yasmin Alibhai-Bro▓▓▓▓▓▓d came to Britain in 1972 as a re▓▓▓▓▓▓n English at Oxford and then tau▓▓▓ for a number of years before turning to journalism. She was the race editor for *New Statesman and Society* and then worked for BBC's Network East. She now works as a freelance journalist and has written for the *Guardian*, *Observer*, and *Independent*. She also broadcasts on radio and television, mainly on race issues. She and her thirteen-year-old son have recently embarked on a new venture: the assimilation of an Englishman into their lives. She lives in London.

Anne Montague is a freelance journalist with extensive experience of writing on social and medical issues. Born in Manchester, she went to university in Newcastle. She has written for the *Guardian*, the *Independent*, and for a number of women's magazines. She also works freelance for Save the Children Fund's Public Affairs Department. She has travelled all over West Africa and spent ▓▓▓▓▓▓ there on her last visit. She is ▓▓▓▓▓▓ lives in London.

THE COLOUR OF LOVE

Mixed Race Relationships

Yasmin Alibhai-Brown
and Anne Montague

ACKNOWLEDGEMENTS

We would particularly like to thank all those people in this book
who gave us so much time and so much insight into their lives.
Thanks to Melanie Silgardo whose patience, firmness and
encouragement spurred us on. Thanks to John and Colin for their
boundless love and support which helped to keep us afloat. And
thanks finally to Ari Alibhai (just entering adolescence) whose
sharp questions forced us to think more deeply about future
generations of Black, Asian and white Britons who will have to
grapple with many of these issues. They will, hopefully, find new
ways of confronting the historical prejudices which still crouch and
lurk around the area of mixed relationships.

Published by VIRAGO PRESS Limited 1992
20–23 Mandela Street, Camden Town, London NW1 0HQ

© Yasmin Alibhai-Brown and Anne Montague 1992

The rights of Yasmin Alibhai-Brown and Anne Montague to be
identified as authors of this work have been asserted by them in
accordance with the Copyright, Designs and Patents Act 1988

*A CIP catalogue record for this title
is available from the British Library*

Printed in Great Britain by
Cox & Wyman Ltd, Reading, Berkshire

> *I have a real dream for the world that everyone accepts everyone for the person they are inside and what they can give. People are always looking for differences – too fat, too thin, too dark – always looking for some reason why they shouldn't accept somebody instead of trying to find the reasons why they should and what they can learn from them.*

– GILL DANESH

CONTENTS

Introduction

'I consider you are not fit to bring up your daughter with your ideas of mating her to a Negro. I sincerely hope that God will cut short your life and that you will *die soon* so that dear little white girl may be saved from the hideous fate you plan for her. A black blubber lipped Negro on top of her.'

'Interbreeding is evil and nobody could be proud of half-caste children . . . The idea of everyone being a wretched khaki colour with thick lips and flat noses in the future is abhorrent to all right-thinking Englishmen.'

– *Letters received by the Reverend Clifford Hill after a broadcast in 1961 during which he said that he would not object to his daughter marrying a Black man*[1]

'He looked at my fourteen-month-old child in his pushchair and said, "Another fucking nigger, another fucking coon".'

'I know how hard it's been and I sometimes wish I had done things differently, but my children? I would never change them, not for anything.'

– *Two white mothers of mixed race children on 'Woman's Hour', 1986*

Three twelve-year-olds watching 'Neighbours' in the room where we were working were curious about what the word miscegenation meant. After careful explanations, which made no sense to them, one of them, an Anglo-Asian mix himself, said in a peeved voice, 'It sounds like something wrong – like misbehave, and mistake, misunderstand . . .'

1

He had put his finger on it. Even the word we use to describe relationships across racial barriers is infused with opprobrium and with the implication that something not quite the norm, something deviant, is being described.

Through the years, most academics and others who pontificate on human behaviour have been unable to break away from this pathological matrix. Interracial relationships, it seems, are a problem (the racist view), have unspeakable problems (the liberal view) or, more optimistically, provide a pretty coffee-coloured solution for all the world's problems. Rich and prolific human experience is reduced to snapshots by these researchers, creeping along with their Polaroid cameras, catching people they define as living in the hinterlands of ordinary life. Popular culture has served to reinforce these views. Anne Wilson, in her recent excellent study of mixed race children, argues that sociological work in this area has been influenced by and has influenced the 'problem' perspective put forth by the media, and that in the United States academics have gone even further, seeing these children as 'marginal':

Apart from the occasional attempt to treat the subject sensitively and seriously, plays, magazine articles, novels and television programmes all tend to return to the same theme: that interracial marriages are fraught with problems and that mixed race children are crazy mixed-up kids who are rejected both by black AND white communities.[2]

We have tried to resist such coarse postulations by asking people with immediate personal experience to talk about the subject – people who, through their relationships with partners, parents and children, have insights that no neat journalistic analysis or ponderous research tome can hope to capture. It has been an illuminating exercise. The conversations were unstructured in a formal sense and self-determined by our interviewees. Their views were taken on board, they had access to us and we did not impose any pre-packaged notions on the people we spoke to. Sadly, time and space constraints meant that we were not able to tackle homosexual relationships – the particular complexities of these relationships merit a book of their own.

But even a venture like this, an attempt to break out of sociological bondage, had to confront certain challenges. Some people saw the book itself as an affront. They argued that a relationship is just that and that such explorations are a meaningless and voyeuristic exercise. 'Would you do a book on blond people having relationships with red-haired people? So why black- and white-skinned people?' we were asked. Of course it could be argued that all journalism and non-fiction is voyeuristic, but we feel that the sheer diversity of experiences we have included, and our collaborative approach, have made it impossible for us to manipulate or make a spectacle of people.

Another more serious objection was that the book itself was based on racist premises. If we accept that there is no such thing as hierarchical racial division, the very notion of mixed race becomes a racist concept and by doing what we were doing, we were declaring ourselves part of the construct. It is an important point but one which rests, we fear, on wishful thinking.

Of course, scientifically speaking, biological differences in inherited characteristics do not denote the superiority or inferiority of any group of human beings. These are false edifices that have been erected, primarily by the white world, to prop up the brutal exploitation of non-whites around the world over several centuries. Our book is in no way an assertion of a belief in the racial ranking of human beings in that sense. But racial stratification has a powerful *social* and *political* existence. Demarcation between groups on the basis of colour, culture and religious hierarchies persists with remarkable tenacity around the world. Wishing passionately that these pernicious divisions did not exist did not seem to us a good reason to assume that they don't. These partitions and the attitudes they engender have permeated the lives of many of the individuals we talked to, although for others they have had less direct effect on their daily existence.

3

But not one interviewee denied that these powerful social forces do prevail around their lives and those of their children.

A book like this is of value for two opposite reasons. The breadth of experience revealed across a wide spectrum of class, gender, age and history proves the silliness of any generalisation in the field of human relationships. On the other hand, this is not simply a collection of disparate ramblings. We *were* interested in testing certain assumptions and exploring connections. For example, is it really possible to overcome potent historical prejudices? Do age-old fears, taboos and fantasies still weave themselves around the private lives of those in interracial relationships?

What became clear as the book developed was the power with which the external world bears down on these individuals. In a society where our reluctance to become 'involved' leaves tortured children at risk in their own homes and raped women lying in gutters, perfect strangers think they have the right to abuse you, or your partner or your child, because you have different skin colours.

In any divided and racially unequal society, people who cross the barriers will always, in some way, reflect the state of that society. They are always located within that bleak racist landscape, whether they succeed in their relationship or not. Susan Benson, who studied multiracial families in Brixton in the early 1980s, puts it aptly: 'to study the everyday lives of interracial families, then, is to study the nature of British race relations as it impinges on the lives of individuals.'[3]

Add to this the many other factors that come into play – male/female roles, sexual myths, psychological factors, religious beliefs, the dynamics of a cultural identity, fame, economic success – and the mixture becomes even richer. But in the end one thing is clear: however society has chosen to label these relationships, whatever impediments it has put in their way – including laws like those in South Africa and the Southern States of America – people from different racial groups across history have continued to have sexual relationships – for better or for worse.

History

Because *The Colour of Love* is concerned with the lives of people in this country, we will not be looking at the global picture. But in any account of mixed race relationships it is important to understand how British attitudes towards miscegenation are inextricably bound up with the history of slavery and colonialism. As Dr Fernando Henriques said in his study of interracial relationships:

Contemporary manifestations of racial mixing have been very largely determined by the historical matrix of colonization. The latter, particularly when associated with slavery, gave opportunity to the colonizer to abuse sexually the indigenous inhabitants of the colony. It is very rarely that this opportunity was not realized.[4]

Before colonisation and slavery there was no evidence of any deep feelings of distaste and prejudice towards certain physical characteristics. Academics who have studied the history of miscegenation – in the West, in the ancient world and during early Christianity – have found that although there was an awareness of colour and physical difference, dark skin was seen as sensuous and attractive. Ovid described his love for a Black slave girl in *Amores* and Herodotus thought that the Ethiopians were 'the tallest and handsomest men in the world'. It is well known that Moses loved Tharbis, also an Ethiopian, and liaisons between the Egyptians and the Romans all reveal an absence of the barriers which came later. Early-sixteenth-century explorers like the Portuguese in Upper Guinea and Goa married native women or had them as long-term concubines, fathered mulatto children and largely assimilated into the way of life.

The change came as the colonial ambitions of the Europeans grew and the demonology of Black inferiority began to – or had to – take hold. Sexual contact between whites on the one hand, and Africans and Asians on the other, were thereafter confined to casual encounters and concubinage. After all, marriage between the races was a mark of equality, and certainly not something to be made available to subject races who had to occupy a servile status. The justification for this abhorrent behaviour depended on constantly reinforcing an ideology of white superiority and Black inferiority. Miscegenation, particularly if it produced children, inevitably challenged that ideology.

Slaves appeared in this country, forming the beginnings of a Black British community. Then, as now, numbers were a racist nightmare and prompted a call from Elizabeth I for the deportation of Blacks from the country. Sexual relationships between Black and white were also seen as a problem and a recurring theme in Shakespeare's plays – not only with the creation of Caliban in *The Tempest*, and in *Othello*, where Iago invoked bestial imagery to describe it, but also in *Titus Andronicus*, where the mixed race child of the Queen, described by the nurse as 'A joyless, dismal, black and sorrowful issue', is defended by the Black father, who says:

> Coal-black is better than another hue,
> In that it scorns to bear another hue . . .[5]

As Black seamen and ever more servants and slaves arrived, there were more frequent liaisons with white women – mainly poor or 'fallen' women, although it was not unknown for upper-class women to unleash their sexual appetites on their Black servants. Children were born from these liaisons, as one George Best recorded in 1578:

I myselfe have seene an Ethiopian as blacke as a cole broughte into Englande, who taking a fair Englishe woman to wife, begatte a sonne in all respectes as blacke as the father was . . .[6]

Throughout the seventeenth and eighteenth centuries the presence of these Black men was recorded in contemporary paintings and other material – for example in Hogarth's etchings 'Times of the Day – Noon' and 'Love – a Discovery: That which was white, is now its contrary'. All this was in stark contrast to what was happening in the colonies. There it was the white men who indulged their sexual passions with Black female slaves, cruelly asserting their power over the women and psychologically emasculating the Black male slaves. Rape and violence against both men and women by their white slavemasters was commonplace and compounded by the fury of many white wives who felt spurned by their husbands and vented their fury on the female slaves. Terrible tales of torture were revealed to the Select Committee of the House of Commons when the abolitionists were arguing their case.

The Black radical activist W.E.B. Du Bois wrote in 1900 that whilst he could forgive white people for slavery and many other injustices, he could not forgive white people:

neither in this world nor the world to come: its wanton and continued and persistent insulting of the black womanhood which it sought and seeks to prostitute to its lust . . .[7]

Attitudes towards the growing numbers of children of these Black–white liaisons were complex. In the early days of slavery, these children enjoyed certain privileges. Having some white blood and a lighter skin colour gave them status. Some white masters provided for them and a few rose to become plantation managers but no higher, except in very exceptional cases where the fathers felt a genuine bond with the child and its mother and tried to give them legitimate rights. Robert Browning's grandmother, for example, was a mulatto who inherited a plantation. But ironically, as slavery was coming to an end and miscegenation seemed more likely, more vociferous views took hold. In certain states, one drop of Black blood made you Black – a law that, in 1781, an amorous British soldier who fell in love with a free Black woman was able to use by swallowing a drop of her blood.

One of the results of this sexual exploitation was the creation of the myth of Black sexual prowess and the corresponding myth of the (virginal and angelic) white woman. This led, inevitably, to the paranoia of corruption by the untrammelled sexuality of Black men – a paranoia which persisted in the Southern States well into the 1960s, when Black men were publicly castrated for the 'crime' of looking at a white woman. Today the knives may have been put away, but in many of these places the venom felt by white men remains. This was and is 'chivalry' unasked for by either party, says Beth Day in her very angry book, *Sexual Life Between Blacks and Whites*:

One of the sad features . . . is that the white women never did ask to be protected from those black men. It was their fathers', husbands' and brothers' idea . . . white women were as much victims of the system as black men. They were allowed no sexual freedom of choice.[8]

In 1772 the white Jamaican writer and slave-owner Edward Long came to Britain overflowing with these attitudes, and exploded with disgust at what he saw:

a venomous and dangerous ulcer that threatens to disperse its malignancy far and wide until every family catches infection from it . . . The lower class of women in England, are remarkably fond of the blacks, for reasons too brutal to mention . . . By these ladies they generally have a numerous brood. Thus in the course of a few generations more, the English blood will be so contaminated by the mixture and . . . this alloy may spread so extensively as even to reach the middle, and then the higher orders of the people, till the whole nation resembles the Portuguese and Moriscos in complexion of skin and baseness of mind.[9]

When Sierra Leone, the so-called 'colony for free slaves', was created in 1797 as a dumping ground for poor Blacks and their 'fallen' white consorts from Britain, there is no doubt that behind the evangelical fervour lay attitudes not unlike those expressed by Long a few years previously.

8

The same appalling bigotry lies behind this letter published in the *English Churchman* two centuries later by a 'nice' lady from Kingston upon Thames:

with their extremely high birth-rate it has been estimated that by the end of the century through intermarrying with us they will completely have mongrelised the British race . . . The irresponsibility of the negro and the fatalism of the Asian will have passed into our make up and we shall never be the same again.[10]

As colonial aspirations intensified throughout the eighteenth and nineteenth centuries, so did the animosity towards Black people. Racial superiority and purity were the pillars on which to build conquest and rule. The Black and brown native was painted as barbaric and sexually rampant. Both implied a need for them to be ruled, to be controlled. The underbelly of this was a sordid and growing fascination with the sexuality that whites claimed was so repulsive.

Crude Social Darwinism backed by missionary ardour fuelled these attitudes. In India, too, things changed dramatically over half a century. In the early days, when the lust was only for trade and money and not for empire, company men had been encouraged to marry Indian women – journeys took so long and it was expensive to transport families all the way from Britain. A wonderful painting of William Palmer and his Indian wife, Bibi Faiz Baksh, done in Calcutta in 1786, shows how relaxed relationships were at the time. Big names could trace their ancestry back to mixed roots. They included Job Charnock, the founder of Calcutta who married the widow he saved from suttee; the Anglo-Indian Skinner, of Skinner's horse, one of the most famous of Indian regiments; and nineteenth-century Tory Prime Minister Lord Liverpool. Alongside this harmony ran the obsessions of British Orientalists and sensualists who found much in the East to titillate them, sometimes grotesquely so – people like Richard Burton, who translated the *Kamasutra* and seems to have made it his business to sleep with women, men, goats and sheep in every country east of Suez and then write about it for all to gawp at.

As the political ambitions for India grew, so did the stereotype of the inept, barbaric and dangerous 'baboo', and by the time white Memsahibs arrived, sexual relationships between the races were confined to white men and prostitutes.

Britain, meanwhile, was seeing the arrival of Indian servants, ayahs and sailors. Many received appalling treatment at the hands of their masters and found themselves destitute. Some men, like the Black slaves before them, had sexual relations with poor white women. The more upper-class Indian arrivals and entrepreneurs who made good also occasionally married white. Then, as now, class made a huge difference to their status. Sake Deen Mohamed, a poor Indian who became 'Shampoo Surgeon' to King George IV, curing him and many members of European aristocracy of chronic illnesses and problems through his special oil massage, was married to a solid Englishwoman called Jane.

Shapurji Saklatvala, the first Asian Communist MP, had a mixed marriage, as did Shapurji Edalji, the vicar of Great Wyrley whose son George, a brilliant lawyer, was falsely accused of maiming horses and whose case was eventually taken up by Arthur Conan Doyle in 1903. There is no doubt that in Britain (unlike India, where the chauvinist impulses of white women were as strong as those of the men) many white women responded at a human level to the Black and Asian arrivals. Queen Victoria herself sent ripples through the furrowed brows of her wizened male advisers and ministers by holding her Indian servants in unusual affection – particularly Abdul Kareem, whose portrait she had painted and on whom she bestowed many honours.

By the beginning of this century there were core Black and Asian communities in Cardiff, Bristol and Liverpool, and significant numbers of mixed race families. But white Britons in these areas did not approve and 1919 saw the first large-scale riots against Blacks. The reason – an objection to the liaisons between Black men and white women, and the contamination of the race:

Flung out into the slumland culture of the port towns, the black seamen focused upon themselves considerable racial hostility as they became linked in the public mind with growing crime rates and prostitution when they cohabited with white women and produced 'half caste' children.[11]

A decade later Cardiff's chief constable, James A. Wilson, made a public plea for South African-type legislation to keep the races sexually apart. There were official government enquiries into the health and hygiene of these 'hybrid' children. Contamination fears were giving way to the syndrome of the hapless passive victim, the hybrid child who did not ask to be born; later this led to the argument that the poor Blacks and Asians simply could not be expected to survive in this sophisticated environment.

A joint report by the British Social Hygiene Council and the British Council for the Welfare of the Mercantile Marine, both keen anti-venereal-disease campaigners, declared in the 1930s:

Morality and cleanliness are as much matters of geography as they are dependent on circumstances. The coloured men who have come to dwell in our cities are being made to adopt a standard of civilisation they cannot be expected to understand. They are not imbued with moral codes similar to our own.[12]

In the First and Second World Wars millions of Black and Indian soldiers joined up, but despite fighting and dying for the motherland in two world wars, these 'coloureds' could not achieve the same human status as their white counterparts. Their contribution to the wars was largely forgotten; few people realise just how much was done by these troops. A famous war heroine, the spy Madeleine, was actually Noor Inayat Khan, the mixed race descendant of Tipu Sultan and a French woman. After her death at Dachau, she was awarded the George Cross for outstanding bravery.

In fact as these soldiers arrived (and many white women found them irresistible) official panic grew, as did hostility against those who chose to have a relationship with these undesirable aliens. It was no accident that many of the women who ventured into these relationships came from disadvantaged backgrounds, and no accident either that the pressure on the couples often meant stress, a lack of trust and a destructive cynicism. Some came through, though, and are still together.

Academic research, official reports and media hysteria scaled new heights in the mid 1950s and despite the war, anti-Semitic feelings emerged. A rash of 'human interest' stories asking 'Would you let your daughter marry a . . . ?' pandered to the racism of the period.

By the 1960s (and because of them) the development of over-rosy views of Third World cultures, coupled with decolonisation, triggered other 'concerns'. Alongside the image of the poor mixed race child who would belong nowhere, caught in the crossfire of culture, race and politics, developed a bizarre belief that intermarriage would be a good thing because it would lead to a useful assimilation of the alien wedge. Newspapers intermittently regaled their readers with romantic stories of Love Winning Through as heroic individuals crossed into this minefield. But these were little more than flimsy covers for hardening attitudes. This was the time, the lovely sixties, when the Reverend Hill was sent the kinds of letters quoted on p. 1 above. Unsurprisingly, in 1963, from 1,000 parishes questioned, only eighty-four had recorded marriage across the races.

This dream of 'a great big melting pot' started to falter with the first arrivals of large numbers of Black women and children from the Caribbean and the subcontinent. Black society started restructuring into its own family groupings. Many women, both white and Black, suffered great distress as they both found themselves attached to the same Black man. Large numbers of Asian women also began to appear, but although there had been some casual alliances between their men and local women, they were over a shorter period and often had a temporary status.

Politicians had also started overtly addressing the issue of Black immigration. The swamping rhetoric which reached its climax in Enoch Powell's 1968 'rivers of blood' speech had begun. Racism was rife. Immigration laws, unfair policing, discrimination – all became a way of life for many Black Britons. But the Black community, especially second- and third-generation Blacks and Asians, were not prepared to suffer the rejection and injustice that their parents had had to endure. Black pride was growing, following the trends in the United States. Mixed race children began to see themselves as Black. And within communities which might once have been more tolerant of mixed relationships there was now anger and rejection, a fight for preservation and much the same sort of purity rhetoric produced by white racists, although this response came out of years of rage and powerlessness.

It is interesting to note that there have been only two major films in the last forty years which looked at mixed race relationships, *Guess Who's Coming to Dinner?* with Sidney Poitier which, for all its subtle racist implications, did begin to portray some of the anxieties, and the recent film *Jungle Fever* by Spike Lee which has unnerved many people in Britain and the US.

The Present

According to the sparse statistics we have, and from looking around major metropolitan areas, it is clear that there are now many and increasing numbers of relationships that are crossing racial boundaries. The last OPCS (Office of Population Censuses and Surveys) Labour Force survey on the issue, published in 1985, showed that 27 per cent of Black British husbands are in mixed marriages. The figure for Black women was 14 per cent. In the Asian community, 10 per cent of men and 5 per cent of women are in mixed marriages. On the other hand, in 1990 a Harris poll conducted for the Asian programme 'East' on BBC television showed that only 10 per cent within the community had married across racial and religious barriers, and only 3 per cent from the age group eighteen to twenty-four had done so. Furthermore, unmarried young Asians were just as conservative about their futures and most said they would not marry into a different religion, race or even caste. Paradoxically, both these developments are occurring simultaneously, making it (thankfully) perilous to prophesy future trends.

Our interviewees had complex, varied and disparate experiences. We talked to couples who began their relationships in the 1940s and 1950s, as well as those who have done so more recently. We talked to the parents of children who have gone into mixed relationships and to mixed race children, many of them now embarking on love affairs of their own. They told us about their lives within and outside their relationship, about the joys and traumas of parenthood and about their hopes and fears for the future. Their lives were shaped by many different factors, including class and economic status; endemic racism in this society; the rise of Black politics; increasing cultural and religious conservatism; the death of the multicultural dream; radical changes in education and childhood development; sexual politics and demographic changes in inner-city areas.

For some people, for example, changing attitudes – at least among thinking people – and the chance to live in mixed areas has provided a richness of life confirming what Anne Wilson says in *Mixed Race Children*:

Contrary to the popular stereotype of mixed race people as torn between black and white, many children seemed to have found a happy and secure identity for themselves . . . This was particularly true of children in multiracial areas who were able to draw support from the existence of other mixed race and 'brown' children in the area.[13]

Interestingly, just as there are many Asian and Black Britons who would now argue against mixed relationships, there are also many others whose lives have been enriched and transformed by them and who see this as the new dawn. These people have reached a new understanding about the direction of their relationships. It can no longer be assumed, as it once was, that white values would dominate – that the Black or Asian partner would turn 'white', give or take an occasional ethnic headscarf, or sari at the office Christmas party, which was commonplace in the previous two decades. It is interesting to see the names of mixed race children then and now. Today, couples seem to think long and hard about how they want their children to grow up and what they want them to be. Nothing is taken for granted, and this, said one woman, exercised the heart and mind constantly, making you more conscious and a better parent. On the other hand, there are many liberal whites whose assumptions about sexual relationships between white and Black still seem to be based on historical stereotypes.

Many white and Black women have had to think through where they place themselves in this very racist and sexist society, especially as these two powerful social forces are so often in opposition. Some of the women we interviewed had resolved this dilemma, others were still negotiating it and others, although obviously aware of it, saw their lives in entirely personal terms.

British racism has changed its face, and couples and individuals spoke of new challenges they had been forced to confront. Some *religious* groups are now under vicious attack; this is why we have included couples who have crossed religious boundaries, although miscegenation strictly refers only to race. In recent years, the new enemy resurrected out of the old, Islam, is also being tested in terms of personal lives and relationships. White men and women married to Muslims have had a whole area of resentment to negotiate, and this has given them both courage and pain. During the Gulf crisis, this is what the *Sun* columnist Richard Littlejohn had to say:

What I can live without are British women married to Iraqis, arriving back at Heathrow and Gatwick . . . in full Arab garb . . . They have chosen to turn their back on Britain, our values and beliefs. They should be left to rot in their adopted country with their hideous husbands and their unattractive children.[14]

Old enmities against the Jews are resurfacing, but many young Jews are not burying their heads in the sand or trying to become invisible in order to make themselves less offensive to the Anglo-Saxon eye. The more orthodox sections of the Jewish community are beginning to fear the rise in mixed marriages, now up to 30 per cent of community marriages. And even people like Jonathan Romain, a Reform Rabbi who counsels mixed couples and no purist firebrand, *is* worried about where it might all end:

at the end of the day I firmly believe that intermarriage is a bad thing. Intermarriage detracts from the religious continuity of Judaism . . . It also endangers the survival of Anglo-Jewry. This community is decreasing frighteningly rapidly.[15]

Many Black and Asian people are also – increasingly – arguing in these terms. But is a plea for racial purity to be condoned when it is uttered by oppressed minorities and condemned when it is put forth by a powerful majority?

Other collusions and confusions also came to light. Many interviewees thought these needed to be approached more honestly and not shrouded in secrecy simply because it was not politically 'correct' to discuss these issues. The nature of relationships between Blacks and Asians and the kinds of prejudices involved was one important issue, as was the increasing tendency of so many 'successful' Blacks and Asians to adopt white partners almost as the finishing touch to their impressive CVs. These discussions were full of fire and fury as impossible questions surfaced. To what extent is this the fault of the myth of the emasculating Black matriarch and the obsessively devoted (to the son) Asian mother? Why is it acceptable for a Black or Asian man to cross the colour divide, but not a woman?

Other discussions about how historical sexual and power fantasies still appear to infiltrate mixed relationships were even more emotionally charged – a taboo subject Beth Day began to explore in her own inimitable fashion back in the 1970s.

The desire for the Black man to prove himself sexually with a white partner has provoked a bitter conflict between black males and black females, just at a time when they most need to consolidate their ranks . . . the competition for the black men has also succeeded in building a wall of distrust and anger between black women and white women, when cooperation would be valuable in breaking down the barriers of discriminatory employment practices and in pressing for more female political power. The myth of black supersexuality also puts the white woman who is genuinely attracted to a black man in the potential position of being sexually exploited – a pawn in the revenge that the black male seeks to wreak on the white male for his history of oppression.[16]

This is also one of the most powerful messages in *Soul on Ice* by the Black writer Eldridge Cleaver who, back in the days of the civil rights struggles, wrote about the inner damage caused to so many older Black men by inhumane racist treatment. A fictional character, the old man Lazarus, muses thus:

There is no love left between a black man and a black woman. Take me, for instance, I love white women and hate black women . . . I'd jump over ten nigger bitches just to get to one white woman. Ain't no such thing as an ugly white woman. A white woman is beautiful even if she is baldheaded and has only one tooth . . . it's not just the fact that she's a woman I love; I love her skin, her soft, smooth, white skin . . . there's a softness about a white woman, something delicate and soft inside her. But a nigger bitch seems to be full of steel, granite hard and resisting, not soft and submissive like a white woman.[17]

In 1952 Frantz Fanon had discussed the same pathology, but had seen the anguish as beyond the personal and placed it in the context of Black/white power inequalities:

Out of the blackest part of my soul, across the zebra striping of my mind, surges this desire to be suddenly white. I wish to be acknowledged not as *black* but as *white* . . . who but a white woman can do this for me? By loving she proves I am worthy of white love. And loved like a white man . . . When my restless hands caress those white breasts, they grasp white civilisation and dignity and make them mine.[18]

Thirty years on, in the United States and Britain, these arguments are still raging, and are reiterated by many men and women in this book.

Other fantasies also play their part. Forbidden fruit takes a long time to lose its magic. Too often these days, white men (repelled, they say, by feminist white women) turn to Asian woman as 'submissive' and Black women as 'whores'. There are other reasons, too, for the attraction. In a recent article in the men's magazine *Arena*, journalist Tony Parsons asked this extraordinary question: 'Why is the blonde all washed up? Why are more men turning to Pretty Ethnics? Why do most men prefer – either in their lives or in their fantasies – the comfort of brown-eyed girls rather than big broad mares with dyed hair and sagging tits? *Why*? Are you *kidding*? . . . would you rather share your toothpaste with some complaining, big-boned, post-fem ballsy chick or a creature of infinite beauty and grace?'

Designer racism and sexism are alive and well, and well paid too. Parsons does not realise these implications and goes on instead to describe these perversions in near-religious terms: 'Rather than sexual imperialism, I believe that a liking for Pretty Ethnics means that in your heart you are embracing the whole of humanity.'[19]

Another issue that emerged – which deserves more time and space than we were able to give it – was the facile way in which culture is perceived by those who oppose mixed relationships. People rightly argued that cultures develop and change, and must do so if they are not to become fossilised. That dynamism is a positive life force and those who wish to preserve outdated notions in some mental attic full of cultural bric-à-brac were going to make themselves and their values obsolete. If this is so, it becomes meaningless to talk in dichotomous terms about choosing one 'culture' or another, because we are all composite creatures now.

But at the end of the day, the overwhelming conclusion was that however mixed race couples and mixed race children choose to live their lives, they cannot shake off historical baggage or isolate themselves from the assumptions and bigotries of the outside world. These attitudes invade their lives. And for many it is the transition to parenthood that brings this realisation most profoundly.

These are just some of the threads which emerged during the course of our conversations and research. We are conscious of gaps in the book. We have no Irish Catholic and Protestant couples, or many other interesting combinations – German and Jewish, for example. These omissions do not indicate neglect or judgement on our part. We had to draw the line somewhere, but we could have gone on for another two years.

We have divided the chapters thematically, but there is obviously some overlap. Occasionally we have separated the conversations into two different chapters. Brief biographies were provided by interviewees, but for those who wanted to be anonymous we have changed some details in order to protect identities. The last chapter of the book is a range of comments and short conversations with young people in colleges, clubs and other informal settings. We wanted to see what they thought of interracial relationships. The results shocked us, both because we realised how little has changed in some ways and also because the polarisation between the

19

groups, with a few exceptions, seemed so much greater than in earlier postwar decades.

The people we talked to gave us endless amounts of time and coffee and allowed us intimate access to their lives, even when it was incredibly painful or when, as well-known figures, they could so easily have held back. Some people found the conversations cathartic after years of burying feelings about the issue. Others talked to each other as we talked to them, often for the first time, about their worries and realisations. Some claimed to have found renewed joy and vigour by being forced to excavate the past and remember what they gave up in order to be with one another. Theirs were exceptional insights. They made the book. Those many hidden voices and seeing eyes show that one can talk about common threads but in the end these are individuals, separate, unique and each deeply committed – even when it failed – to their relationship. That strength and joy emerged as we went through this unforgettable journey.

Lucy Addington, one of the mothers we interviewed, asked us if that journey had changed us. Yes, profoundly. And the one image that most clearly symbolises that change is her own elder daughter, with her lovely plaited hair, clear eyes, tawny skin, limitless energy and radiant personality; Franka-Rose Crichlow, eight going on twelve, who played the tired old piano beautifully after five lessons, whose paintings are so extraordinary that they were featured on a BBC educational programme and whose appetite for knowledge is so insatiable that it thwarts her teachers. In fact, it was almost impossible to carry on the interview because we ended up busily discussing the evolution of skunks and where bears come from whilst Franka did her somersaults. So much for the mongrelised mixed-up mixed race child.

Notes

1. Clifford S. Hill, *How Colour Prejudiced is Britain?*, Gollancz, London, 1965.

2.   Anne Wilson, *Mixed Race Children: A Study of Identity*, Allen & Unwin, London, 1987, p. v.

3.   Susan Benson, *Ambiguous Ethnicity: Interracial Families in London*, Cambridge University Press, Cambridge, 1981, p. 21.

4.   Fernando Henriques, *Children of Conflict: A Study of Interracial Sex and Marriage*, Dutton, New York, 1975, p. xii.

5.   *Titus Andronicus*, Act IV.

6.   Quoted in Susan Benson, *Ambiguous Ethnicity*.

7.   W.E.B. Du Bois, *Darkwater*. *Voices from Within the Veil*, New York, 1969; quoted in Fernando Henriques, *Children of Conflict*, ch.6.

8.   Beth Day, *Sexual Life Between Blacks and Whites*, Collins, London, 1974.

9.   Edward Long, *Candid Reflections*, London, 1772.

10.   *English Churchman*, 10 April 1964; quoted in Susan Benson, *Ambiguous Ethnicity*.

11.   Paul B. Rich, *Race and Empire in British Politics*, Cambridge University Press, Cambridge, 1986, p. 121.

12.   Quoted in ibid, p. 138.

13.   Anne Wilson, *Mixed Race Children*, p. vi.

14.   The *Sun*, 10 September 1990.

15.   *New Moon*, the Jewish Arts & Listings Monthly, May 1991.

16.   Beth Day, *Sexual Life Between Blacks and Whites*, p. 8.

17.   Eldridge Cleaver, *Soul on Ice*, Dell, New York, 1970, p. 159.

18.   Frantz Fanon, *Black Skin White Masks*, Pluto, London, 1968, p. 63.

19.   Tony Parsons, *Arena*, Spring 1991.

1. In the Public Eye

> *We have had racial attacks. We've had police guards, break-ins, death threats, telephone calls, my car nearly pushed off the road during the last election. I was spat upon in the road and called 'nigger lover' and Richard was asked what it was like sleeping with someone like me . . . You have to accept that if you're in public life, you are a target for nutters and racists.*

– ZERBANOO GIFFORD

Frank Crichlow and Lucy Addington

Frank Crichlow came to Britain from the Caribbean in the 1950s and settled in the Notting Hill Gate area, where he lives to this day. A pivotal figure in the Black community, Crichlow was involved in many key projects and also ran the popular Mangrove Club, which he was finally forced to sell in 1991. His partner, Lucy Addington, is from Wiltshire; she was a community worker and then a teacher before their children were born.

In the late 1960s Frank Crichlow was tried for organising the first demonstration against racist policing in the area. It was to be the beginning of a long, ugly relationship with a series of false arrests, unproven accusations, court appearances and acquittals. The climax came in 1989 when Frank was charged with drug dealing from the Mangrove. After what seemed like an endless nightmare, he was eventually acquitted of all charges and an 'Open Space' programme on BBC television, following the trial and reconstructing the events, showed the extent to which Frank Crichlow had been the victim of a frame-up.

Yet all these years, Frank has been loved and respected by the Notting Hill Black community. He has worked tirelessly on their behalf. He has won the respect of authoritative figures in the white establishment, too, and he has survived the long vendetta against him. Lucy Addington has lived through these years with him, and now their four children – Franka, Leah, Knolly and Amandla – know what it is like too.

Frank: Why me? I think it is because of my role in the Black community, where I complained very seriously against the way the Black community was policed. So they have had it in for me personally, and for the Mangrove, which had become a symbol of that resistance. I don't want trouble. All I am against is injustice, dishonesty and corruption, particularly in the police force.

Lucy: It was such a ridiculous suggestion – Frank Crichlow found with drugs in his pocket! We just had to assume that it was *because* it was Frank that this was happening. Because of his increasing credibility. But although Frank was acquitted of the conspiracy, they win in the end, you know. The Mangrove was shut down throughout the trial, Frank was not allowed to go near there for months, the debts grew and it proved impossible to refloat the business.

I'll never forget the day he was arrested. I got a phone call that they had taken him, it was the day Franka developed chickenpox. I was used to *that* happening to Frank ever since I had known him, it came with the job. But when he still hadn't come home quite late, I was worried sick that this time maybe they would get him. We finally got to see him on Monday, and I remember feeling a real panic. By this time all the children had chickenpox and we decided not to tell them and not to take them to the prison even when they were better. But you can imagine how terrible I was feeling. So much had happened to Frank in his life, because he was Black and because of what he had been doing in the community. The outside is always knocking on your door.

Frank: It was terrible, but I had some amazing support from the Black community, and from powerful white people. When they were trying to fix bail I went to court and the judge was really confused, because he couldn't understand how my backers were people from the Home Office, magistrates.

Lucy: It is true. There is incredible folklore about Frank in the area – there is this drip, drip, drip of Frank stories which sometimes amuse and sometimes anger me. You know: Frank the Godfather, Frank the Drug Dealer, that he is this all-powerful guy who controls All Saints Road. It feels like I am the moll of some charming bandit! You can see all the loot around you in this house, can't you?

The children do remember a great deal. And what they can't handle is that this whole year, suddenly after twenty years, Frank is home all the time. Frank has had to assume the mantle of the New Age man, and he has become very skilful at it all. I too value his fathering role now that his life is changed.

Frank: Yes, after all this time, Crichlow goes to bed at nine o'clock! It changed my life completely. Having a family also changed my life. The first thing that came into my head when I was arrested this time was thoughts of my family. You worry about things in a different way from before, when you only really had yourself to worry about. I had stayed single for so long, but I knew my family would suffer. Not Lucy being white, that didn't feature. But this happened when I had her and the children to think about. That made it so much worse. Lucy was strong and stayed with it, but so much could have been destroyed. It was hard for us both. They even tapped the phone. These people in positions of power have such power to destroy your life.

Lucy: The children were affected, although I tried to protect them. What blew the gaff was that they saw Frank when he was acquitted on the television news, and that was a shock because they showed a photograph of him lying down with his wrists handcuffed at the back. They have never forgotten that. It was a horrible picture.

If we had been living in some white suburb, it would have been even more awful to go through what we did. Here, all our friends, white and Black, were such a tremendous support, often in a practical way. I suppose you could look at it as a positive demonstration of how Black and white people can get it together in this way in spite of all the racism out there. I don't know what my feelings would have been if only Black people had come forth. Even people like the Dean of Kensington came up, and he is a heavyweight. We were – and have had to be, with all those nightmares going on – very supportive of each other. It makes your relationship very strong. In fact maybe it is more difficult now that the pressure is off up to a point. And you also think: I am not going to go through that again and the kids are not going to go through that again. I think I now feel that Frank has done enough for the cause and maybe it is a case of handing over to whoever takes it from there. The way he has dealt with losing everything is amazing.

Perhaps, having been pushed to the edge of things so

much, our relationship has been at a different level from most other people who lead fairly straightforward lives, worry maybe about money or something more normal. At this stage, perhaps that is what I'd like to try – a boring life! You can't be bored with four little children who are very demanding. That too helped us through, because I was pregnant with our fourth child.

I have no regrets about being with Frank. I have had to find hidden strengths and ways of thinking and living to deflect the stress. Between my upbringing and my personality I was not easily able to express anger, disappointment or frustration. But now I can, and it is healthier.

I do have resentments about the time and energy that all this has taken from Frank and me. Life was always very emotionally draining and we have always had serious financial difficulties. We always had to be on our guard about what would happen next with the police; it's hard to express the tension that causes. It's like living in a war – nothing can be planned or organised.

Frank: Lucy was really fantastic: carrying our fourth child through those terrible days. And when the trial came up we took the three-month-old baby into court – I wanted the baby there, but I also didn't like it.

Lucy: We met, funnily enough, at a court, since courts and police stations have loomed large in our lives – Frank was with someone and I had brought in some kids I was working with. We talked and tried to get into the court. And then, a few years later, we met on Portobello Road. I was shopping and he was in the same shop and he was nosy, and I was nosy, and we both started talking because we were both community workers. I lived round the corner but I came from the country, from Wiltshire. I grew up on a farm, so it was quite different.

But it is strange. Although you might think that I would never have thought about ending up in this way, I did. The irony is that after my grandmother died, one of her daughters, my aunt, actually said that she thought, long before I knew any Black people, that I had had a child by somebody Black. She thought this because I came to the farm with some children from an adventure playground and she looked out of the window and saw me hugging these little Black and mixed race children and thought that I must have had one somewhere and was missing it, or that one of them was mine.

The other irony is that my mother and I – she died twenty years ago – used to talk a lot about mixed race relationships. We would talk about the difficulties and I would always press to find out what they thought, because my parents never talked about difficult issues like race or money. I think they would have been like those people in *Guess who's Coming to Dinner?*

Frank: What has happened – and it is important to stress – is that a lot of white people who are political and involved in community politics do think of themselves differently from in the old days. They turn up at meetings and demonstrations – they like to show that they are not all like the rest. That took off in the sixties in the hippie days. Relationships across the races, like mine and Lucy's, began through that. We worked together and had very similar views on the effects of racism. But I have always had kindness shown to me by all sorts of whites; they have been in the struggle. That is why I have no personal bitterness towards whites at all.

If you ask me if I felt a sense of guilt or impurity being with a white woman the answer is no, emphatically no. I think people talk about that now and did twenty years ago, but my view when I looked ahead was that this would be a melting-pot time. It can't be stopped. It is early days yet, but they can't stop it. We were talking at the Mangrove, for example, about how Asians have changed and how many of them can now be seen with white partners. I think in certain political circles it is not considered right for a Black person to have a white partner. But the really uncomfortable time was during the Black Power days. Even to have a white woman as a friend was not acceptable. Many Black people accepted this without a problem. Those days are over now, although Lucy may disagree.

At the first meeting we had, after the New Cross fire in which Black teenagers died, some people said that no white people should be allowed, yet some of those mothers of the kids who died were white. So what were we going to do about that? There was a lot of confusion among people who felt very strongly, but this thing is not simple, however hard we try to make it so.

Lucy: I think it is still very very difficult because there are still Black political meetings which don't want white people there and I think that is perfectly valid. Like with the women's movement – I think there is a time and a place to operate separately. It can get very difficult, and there will always be people who get left out. But I am not sure where that leaves the children.

I feel in some ways that in spite of my upbringing I am different. I have never felt part of the system at all just because I am white. I hadn't felt that for a long time, obviously, or I wouldn't have gone for this life. But I have never wanted to become Black either. That is not the way. I have kept apart from Frank's lifestyle in some ways: I have my own political involvements. I feel that Frank's struggles must be fought by Black people. I can't really do that. I have been in the background, supporting things before the children were born.

I didn't learn all this from my life with Frank. Even before Frank I was teaching and was aware that things were happening: the Black kids in this permanent state of being harassed and picked up and blamed. They had no voice at all and I realised then the work that Frank was doing for them. So when my relationship with Frank developed, I guess he was fairly heroic, so it wasn't difficult to get involved with him. But I was attracted to *him* more than his colour. I did not appreciate the significance of colour until much later.

But you know even in the Black community then, the Mangrove reputation was very dubious. The kids I used to teach would be really shocked and a bit impressed that I knew people from the Mangrove Club. I talked to them to dispel some of these myths and spoke about the work we did and the issues that Mangrove campaigned around.

It has been a shock to experience firsthand what life is really like for a lot of Black people in this country. For me, I am just another white middle-class lady; people listen to what I have to say and behave respectfully towards me. What is so horrifying is that these great British institutions that I have been nurtured on – and I suppose must have believed in – are this corrupt and this vindictive. Most white people don't have that insight. They disbelieve the stories that Blacks tell about the police. I can never do that. In that way you feel funnily privileged, less gullible, maybe more grown-up than most other people. You become so wary. For two years I made no new friends. When your partner is on bail for something and anti-social as heroin, you don't feel like offering friendship. You feel like a problem. The thousand tiny, subtle ways certain doors are closed, a certain quality of life that is simply not there for many British citizens! I know it is better here than in the USA; there Frank would probably have been killed for being so troublesome. But it could be a lot better here. I really don't want my children spending all their energy on defending their Blackness and their right to be here. I feel sad that there is so much creativity and beauty in different cultures to be shared, which is belittled and ridiculed.

It was fantastic going to Trinidad and meeting Frank's family, and the children began to feel much more a part of that side. It was lovely. We got on really well with all the uncles and those people. They never made me feel like an outsider because I was white – never.

Frank: Lucy's family treats me fine too – maybe I am just lucky in some ways, not in others, and I am spoilt by where we live. There are so many more mixed race couples, and at

29

our parties we are just one big family. Maybe my views are coloured by the experiences of living in this very mixed and vibrant area, Notting Hill has always had mixtures who got on very well. We should look at the number of white women who have been in with this from the beginning; it has not been easy for them from both sides.

Lucy: Frank has always said that – how brave those women in the sixties were. That you are in a no-win situation. You are in no-person's-land. You are not part of the white community and you are not part of the Black community. You are caught in the middle. I know there are many white women who do find that difficult, especially if there is a politically aware Black group around, or people who are very angry with the white establishment. It doesn't bother me because Frank and I have similar views on these issues, and also because I don't expect to be part of anything. I never was. Some people grow up feeling very much a part of a group; I didn't. Our farm was in the middle of nowhere. I have close friends and I am not too bothered about belonging. I am not too bothered about belonging to Frank's world either.

I think there is always a type of white woman who braves it. Maybe it is to do with rebellion. I have always been a bit of a rebel. You are made to feel it. When I met Frank I was working in a school in White City and there were kids there I bumped into in the market a couple of years later and one of them said, 'You still like Black prick, Miss?' And of course there are always people who are cross about it; we go to the country often and I am always surprised at the way people look at us.

We both feel that it is crucial to start thinking about the children. Our children are interesting. We are able to give them a sense of roots from both the white and the Black side, and there is no conflict about that. They know they are Black but they call themselves brown. Franka, the eldest, is very colour-conscious and really articulate – she feels things the most and talks about them. She knows her colour is brown,

30

not Black. Leah, the second, who is also the fairest, is very pro-Black, funnily enough, and very comfortable about it. Franka was very worried about being not white. I remember she had a fever once and she was crying and said she wanted to be white. Although we live in a very multiracial area, there weren't many Black children in her nursery and all the workers were white; I think she really picked up on the power structure. But since then she's been in schools that are more Black and she's met Black people in power, doing really constructive and positive things. I notice she gets very excited and says things like 'A new Black boy came today', and also when there are new Black children in the street. She has a real sense of solidarity with Black people.

They are also talking a lot more about Frank and what happened to him and what it means about authority. We have to talk to them so they can be prepared, otherwise they will be damaged. We have all become more politicised and more aware because of these experiences and we have to use that – I don't mean cram their heads with hate, but explain things.

The other day we were going through Holland Park, which is a route we took every day when we used to go to the court. Leah – who is now five, but was three at the time – ran on ahead and said, 'This is the route we took to the court.' And then there was this big discussion about the court. Another child who was with us said, 'My daddy is Ethiopian and he didn't have to go to court.' And the girls got defensive and said, 'Why did the police have to go and arrest Daddy? Just because he's famous and got the Mangrove. So they went for him.' What is so surprising is that they were very young but they had noticed, especially when he disappeared for six weeks. After those sorts of experiences you do fear for your kids very much.

It is important to talk about these things, because as we have been political people and been the targets of the police for so long, we know better than many what is happening out there to Black kids, and it does worry me. Even in my own family some of the relatives won't talk to my children because they are Black, although most are all right.

Frank: But I think we have to be a bit careful about this thing. If Black and white people are now keeping to themselves, when this is a multicultural and multiracial society, what confusion for a kid at thirteen and fourteen! I am so cautious about these things, especially when they are being made public, because anything we say could be a wrong signal and dangerous, because the melting pot is going to find its way. There are now thousands of mixed race children and adults in this country and they will have to find an agenda that they can relate to, because their experience is something different again. Both Black and white people must respect that if we are to avoid yet another 'under'class or 'sub'class. The world narrows its options only when people become judgemental. People are people, and the beauty and interest in life is in the enjoyment of the uniqueness as well as in the commonness.

Lucy: I know a lot of Black women think their men have an easier time with white women and are really shocked when they hear that we have the same problems as them. Because it is a male–female relationship as much as anything else. It is a myth that it always goes that easily. But this race issue is very complicated. Too often racial differences are focused on in relationships when something different is happening. Many of the women I work with, for example, Black and white, understand when I'm talking about Frank that it is to do with the fact that he is a man, not that he is Black.

Frank: It is still less common to see Black women with white men, though it is growing – it got very fashionable in the seventies, and there are often many moans about it from Black men. But those couples tend not to live in very Black areas, I think deliberately, because of the attitudes of Black men.

In the early sixties when I first started the Rio Club in these parts, and people were still coming over from the West

Indies, the only women who were available were white. The Black women who were around were nurses and you had to find out where they went to parties, and that sort of thing, but the white women were there all the time. There would be sixty men and all the women would be white. Some were prostitutes, but not all of them, although prostitution was very common at the time. That is where the Christine Keeler – she used to call me Dad, you know! – story came from. She used to come to the Rio with her clients and friends, because our clubs were not boring and dry like the English ones; there was life in them, it comes from a love of life. And the racism that came into the area at the time was not among the white women.

Things changed as the young Black youth explosion reached the streets of this country – that was a dividing line between what happened before and things now. You don't get the same mixing now, even in this area. You must recognise the guts that these women needed to come out on the streets with their Black men. Nobody talks about that but they paved the way, they were brave women. Because they get it so badly, you know. It wasn't a political thing but a sex thing at the time. They liked the young men who came over, with all their fancy clothes and good looks. I remember when I had been here a couple of weeks and these two white girls started following me around. They were very young and – how can I say this? – very forward. They really wanted to pick me up. And I couldn't handle that! Many times I would be ready to close the club and a girl would say, 'Are you ready to go?' That used to bother me. So Lucy has a long tradition to follow.

Patti Boulaye and Stephen Komlosy

Patti Boulaye, an international singer and actress, was born in Nigeria but has lived in Britain since she was sixteen. She has played several leading roles in musicals, including Yum

Yum in *The Black Mikado*, has released seven albums, and has also been very successful in the international cabaret scene.

Stephen Komlosy is English. He is now fifty and has been in business since 1958, previously in leisure and now in property. His marriage to Patti is his third.

Stephen and Patti have two children. Their eldest daughter, Emma, is a talented swimmer and now takes part in international competitions.

Patti

I can still remember my shock when I saw Britain for the first time as a teenager. Over in Nigeria all we saw were these upright English administrators and respectable teachers. I saw the country in a mess, a degrading mess. When I landed a part in the musical *Hair* it was a revelation. Free booze, free sex, drugs, people with torn jeans – I couldn't believe it. And here I was, a proper convent girl who would never do any of those things. So I came across as stuck-up, because I thought they were not as good as I was or people I knew. Being that way helped me not to feel any of the animosity, I sailed proudly above it all. I knew there were certain attitudes towards me but I never allowed it to disturb me, or to think it was just because I am Black. I was so rooted in my religion that I had a purity in my way of thinking. So if anybody did anything to me, I made excuses for them. It wasn't difficult as a young girl in England who sees most people around her messing up their lives on some kind of substance in the name of enjoyment. That attitude and a certain realism carried me through.

It was probably a strategy for survival. But in another sense, it was because I couldn't understand how anyone could look at another human being and see that much difference. So when things did happen, I handled them better because of the way I saw things. I remember a show in Windsor when a man started to hassle me. He came with a coachload which included one Black guy. He started saying things like 'You both came together on the banana boat, I expect.' I looked at the Black guy, threw my arms around him and shouted 'Uncle!' Then I turned to the guy who was hassling me and asked him where he came from. He said, 'Bethnal Green', and I said, 'I thought so, that is the sort of place for people like you.' Some people are so stupid. I was important enough to come and see, but I was Black.

So I never imagined I would marry a white man. I had been out for drinks with white men but had never found them that attractive. My illusions about the great white man had gone, and those stoned people in torn jeans were no substitute. The gentleman I saw in Africa was not the person I saw here. Stephen was totally different from any other person I had met in this country. He put the gentleman back into the British.

I was frightened about what my parents were going to say. My father already knew who I was going to marry: a good match. Somebody from a family as important as the one I came from.

At the time colour was the last thing that came into it. It was all pretty difficult. Stephen had been married twice before and getting married would mean a second divorce. If it didn't work before, why should it work now? I was pregnant but having the baby was not a problem, because in Nigeria things don't work like that. But it made things more difficult for me because I didn't want him to think we should get married because of the baby. That would have been the wrong thing to do. The pregnancy was a complete surprise because I had been told I couldn't have children. So I didn't want Stephen to think I had done this purposely either.

And as a Catholic, getting married to a divorced man was difficult and it tortured me for years. For years I didn't go to Communion and used to pray for God to forgive me. I decided that the sign of forgiveness would come if Stephen came to church and we could get married in the Church, which we did four years ago, nine years after our civil ceremony.

I remember when Stephen had to meet my mother for the

first time. I said to him, 'You will never understand this, but if she doesn't like you, I cannot marry you. I don't care how much in love I am with you. My mother is my best friend and if she feels that there is something wrong in this I will keep seeing you, but marriage is out of the question.' You know my mother always told me: there are boyfriends and there are husbands.

I was petrified. I left them alone for two hours and when I came back, I saw the relief on Stephen's face. He thought she was wonderful. My mother had been worried – not just about the prejudice we might meet; I could hear her thinking, 'How could it work? Your customs are different.' In the end she said, 'If you can find someone who loves you more, you will be lucky.' All my sisters married Nigerians, but my mother didn't object. What mattered to her was whether this man would make her daughter happy and love her. In fact not one member of my family objected. My father met Stephen only after we were married, I thought my mother was more important; in our society the female voice is more important. When they met they got on very well. Stephen found my father, with his old-fashioned English – that quaint proper English that existed in the colonies – fascinating.

Stephen didn't worry how his family would react; he was more concerned about my family's reaction. I didn't think I would have problems with them. I thought: unless they are horrible, miserable people I will get on with them, and I did quite easily.

I don't think I could have found a companion like Stephen if I had married someone of my own background, although I don't know what could have been, so maybe it is not fair to say. I couldn't have found such a friend, someone I feel totally at ease with. In Nigeria – and of course this is a generalisation – male–female relationships are strained because men feel that they can go and marry anybody. With Stephen, the real me, the hidden me, has completely come out. The fact that we are different has enhanced our relationship. I have a very close family and a large family; Stephen is not used to having a lot of people around him. So he has had quite a shock – the minute he married me, he married my family.

He feels he has to protect me. I can't understand girls who want to be too independent and grown-up. My mother still protects me, my sisters protect me and my husband protects me. His love and support help me deal with the people who make hurtful remarks. He stops me falling into the destructive idea that people as a whole are like those idiots. Sometimes it is thinking people who should know better who say or do things, and when that happens I get really heavy in my heart. I have a white friend who finds it a constant surprise that I can dress glamorously and that my home is the way it is. I used to be so sensitive before, and would cry over these things. And just like a father or mother, Stephen is always there for me to come crying to.

The last time I was abused a taxi driver called me 'a Black bitch'. But things like that have never happened to us when we are together. No one has said anything to our faces, although they might say it behind our backs, perhaps because we don't meet the kind of people who would come out with that sort of line. We don't mix with people with a low mentality, you know, fools. Class makes all the difference.

Some attitudes do make me very angry. Stephen doesn't agree, but they are there. The way the media portray Blacks, for example. It seems that if you are a Black person, a finger will be pointed at you on any excuse. If a woman is raped by a white man, it is a man, but if it is a Black man, *that* is the problem. We disagree on South Africa. I grew up in Nigeria, where we had a lot of coups and political problems. I know that governments, white or Black, are crooked and can plant anything. Stephen dislikes Winnie Mandela, but while I am not saying she is innocent, I do not want to judge her because I know what can be done. I have seen it done in my country – too many times.

When I watch things on TV about how Black people are seen in this country or elsewhere, it affects me. It makes me feel angry. It also strengthens my belief that many white Britons really have sunk. I was parked in Richmond some time ago and all the police could see was a Black woman in an expensive car. The policeman came up to me and, not looking at me, said, 'Your licence, please'. I gave him the licence and he said, 'Can you tell me what you are doing in the car?' I said, 'I am sitting in it.' So he asked me who was the owner of the car. I told him I was. That is when he looked at me. His face changed as he realised who I was. Suddenly it was 'Oh Miss Boulaye, it is you.' So I do know it happens and I know that if I was a man it would be worse. Stephen cannot believe that such things happen; I think he would rather not believe it.

But I can't understand how some Black people think either. I have a friend whose defences have been up for so long, her need to protect herself has been so strong, that it has really affected her – I think because she has been told by her friends in Brixton that she has sold out by living in Richmond with a white man. When I drive my car, the Rolls, she says, 'How can you, a Black girl, drive a car like this?' – as if people who drive Rolls-Royces cannot be Black! I tell her that it is even more important as a Black girl to drive a Rolls so people can stop thinking we all live in slums. The first time the people at my daughter's school saw the car, there was disbelief. Now they have accepted it, and me, and learnt something, I think. If we are all frightened of going out and looking good, we are letting ourselves down.

I have no hang-ups. I like myself – the way I look, the way I am. I would never want to be any other way. I like being Black, I couldn't be another colour. Who wants to be another colour? I feel totally blessed in every way.

Stephen

I grew up in this country until I was nine – some of those years during the war – first in Shrewsbury, where I was born, and then in Essex. Then my parents moved to Singapore because my father was the Chief City Planner there – that is when I realised that there were more places in the world than

38

Brentwood in Essex. I loved Singapore; I went to the local Chinese rather than the expat school, and that made a huge difference to how I saw the world. It didn't do me any favours academically, but it did mean that I had an important experience in my childhood of being a minority in a society; there was only one other English person in the school. Singapore is a totally mixed society – there were Indians, Malaysians, Chinese, Americans: a real mixture. There was a colonial attitude, but my parents refused to get involved in the English Raj thing. They insisted that we had local friends and they integrated fully. So coming back and going into the closed world of a boys' boarding school, Highgate School, was very difficult after all this richness.

So my images of brown people were that they were very attractive, although my images of Africa were the usual ones and I must admit I am still a bit nervous when I meet groups of teenage Black boys. I think that comes from the fact that when I was in Singapore there was an uprising by the Communists. They started shooting at British administrators, farmers, and so on, and killed a few people. So I was aware of that kind of colonial struggle. When I came back to school here, the Mau Mau struggle was on and when you read stories about people being hacked to death, you do feel threatened in a way.

But colour never occurs to me when I am looking at a relationship, just whether the person is attractive or not. Patti was the first Black woman I had ever had a relationship with, but for me she was just a very attractive woman, nothing at all to do with her being Black.

When I met her, I was quite happily married. I had already been divorced so I wasn't terribly keen to get divorced again. I was running a theatre where Patti was appearing and noticed how attractive she was. For eighteen months I was very aware of her, but I decided that I must avoid her or there *would* be trouble. But before going home I used to watch her singing this beautiful number from *The Black Mikado* and I was deeply struck. But that was it. Later, when I was making an album, I asked Patti to work on it and it went on from there.

I don't know if my marrying Patti was an issue for my family. They haven't mentioned it, perhaps because of my attitude. After we started our relationship, times were torturous. I tried to stop the relationship, or rather myself, but by that time Patti was already pregnant. Even when she had the baby, I tried to stay with my other life. It was a very difficult thing to leave one family and start life with a new one. It was and is dreadful, I know I have damaged the children and I feel very bad about it. So the fact that we were different races didn't come into it. With all that was going on, the fact that Patti was Black was the last thing on their minds. As for my friends, I have no friends. Patti is my friend; I am not a 'friends' person.

Her being Black is not a problem, although I do sometimes find it difficult to deal with some of the male members of her family. I find them difficult to get on with and they find me difficult. But that isn't to do with being Black. Some of them are teenagers and are naturally aggressive and rebellious.

Patti got me back to the Church. We were originally Catholics, then my parents changed to the Church of England, so I was Church of England – or probably agnostic – by the time I met her. She used to drag me with her and I was rather impressed by her nature and attitudes, which I related to her Catholic upbringing – that natural sort of faith which produces a deep quietness and self-confidence, because there is always something to fall back on.

Men do find her terribly attractive, especially white men. I know it is there, but I don't react to it; in fact I am quite immune to it. It is lust, I suppose. Part of it comes from the simple fact that Patti is very attractive, but as a Black woman maybe she evokes some folk memories in white men: of slavery, of Black women being available, being forced. I think that, maybe, is what makes a lot of white men sexually attracted to Black women – they were slaves; you could do what you liked to them. And of course because Patti is on the stage, all this is heightened because she is the centre of attraction.

40

Some funny things have happened. I was once standing watching Patti on stage, and the man standing next to me turned to me and said, 'I would really like to give her one.' I turned to him and said, 'Well, I frequently do!' I didn't say anything else. It suddenly dawned on him what I meant and halfway through the show, he came up to me and apologised. I suppose because she is so attractive I expect this sort of thing anyway, and don't get jealous. But I don't expect her to get abuse, and when Patti comes back and talks about some foul-mouthed taxi driver, I am really surprised. I expect them to look at her and not think 'Look, she is Black' but 'Look how pretty she is.' Prejudice surprises me and when we come across it I tend not to believe it, which irritates Patti. I tend to find some other reason, which of course it could be.

I have had a lot of experience in my life. I have worked for myself and gone through all sorts of businesses. I know about the system and how to get through it better than Patti does, which she finds useful. I also feel that because she is Black, she is more vulnerable because there are the 10 per cent of people out there who are idiotic, so there is always a risk that something could happen – that she is at greater risk than if she wasn't Black and so attractive. I want to protect her from it but it is very hard to do, because you can't be there all the time and often it's just hurtful remarks, usually made out of ignorance.

We do divide on Black and white lines on South Africa. I am very impressed by de Klerk and what he is doing and feel this should be encouraged. I have a great dislike for Winnie Mandela. I think she is dangerous and will do nothing but harm to everybody, including her own people. Patti can't see this and whenever she sees something which says Mrs Mandela is guilty she will immediately assume that it is white propaganda.

We do occasionally have cultural differences, but that is almost always a question of language. It is a question of difference. People come and stay, for example, and there is no idea of privacy in the way that we have – bedrooms are open and people walk in and out; space has a different meaning.

We have had only a couple of rows in the entire fourteen years we have been together. I am quite tolerant – or maybe a better description would be conceited. I don't really care what anybody thinks, so I can ignore other people's foibles. I find Patti's view of the world and her relationship with the family very interesting. It is different, and it is enhancing to see the contrast between our lives.

Zerbanoo and Richard Gifford

Zerbanoo Gifford was born in India in 1950 and came to Britain at the age of three. She was educated at Roedean and the Watford College of Technology. In 1982 she was elected on to Harrow Council and has twice contested parliamentary seats. She has chaired the Liberal Party's Community Relations Panel and their 1986 Commission looking into ethnic minority involvement in British life. She is now Adviser in Community Affairs to the Right Honourable Paddy Ashdown MP, leader of the Liberal Democrats. She is the author of *The Golden Thread – Asian experiences in Post-Raj Britain*.

Richard Gifford, whose nominal ancestors arrived in England with William the Conqueror, was educated at King Edward VI School, Norwich, before reading law at Trinity Hall Cambridge. As a senior partner in a solicitors' firm Richard specialises in litigation and private client work, representing clients from all corners of the world in civil disputes, divorce, nationality and international claims.

Zerbanoo and Richard Gifford have two sons, aged fifteen and twelve.

Zerbanoo

We met at my twenty-first birthday party. I don't believe in testing and trying; if you test and try too often you get dissatisfied. I knew exactly what I wanted, and Richard was it. I felt as though we had been friends for lifetimes – this was just another lifetime together.

Marrying Richard was the very best thing I ever did. We went out together for about two years because he wanted to be quite sure. I think he was more cautious than me – I was sure from the beginning. Who you marry is the most important decision you make in life. How people can go into marriage thinking 'We can divorce' is quite incomprehensible – for me it is for eternity.

The fact that he was white British and I was Asian was an issue; that's why we waited. I didn't have any reservations but I think there is a fear that it has to be successful, you can't let it be a failure, there's so much more pressure on you. Although if a marriage doesn't succeed, it's usually to do with individual incompatibility and not so much with culture.

Richard thinks culture does make a difference and that our psyches are different. Having been brought up in this country, I have the same sense of humour and the same expectations of life. But the basic discipline in the mind, the way I think and verbalise and perceive the world, is still slightly different. Richard won't have any talk of astrology, it's a very Indian thing. Most Asians will talk about their Kismet [destiny]. In India when they read my stars they always say how lucky I am. They say it was my good Karma – good luck – that brought my parents to this country. Only the fortunate come to England.

I feel I had to come here to marry Richard. He'll laugh and tell you he married me because I was such excitement. I think it was inevitable. He's made me so happy. I don't think anyone else could have made me happy like this. For many people the next best thing to God is an Englishman, and when I say Englishman I mean an English gentleman – Richard is what you would typify as an English gentleman. He's a civilised man. I don't think anyone else would have allowed me the freedom to do the things I want to do, and the trust. The first summer after we got married I went off to

43

China by myself; everyone was shocked, even his parents. But he never questioned my decision to go.

Everybody would have liked me to marry a Zoroastrian, but I never found anyone I remotely liked. When I started seeing Richard my mother was very good – I think she thought it might wear off, she was very sensible. But at the end of the day both my parents are sensible and my father now says Richard is the perfect son-in-law: if only he was a Zoroastrian! In The *Sunday Times* recently he talked about his original sense of shock that I had married an 'outsider'. I said to him, 'I don't think you understand – *we're the outsiders.*'

My father didn't attend my wedding because he wanted me to marry a Zoroastrian. He was the Founder President of the World Zoroastrian Organisation and he's very religious, very orthodox. I would have liked him to be there, but instead his elder brother, my uncle, gave me away. I was determined to have a religious wedding, I didn't feel I was married unless we had been blessed by God with our friends and family there. We couldn't have a Zoroastrian wedding so we had a Christian one, a church wedding at St Mary's, Harrow-on-the-Hill. Having been brought up in school here, going to chapel every day, it was all very familiar.

It was years later, after Mark was born, that my father came round – I didn't see him at all during that time, although now we're terribly close to him. But I made it quite clear that the most important person to me was my husband, there was no allegiance to anyone else; if I had to make a choice, it was my husband.

His process of coming round was a gradual one of seeing that we were happy, we stayed together, and we've done something worthwhile in life. We haven't just been self-obsessed. I don't think my father was worried about me losing my identity, I've always known my heritage. I think he might have worried about Richard leaving me, us having children, me being stranded. The point is that if you marry into your own community, you have a sort of control: everyone knows who you are and there's a support network.

If you marry out, you make your own bed. I realised that once I left home, that was it. Life is not neat. If there is no tension or vulnerability, the relationship is not really meaningful.

Of course you can make a mistake, even now everything is evolving and changing, you might have a happy marriage and tomorrow something may change – who knows? Anything might happen. So you cherish the days you have and enjoy it. You can never be too sure of anything.

I knew everyone would think Richard was marvellous. After we were married we went to India. My grandmother, who's dead now, thought he was wonderful, and that was what mattered.

And the differences can be challenging. Our thought processes are different. I'm very lateral in the way I think – I think in stories, in concepts. Richard thinks in words; his thought processes are linear. I think Asians live in a sense of muddle and chaos but there is a discipline to it, that keeps it all together.

Another thing Richard had to get used to is that there is little concept of privacy in India. When we were there everyone would walk into the bedroom and Richard would say, 'What is this?' In India there's not enough space; in England everyone has their own private bedroom, time to be on your own. When we first got married, we always had an open house, always had people to stay. Initially he was intrigued and would ask what was happening. I'd say, 'This is a *dharmsala* [free hostel], you've just got to accept it.' Now he expects it.

Both our psyches have shifted slightly to accommodate the other as time has gone on. You can treat differences either positively or negatively, it's up to you. If you want to see life negatively, then you're going to be miserable. I've never expected other people to do things for me. If there's discrimination, I think you should get off your own butt and change it. If you wait for somebody else, nothing will ever happen.

As for how the children were going to be brought up, I

never positively decided anything. Take religion: it just evolved. Mark, the eldest, is going to do religious studies for A level, but didn't want to learn Zoroastrian prayers. The younger one, Wags, is learning Zoroastrian prayers. He wanted the story of Zoroaster painted on his bedroom wall, and he is a Zoroastrian. In the same sense, I cannot help being a Zoroastrian, I do see life as fighting evil. If there's racism, ignorance or greed, I see myself as being here to challenge and change it.

I've never been concerned about racism and my children. We have had racial attacks. We've had police guards, break-ins, death threats, telephone calls, my car nearly pushed off the road during the last election. I was spat upon in the road and called 'nigger lover' and Richard was asked what it was like sleeping with someone like me.

When it first happened I went to my father, I was quite shaken and I had to make a decision. I was a mother with young children. My father said that nobody would think any the less of me if I gave up politics, but, he added, 'If you do you will never be able to do anything in public life. You've dedicated your life to fighting evil and this is a form of evil.' Once I'd decided, that was it.

Richard was wonderful about the attacks, but if he ever asked me to give up politics, I would do it tomorrow. He thinks just taking the stand with these people is important. We both know if they really want to get rid of you they can.

The kids went through it too, but I cannot be a crybaby politician. You have to accept that if you're in public life, you are a target of nutters and racists. People think racial attacks happen only to Bangladeshis in the East End of London; they don't understand that it happens to middle-class people. In fact it was cleansing to go public about what was happening. I didn't for a long time because I didn't want people to say, 'Asians go into politics and then give up at the least difficulty.'

Richard comes to all the Asian functions – he's an honorary Asian. They all say to me, 'We know he's an Englishman, he's a perfect gentleman, but he's really an Indian, isn't he?'

I think we're both at ease in two cultures. I go to English functions in a sari or in whatever I want to wear. If you're relaxed then other people are relaxed. If you're very tense and worried then they get the vibrations.

Is our 'mixed marriage' a positive thing for others? I could say, 'Oh yes of course, we're bringing two cultures together', but at the end of the day you're two individuals and that's what matters. You can be at ease in two cultures, but it's being at ease with each other that matters. We're very happy and I can't think of anything better than being married to an Englishman.

I would not have done what I have, or been what I am, without Richard – not because he's given me permission, but because he's allowed me to grow. I don't think I would have found someone from my own community who would have nurtured me – I would have probably been 'allowed' to do it, but not by someone who would have directed me along the right road, someone who saw my qualities. I know the only thing that matters is a happy marriage. Winning elections, writing bestsellers – everything else is outside it.

I think it's important that on the 'Eastern Eye' programme I said openly that it was the best thing I ever did to marry Richard. A lot of people wrote and said that they were married to English people and how pleased they were for someone to say positive things about it.

Even my own community will now write about us, which caused a big stir because it's very inward-looking. They won't ever write about anyone who hasn't married a Parsee. But I've made it quite clear that for photos, etc., it has to be the whole family. It's a slow process of educating people, it's fear of the unknown again.

I think the eighties were an era dominated by Thatcher, 'Pride and Prejudice'. And that was true of all cultures. You thought your culture was the best and felt prejudiced towards others. Now we're going into the nineties and 'Sense and Sensibility', where you look at other people and see what's good in others and the commonality. That is difficult because it is a more sensitive approach and requires more understanding, more confidence.

I hope a marriage like ours helps people develop a greater understanding. A lot of people are now interested in Zoroastrianism and want to know about my culture – and know about Asians. That's nice; they get a different viewpoint which they wouldn't have had. People always say to me, 'You can't be Indian, you're not like them.' It seems like a compliment, but in fact it's very insulting. I always tell them, 'It's because you know me – when you know "them", whoever "they" are, then you'll understand.'

I don't see that I have to get acceptance from anybody for the man I marry. If it's that important to people to be accepted, that's their problem. The Asian community are going to admire you and accept you only if you're somebody.

Having said all that, when I was told by an astrologer that one of my sons would marry a Zoroastrian I was absolutely over the moon. Now, after all these years, it is still so instinctual. I found it very comforting and it amused me that I was comforted – I thought it would be like having my own daughter.

Richard

Zerbanoo is an original in anybody's language or scale of values. There's a history of them in her family, a strain of oddballs. She's immediately attractive and a dynamic personality, an extrovert who galvanises and motivates people. Essentially there's a vitality in her family, which is partly individual, the mix of genes, but also cultural in their views about society, being an immigrant community in India and on the fringes of English society.

It seems to me that there's one basic thing that applies to mixed marriages – that it satisfies the instinct for what the anthropologists call exogamy, which is to cast your genetic net wider than the immediate circle. That instinct is about more than the desire to open frontiers to explore and examine something fresh and different. It is as basic an instinct as the infant suckling on his mother's breast, it's inbuilt and has nothing to do with choice or decision. It derives from the basic need to reproduce outside your immediate peer group purely in order to preserve the genetic stock. I am very conscious of broadening the gene pool in a very wide and comprehensive way.

Zerbanoo's community is extremely intermarried, they are very exclusive, they can't marry out and children of those who do are not accepted into the religion. So it was extremely difficult for her to marry outside her religion. They've never accepted any kind of convert into the religion since the days of the old Persian emperors.

When I met Zerbanoo she was twenty-one, and very anglicised; she'd lived here since she was three and at that stage had little concept, I think, of culture and community. Her group was basically English. Her very acute sense of community really has developed since we got married. Now she spends a great deal of time and mental energy thinking about Asians in England, India and around the world. That involvement, in retrospect, was partly a function of us getting married. It was cause and effect; she felt the need to reidentify with her cultural roots. It's been rewarding and enriching for her. She has built up a great presence in India and is seen as a bridge between the two communities.

It didn't really concern my family too much who I married. They take the rational, liberal humanist approach that it's up to the individual to establish his own destiny. My mother, who is religious, took the view that she was there only to achieve the happiness of her boys. But she made it her business to get on with Zerbanoo even though she found things puzzling because she is a little more reserved. My father, who was a good deal older than my mother, was a little troubled and didn't take to things very easily.

There was no opposition at all to me from the community here; the only people who were unhappy about it were the two fathers. My father is quite elderly now and I'm extremely fond of him, but he was brought up in a different age and way of thinking where things weren't as international – you stuck to your own. He was no doubt brought up to think that the English education and way of life was the finest in the world, a hangover from the days of empire when everybody was a little suspicious of anything that didn't fit in. I think he had a slightly cynical, rather unenlightened view about how Asian girls would be delighted to marry Englishmen. You invest your own beliefs with a far greater significance than they have and feel you're doing everybody else a favour. He's fine now.

Zerbanoo's father had real difficulties too. He had a very intense sense of community and it was unheard of for anyone in his family to marry out. It was very upsetting for him. When I asked him if I could marry his daughter he was quite shocked. To be fair to him, he was extremely decent and kind and never hostile. He didn't say it was a matter of shame, but I've no doubt he felt it. And he felt he had lost a daughter. But he took the view that his daughter's happiness was her own decision, even though he couldn't condone what was happening. Her mother was very sweet and helpful and supportive.

It is a tough way to start a marriage, without both fathers' support, but it's part of the process of making your own life and your own decisions; you have to leave something of your background behind. It's not really different in kind from any other marriage, just in degree. You say, 'I'm acquiring a new perspective, I'm acquiring a different way of thinking and a vast family spread across the world.'

When we got married and went round India, the family is so Anglophile that it was regarded as natural and positive that she should have married an Englishman. It was fascinating becoming part of the family and community, an incredible experience for me. After our wedding we were fêted in a way that people just don't do over here.

On the level of things like privacy it was a culture shock. And there is quite a cultural divide because if you're brought up in India you're used to tolerating muddle and mess and social decay and starvation. Things don't work in an ordered manner. You don't believe that administration works, for example, because administration doesn't work – maybe because the resources aren't there and the administrative mind isn't the same.

We're all a product of our culture, and Zerbanoo's culture imposes very little in terms of intellectual restraints. You are not tied to preconceived patterns, you go and do it. With my upbringing and temperament it's a completely different mental process. But I have to say that I regard personality as infinitely more important than culture. It wasn't really of any concern to me that Zerbanoo came from a different culture or religion. Coming from a Free Church liberal tradition, I wasn't bothered at all by the fact that my intended wife had a different religion. It happens to be monotheistic, they happen to be related, so we're not talking about somebody with a tribal concept of God.

If, for example, I'd fallen in love with a Hindu girl, I think I would have had considerable intellectual difficulty grasping what might have been at the back of my wife's brain. As it is, the Zoroastrian religion is based on good thoughts, good words and good deeds, and the idea that there is an everlasting struggle between good and evil. These are such easily recognisable Old Testament concepts that you don't have any worry at all that your spouse is wrestling with odd deities.

If Zerbanoo came from a mainstream religion there might have been more difficulty, but basically she comes from a sort of boutiquey religion – maybe seminal is a better word – of a microcosmic community, delightful, charming and cultivated. I couldn't have coped with a relationship where the other person expected me to become involved in their religion – I would never expect anyone else to do that. Religion is so much a part of upbringing, you can't possibly change it. I find changing religion as a gesture to the other person's culture very odd. It makes you wonder whether people fundamentally believe in anything. I find it extraordinary, for example, how a Hindu could convert and become Muslim in order to marry a Muslim. And I cannot understand people who turn native, people who marry spouses from different parts of the world and take it all on, even moving there.

It is fascinating to see how different values, a view of the universe, translates into day-to-day concepts, actions, thoughts and motives. People like Zerbanoo and her father really see life as a struggle between good and evil. It's a daily driving force. Zerbanoo also has what very few people have: a pride in projecting her own inheritance. She doesn't pretend to be anything that she isn't and takes pride in telling strangers about Zoroastrianism. You always find that because she's so positive about it, people are interested.

She goes in for the extended family. Although she comes from a very small community, the links worldwide are tight and humming. Every day she'll be on the telephone to relatives in Poona or New York or Florida or Bombay. I telephone my dear mum, whom I'm extremely fond of, once a fortnight, and go and see my family maybe once a month and they're only one hundred miles down the road. That is all quite refreshing. I did get to think that decent middle-class Nonconformist people in semi-detached houses really didn't know an awful lot.

The racial attacks were very worrying. It was the first time anything like that had happened. It started almost immediately she was adopted as a candidate for the seat in Hertsmere in 1983. She was adopted on a Thursday. On the Saturday I took the boys to Norwich and from that night on she started getting dreadful phone calls. It was a sniping thing; they would get her when I'd left for the office, I was never the recipient of any of the calls and knew about it only from the dreadful effect they had on her. Her calls would be interrupted, presumably by someone who worked in BT, because someone would cut into the call, and threaten to kill her.

The callers were almost certainly members of the British National Party who had their HQ in Watford, close to Hertsmere. They knew exactly what all her movements were. It was all racist abuse: 'We don't want fucking wogs in

Parliament, we're going to come and slice you up and kill your children, we know where they go to school, etc.'

Zerbanoo is very sensitive but was extremely courageous and realised she had to see it through for the sake of race relations in this country. In the end they backed off because she stood her ground. It made me wild, I was dying to tape-record the conversations and track the person. One of the difficulties was that Zerbanoo was always so terrified of contemplating a method of coping with it, she didn't want to know, although at one stage we had a break-in where a death threat was left and the police managed to get finger-prints.

I think our marriage makes people who are sympathetic to it become more so, and people who are basically suspicious or hostile become more so. It might help to change people's minds, but probably subliminally. I don't think most people are hostile on principle. I don't think they object to a mixed marriage as such. They evaluate these things on the basis of their own preferences. Zerbanoo is so charming that no one has ever said, or even intimated, 'Why have you married someone of a different race?' I suppose it might have been different if I'd married someone very different – from the Caribbean, for example.

Elean Thomas-Gifford and Tony Gifford

Elean Thomas-Gifford, who is Jamaican, is a radical journal-ist, campaigner, poet and novelist. Her work includes her prizewinning first novel, *The Last Room*. She is married to Lord Gifford, who is a Queen's Counsel, well known for his defence work with the disadvantaged members of the com-munity, including Black people, Travellers and gay people. He was one of the barristers involved in the Birmingham Six case which resulted in the acquittal of the six Irishmen who had spent over twenty years in prison for bombing a pub in Birmingham. The Giffords now live in Jamaica.

Elean

Tony and I love each other. We have many joyous times together. Yet had I been born, grown up or lived in England for any extended period, we might never have met in a non-antagonistic way. Such is the distortion of human relations which inevitably arises in everyday-racist societies. As it was we met in the Caribbean, in Jamaica and, I think, had a better atmosphere and social environment in which to assess each other's worth as human beings.

This is not to say that racism does not exist in the Caribbean. Racism has been institutionalised over some five hundred years as an international phenomenon by white European enslavement and colonisation of African and the majority of coloured peoples of the world. In the Caribbean, and in Jamaica in particular, racial discrimination is further complicated by a hierarchy of 'shades'; a reality which is reflected in the saying:

> 'If you White – you right
> If you Brown – stick around
> If you Black – stay back.'

At the same time, there is a difference. Black Jamaicans are the majority in our country. My experience of living in England confirms that it is much more possible for a Black Jamaican child living in Jamaica to aspire to and achieve any position in that society than it is for a Black child living in England. Also, European racist culture is undermined by a more humanistic African culture, which is still strong in the Caribbean.

And it does make a difference to our sense of security, to the mind-images of our hopes and aspirations. To our achievement of self-knowledge. To our greater willingness to accept people just as human beings and to judge them on their individual merits or demerits.

Tony and I first met in the heat of the aftermath of the United States invasion of Granada, which itself had been followed by the split in the New Jewel Movement (Grenada's governing party) and the traumatic, fatal events of 19 October 1983, when Prime Minister Maurice Bishop, Jacqueline Creft and others, including children, were killed. I had been in Grenada during the American invasion and on my return to Jamaica I worked with others to bring together a Committee for Human Rights in Grenada. At that time about 3–4,000 of that island's population of 110,000 were interned in concentration camps by the American forces. It was very difficult to get the attention of influential people because very few people cared. I had even then come to learn that it is at such times, when the whole world seems to turn its back, that help is most crucially needed. Tony had gone to help when it was not fashionable to help, and he had accepted our Committee's invitation to come on to Jamaica and let people there know what was happening in our sister island. His courage impressed me tremendously.

Up to that time a British 'Lord' was, in my mind, some old codger, laden down with the blood, guilt and the stolen wealth of my people. It didn't take me long to realise that Tony was different. He was not only a normal human being but also one whom people who knew him could not help liking. We were friends and comrades for over three years before we had to face the fact that there was something more there.

I myself agonised about this reality of feelings for nearly a year. I was living in Europe by then, and everywhere around me were the 'monuments' of the plunder of my people – the European pirate-heroes, the slave-built castles and the continuation of the subjection of the Black and coloured peoples. Tony wanted to get married from the moment he realised how we felt about each other. He said he didn't want anyone to be confused that this was the slave-plantation type of situation all over again.

I was never the marrying kind. Not that I did not think that I needed a close, loving relationship with a partner, but I was not willing to pay the cost where this meant suppression of myself, my own creativity, my development, to become some wifely appendage. I never did accept (and still don't) that my mission in life was to nurture, to fetch, carry, clean, cook and be nurse for some man, in the name of 'love' and marriage.

But then, the decision that was facing me was complicated not only by the gender element but also by the race and class element. By now (1987) I knew that Tony was a good man. I knew that I admired him deeply. I knew that I was attracted to him, sexually and otherwise. I liked his keen mind. I could be myself with him. I liked the things that he loved about me – some of which had made other men feel 'intimidated'. I remember, on one of our first visits to Jamaica as a couple, having a raging debate at the university bar with a male lecturer. When I wouldn't accept what he was saying to me and held my ground strongly, the man turned to Tony in male solidarity and said: 'How can you stand to deal with this woman?!' Tony looked at him with a smile and answered: 'I don't "deal" with her, I love her and live with her.'

I had seen this in him from early on, but I still agonised over the decision to commit myself to him in that way.

Here, the intervention of three close friends helped me a lot to clear up the issues in my own mind. One said: 'Elean, he is a good man but no matter how good he be, you can't make people know that you going with a white man. If it was me, I would meet him in private.' The other said: 'You can kiss goodbye to your political career if you marry this man. Oh yes, everybody who knows him knows that he a good comrade. But that is quite a different thing from him being your lover or husband. Black people would believe you sell them out.' The third friend said: 'You know, Elean, I have never seen you like this about a man before. You must love this man. Tell me, if he had all the qualities which you have seen in him in a Black skin and from a different class, what would you do?'

'I would grab him,' I answered. 'Well? . . .' my friend said, and rested his case.

The rest is now history. We were married in my father's church in Kingston, Jamaica. Only the questions I grappled with then are not questions which are answered once and for all time. Because in a Black–white relationship, despite whatever deep feelings bond the two together, the relationship is being tested almost on a daily basis. A decision as to where to live and where not to live is determined not only by your economic circumstances but also by the racial and social environment of the particular neighbourhood. I myself believe that mixed couples who choose to live in all-white neighbourhoods either have a death-wish for their relationship or the Black partner nurtures a need for self-suicide. One of the things which worries me about some of the mixed couples I've seen is how much the white culture dominates the African culture even in the home. This becomes most marked in the raising of the children, where the mother is the white partner.

The truth is that white people have been moulded over hundreds of years into a culture that is not only racist but also mechanistic (as against spiritual), materialistic and anti-human. While many Black people have also been reared on and adopted this culture, it is not of our essence. And one of the main ways that this culture persists even in good white people is in the conviction that their ways of thinking, acting and doing things are inherently better than ours.

Tony's and my relationship could not survive, and will not survive, unless we are totally honest with each other on all the really fundamental things. First of all, we talk about racism together – not only as something 'out there' which negatively affects my people but also as something 'in here', inside the relationship. I do not hide my pain from him, and I do not hide my rage from him. I once told a very dear white friend of mine that she cannot really consider herself friends with a Black person unless that person exposes her/his pain to her. If the friendship survives this, then it will be firmly rooted.

I do not pretend that I like castles because he likes them. I respect his family and friends but I treat each of them as an individual whom I like, dislike or am indifferent to. I have never known him to be consciously racist but there have been times when he has not been quick enough in recognising racism in its myriad forms and acting accordingly. For instance, it was quite a shock for him when he saw how racist some of his 'right-on' political associates were. I think that more intimate contact with my people and me have helped to develop his own genuine humanism and at the same time he can recognise more those of his own people – and my people too – who possess this quality, whatever their class or gender.

I have also learnt a lot from him. I have been put in contact with many true-hearted people by him – Black and white. By his own example, he has taught me to strive for more personal discipline as an integral requirement for the attainment of one's goals. Despite my many years of schooling, including in a subject called Geography, it was he who taught me how to read a map. He has taught me to be more tolerant of people because he always strives to see the good side of a person.

In our relationship, I have found that honesty and a genuine caring for each other are indispensable. It is not a 'storybook' relationship. It is a working-through-together of the difficulties, a sharing of the joys, while at the same time realising that not all one's journeys and not all one's space can be shared with each other.

Jamaica is a good place for us to be and a base from which to continue our mutual and individual growth. Jamaica is not a beach/palm-tree/marijuana/dreadlocks/reggae-music 'ethnic' paradise, as some people stereotype it. It is a country, just like any other, and at the same time it is a place of contrasts and extremes. The life is very real here. People are very real here. And anyone who seeks freedom, in the sense of the liberation of the mind and the spirit, can find it in Jamaica.

That is why we are here.

Tony

I was born to two very kind people. My mother was the daughter of a leading Australian family, so that although there was a lot of privilege in her background there was a lack of stuffiness. My father was an extraordinary man with great humanity, a liberal Tory who, although he went to Cambridge and public school, thought public-school attitudes were appalling. Having said that, I admit that they were also prisoners of their class and surroundings. We lived in the South of England in a comfortable house, not lords in the sense that you might imagine. They were both liberals, but ironically, that branch of the family were also terrible imperialists. On account of that I was recently moved to tender my apologies to the Queen Mother of the Ashantis when I was over there with my wife because one of my ancestors led the British army which slaughtered a group of these wonderful, proud people.

To understand the decision to get married to Elean, who is a strong Black woman, you have to go quite a long time back into my own life. You have to understand that my marriage, my decision to go and live in Jamaica, is not something that just happened; it grew out of an approach to life that had been developing in me over the years. And meeting Elean and feeling as I do about her has been, in a sense, a climax to that.

It probably started with the influence of the Mozambique Liberation Front (FRELIMO), for whom I had worked. That, together with legal work in Notting Hill in the late sixties which got me involved with the British Black community, started changes which have gone on ever since. I think the first had already influenced the second; these things happen cumulatively. Maybe the reason why my approach was already different from that of some other progressive lawyers working in those sorts of areas was that I also had an African grounding from very close relationships with FRELIMO. In 1966, in the fascist days, Amnesty International sent me to Portugal to observe a trial. That made me examine the situation in the Portuguese colonies, and my interest in the area grew. I was then asked by FRELIMO to form a solidarity group in this country and look after their interests. It was felt that people were so abysmally ignorant about what was going on that they needed to be informed and involved.

It was an extraordinary period. FRELIMO were making enormous advances through Mozambique and a delegation of our Committee were asked to march with them into the liberated areas and actually see the life, the new society, they were trying to build behind the lines. So it wasn't just solidarity at a distance, but a close involvement with a group of people whose ideas were so obviously right and carried out in such a human and caring way that it gave me a kind of friendship and comradeship with Black people on a footing of total equality. That was very important, because so many Black–white political relationships, let alone personal ones, are so one-sided and patronising, they really can't grow.

I met Elean, who is my second wife, through Grenada. After the American invasion in 1983, I was asked to go to Grenada to act for dozens of people who had been detained without trial. Although they didn't admit me to the Bar, I worked with a Jamaican lawyer and we had some effect – we took habeas corpus actions and put a lot of legal pressure on to secure their release. I went on to Jamaica to report on the trip.

Elean, through her work as a journalist and her previous involvement with Grenada, was the organiser of that visit. Soon afterwards she went to Prague to work as one of the editorial board of an international magazine. She visited Britain quite often, and we became friends. For three years we didn't have any relationship other than as people who very much admired each other. I assumed that she would eventually go back to Jamaica. My first marriage had broken up just before the Grenada visit.

One thing I was very clear about as soon as it was apparent that Elean and I were going to spend the rest of our lives together was that we were going to be married. Marriage is a statement which cuts through any idea that people are going to throw at you that you are just taking a Black woman for some fun, as a mistress. It would have been unacceptable, here or in international circles or in the Caribbean world, to have any other kind of status. And we knew how we felt about each other and what that meant.

Because of my background, my marrying Elean and moving to Jamaica was in a sense also a statement about where I wanted the direction of my life to be. I had spent so much of my life working at one remove with people in the Third World that the move to actually live there was just a climax of that.

I am very aware that it is a Black–white relationship – particularly in Britain, less so in Jamaica. Jamaica is a more human place, a place where people are more ready to respond to you for who you are, not as a stereotype. Once it was clear that I was not there as some superior white person who thinks he owns the world and that I deal with people in a normal way, people dealt with me in a normal way. Jamaica is full of laughter, courtesy and an intensity which I love.

People in this country are different, and we have seen this very markedly in the last three years, particularly in the way many have responded to our marriage. Some of the more gossipy people – including some of my friends and acquaint-ances – have, in some cases, reacted extremely badly. Others have reacted in that rather neutral way which tells you a lot. Nowadays many of our close friendships in England are with Black people, but there are wonderful exceptions who have stuck with us through thick and thin.

One of the funny but saddening experiences in Jamaica is to listen to people recounting their experiences while visiting Britain. Everyone will tell you the most ridiculous stories, stories which would be ridiculous if they weren't tragic – about the way they were treated, particularly by people who should know better. People far preferred to go to the United States.

Once the decision to move to Jamaica came out in the open, it seemed to be so obviously right. Anyone not born in England can see what a sensible thing it is, but a lot of my white English friends think it is rather extraordinary. For white Britons it is a problem and a reflection of how they see Britain and Europe as the centre of the world – that somehow, although we can go to Jamaica for holidays and show solidarity with the ANC, we have a position of superiority. So many, even enlightened white people don't open their eyes to learn; they think they know better. I have appreciated this much more since being with Elean – the approach is always 'How can we help you?', 'Is there anything we can do?' Never the other way round. I think it is about time people started to reverse that, and if my going and how I fit in there serve to show that a different relationship is possible in this shrinking, multinational world, then so much the better.

Of course many people don't understand the seriousness of our decision – some probably think I am less than sane. Not that they would say that openly. Many white friends have said things like 'Oh, you are such a loss,' or 'You are so irreplaceable' or 'Why are you leaving us?' There is also a kind of envy that comes into it: 'Did you have a nice holiday in Jamaica?' or 'You don't look very brown.' As if the purpose is just to get a good tan.

In this situation, the white member of the partnership almost has to see himself or herself as a Black person. Elean said this to me and at first I didn't understand, but I am beginning to. People haven't been able to marginalise me professionally. Politically they would have done so anyway and personally there has been some sort of unspoken distancing. I am trying to speculate what people are thinking and that is very difficult, because these views are so extraordinary and a denial of a loving relationship.

So I think the white member of the partnership has to recognise that all the natural humanity evidenced in your relationship is in fact not shared by the vast bulk of your own people, although it is shared by your partner's people. In spite of this, I think what I am saying is positive rather than negative, because you have to enter into that spirit, to embrace it and be prepared to be loved by the people who *do* cherish the relationship. One of the most exciting things for me has been the amount of warmth and love that has come from people, many of whom were already my friends, clients or colleagues in the Black community, who have become rock-solid friends.

This is a very significant change from what happened before in Black–white relationships. It used to be assumed that the world of the white partner would dominate, but that is no longer the case. A number of those sixties relationships imploded because of the strain placed on the Black partner. That way of doing things, while people had no option, was a product of a racist approach to society, which the couple couldn't challenge except by the statement they were making to each other.

All this means that Elean and I have a very equal relationship. For me a relationship is possible if within it people are able to be strong, not dominated. A good relationship must allow people to grow into something and have the chance to feel that strength, and help each other build up that strength on both sides. That has definitely happened to us. But this could lead to a whole new conversation about man–woman relationships and how it is normally the woman who has to subordinate herself, and with mixed relationships it is the woman who has to move to the white country, or to the white area and to the white way of life, and that is an unbalanced attitude not just towards race but also towards gender.

Meeting and marrying Elean has undoubtedly been life-enhancing for me, in the broadest terms. We have a deep commitment to each other but also to a different and better way of looking at the world. When you then take that into Jamaica – and I am sure it would be the same in any Third World country where those values are shared by the larger community – something very important happens. I am not minimising any of the problems – the violence, the crime, the racketeering – but the dominant values are still very caring – deeply so. And that is less and less so in a country like Britain.

All this leads to a kind of evaluation of human relations and learning how people can treat one another. The people in Jamaica and Africa deal with you as they find you, without those stupid preconceptions and categorisings. In Jamaica people deal with me without putting me down or putting me up; it is a very equal and natural relationship. So you get by on your own merits. It seems that in these places human values like kindness and compassion have been retained, and this gives the people a great strength.

I think I will be better able to analyse what is going on in Britain when I am no longer part of it. One of the problems about living as part of a society when you are not personally oppressed by it is that you survive, you know you have your pursuits and you don't realise what you are doing. You are spending your life in a culture which is permeated with a terrible arrogance and inability to learn – even an inability to think that there is anything you *can* learn. That particularly exists among people who say that they are full of solidarity and socialism and support for the struggles of oppressed people. For example, it is only very recently that I have really understood the way many people deal with race. I had a number of colleagues and friends who seemed, intellectually, to be contributing far more to the race scene, writing learned books and 'right-on' articles, than I was. At first I was taken in by all this, until I realised that their human relationships with Black people were all wrong, they couldn't extend it to their emotional lives. Isn't it surprising that people cannot just behave in a human way? But I think it is because of the impact of centuries of indoctrination and education and the way in which you are brought up to think that and to take these attitudes about Black people.

There is nothing about being English that I miss, nothing deep that I feel attached to. Last winter, when we were in Jamaica for a few months, the only thing I missed was the family, my children and my mother. Institutionally, I didn't miss anything. This is probably because my English roots are a little shallow – commuter belt and public school are not exactly a solid footing, especially as I rejected most of those values and have spent a lot of my life trying to change unjust and antihuman aspects of England. If I had been part of an English culture with genuinely deep roots, I would miss it, but I am going somewhere which will be supportive in every sense. The difference between the nuclear family and the extended family, for a start – the difference between living in a house with one person and children as opposed to living in a house with different generations, and other people, in a larger compound. It's a whole new world. I think I am finding a culture, not losing one.

2. Blind Prejudice

❛ *There are two types of reaction to you
as a couple. There are the remarks that you
have an opportunity to respond to, and then
there are the unspoken gestures and actions
that hurt the most.* ❜

– RIFAT WAHHAB

Ethal

Ethal was born in the North of England, the youngest of five children, four girls and one boy who was killed during the Second World War. She left home, came down to London and worked as a prostitute for several years. She is now in her late seventies and lives in an old people's home in the South of England.

You will change my name, won't you, and you won't tell them where I live? You see I am seventy now and I live here in this home, but they don't know nothing about me. But I have had a life, I tell you, a real life. Back then, when the war started and all those handsome men went off. My mother cleaned and my father was sickly for quite a long time. Then he died.

66

I had to leave home and come down to London, where there was no work. I did try. I remember feeling as if I was alone in the world. London was like that. I found a job with this gentleman, next to the lodgings; he was very kind, he introduced me to other nice gentlemen. I didn't walk the streets then, you know. But then he died and I had to leave. But one of my customers was this Black gentleman – the first one I had ever had. He wore these polished shoes and looked after himself really well, and those hats! Harry was his name, I think. I think I fell in love with him a bit, but one didn't, you see, not with a Black, not even a girl like me. He used to visit me well into the night after he had been in one of their clubs, and he would tell me stories about the gambling and the drinking. He sang and the neighbour didn't like that. Not one bit. He didn't come back one day and that was that. Then things were rough and I had a few Black sailors and even an Indian sailor who didn't speak any language and didn't know much about anything else either, you know? He was so skinny and had these dark hairy legs. I knew I couldn't tell my English customers about it, they wouldn't have liked it very much.

Then I met Frank. He was in the RAF, a dashing pilot, from Jamaica I think. He spoke so posh and he would bring me flowers and treated me like a lady all the time. He had a lot of money to throw away and he hated it in the service. But I knew he was getting attached. Anyway, a few months later I knew I was . . . you know . . . in the family way. I didn't know for a long time and then when I did I couldn't get rid of it. I was a Catholic, you see, my mother was. I didn't know whose it was. But when it was born it was as black as soot. They were shocked, all of them. I was too. I couldn't even hold him. I told Frank and he was a gentleman. Others would have run away. I was going to put the little one up for adoption, but Frank would have none of it. He called his mother over and we all lived together in this small place, there was no shutting of doors. She was a good woman. I couldn't understand what she was saying at first and then I fitted in. They were all marvellous to me – the aunts, the girls. The men would tease, but never flirt. I was Frank's girl. Nobody made me feel low.

The white neighbours took it rather badly. They would turn away when we came down pulling the pram. The children used to call me a 'nigger' and I saw such hate in the eyes of the women. I sometimes wish I could have told them how these people had helped me to find a family again. And my Black family was better dressed, though we could not get a decent place to stay then. They had those white gloves, those long nails, hats. And on Sunday they dressed in their best as they went out to church. I still couldn't get close to the boy, though. I didn't feel he had come from me. Mothers want their children to look at least a bit like them. He was just Frank's mother's boy, I think. He thought I was his aunt or something. Frank was good to him. But he was a good man. He suffered when the war was over. Couldn't get the work he wanted – he was an engineer and so proud. But all he could get were these low jobs. But he never thought he was too good for them. He worked and kept us all going. Me, the boy, his mother and sister. Then the uncle would come over sometimes. On Saturday the small place would be full of them and they would play cards and talk about back home.

At first I felt strange, a white woman living with Black folk. I think it was like changing colour. And I found the food and the noise terrible at first. But at the end I thought they were my people. And they were. I had no white friends. One friend, Martha, who used to be very nice, did come a couple of times but she soon stopped. I remember once going to a market with a group of West Indian women, and this man asked me why I was so white and did I have any white blood in the family! And I must have started talking a bit like them – you do, don't you?

Frank kept from them what I did before. Them being so religious, he didn't think it would go down very well. He used to say to me, 'Ethal, I see human beings. Others see what your job is and the colour of your skin.' He was marvellous. So wise, so educated. I often wondered what he was doing stuck with someone like me. I had never read a book. He would read all the time. But it was an honourable thing to do, to marry me. Not love, not the way it happened. But we did love each other after. I thought it was very funny. My white friends could accept me when I was a woman of the streets, you know, but not when I was married to a nice educated Black man. I hated the way the family was treated. At first I would say things in shops and cafés. But the insults would get worse, so I just gave up. I mean, we are supposed to be civilised and they were not – to me in my life it didn't look that way.

And I suppose people *were* shocked to see us all out together on a Sunday morning, dressed in our Sunday best, going to church. At first I found all that moving and singing in the church a bit funny, and I never really joined in, even at the end. I was the only white person there. But those people believed so much, they would cry, it was marvellous, simple real faith. I think all this made me more religious. They were good for me.

I am sure the family was disappointed that Frank didn't marry one of his own. I remember his mother showing me this old picture of a young West Indian girl standing outside on a balcony, with this swinging skirt on, she said it was one of his girlfriends a long time ago. I didn't feel jealous or angry. It wasn't like that for us, you see. You learn a bit about men when you have entertained them. You know that you can never get inside them. And all those promises are always broken, so I never had that much to expect.

I enjoyed my life in those days. We used to go to Black clubs and dance, I felt really quite proud on his arm there, when they called me his girl. Not like out on the streets. There were many of us white girls there, but I never became friends with any of them. I don't know why. Once when we were coming out of the club, a policeman, a big man, stopped us and asked what I was doing with 'the nigger'. He would not believe we were married and thought I was picking him up – it was funny when you think about it. And then he came to the house. I could tell he was really more shocked that I was married to him. Frank was so strong when this kind of thing happened. He would say nothing, but I could see how he was controlling himself. 'Yes sir', 'No sir', but his eyes were like red fire. Even when we got married in the registry office, they were all so shocked, you could see, nobody was smiling and when the registrar had to shake our hands it was like he was touching dirt.

Did I feel sad at the way white people treated me? Yes, sometimes. I remember when one woman had been very rude to me when I had the boy with me. She pulled her child away when she came to play with him, she said I was dirty and I really felt that. I cried when I got home – I think it was because of the children. I was used to being called names even before.

I think a lot about those days now and about how life has been. I have always been outside, you know, not a part of anything. Not because I wanted to, it just happened like that. When I saw the gentlemen, I had to keep it from my family. People would reject you if they knew, so I used to say I was an office worker. All those lies. Then living with Frank's family I was more of an outsider and even within the family I was not quite one of them. They were always so kind to me, not like the whites, but I was outside. Now here I can't even show these ladies my pictures, I have them locked up and if they could see – my, my, they would be so shocked! So here too there is all this hiding. I think they are curious why nobody comes to see me. I read a lot of books now, Frank would have been proud. But then I was so full of dresses and music and fun. I missed him so much when he died, just like that, suddenly, twenty years ago. I stayed on, they were my family, but it wasn't the same. The boy, Randolph, had gone away to America, and he still sends postcards. But I haven't seen him. I wasn't that close to him. It was his grandmother and aunt he felt were his family. I think I was ashamed of him.

I left the family and went up North and started cleaning for offices and lost touch really. It was another life. I do miss Frank, though, he was such a gentleman. He gave me this brooch once, the only present he gave me, we were quite poor. But this was special and I still wear it. It is a rose, you see, and he always used to tease me about my white skin and being an English rose.

Andrew and Betty Shepherd

Andrew Shepherd came to Britain in the 1940s and was in the RAF. He has lived here all his life since then and has been involved in the life of the Notting Hill community for many years. He is a member of the West Indian Ex-Servicemen's Club. His second wife, Betty, has also worked in the community for many years and now works at an advice centre. They have two sons.

Andrew

A vast number of Caribbeans were in the Royal Air Force and working as engineers and munitions workers. So there we were, in 1945 in Sussex, with all the WAAFs. We all used to have medical examinations, what was known as 'Free From Infection' parade – we would wait with our underpants and overcoats on while the doctors examined us.

I remember very well the hostility towards us then. Both Tories and Labour used to say that Blacks would corrupt white women and live off their immoral earnings, that that was their stock in trade. High Tories took it further and said that we would take their women and hide them; they said this even when we were fighting with them in the war.

The WAAFs were told not to sleep with Black men because they would have mulatto children and would harm themselves. One girl, who was quite precocious and pretty experienced, demanded to know how sleeping with a Black man would harm her. She was told that West Indian men were unusually large and that our lovemaking had no sophistication about it, we were animal-like in our behaviour. That was the kind of nonsense that was pushed down these girls. The irony was that I was twenty-one years old and a virgin – I had never had sexual intercourse in my life. So when I did have sex, it was an experienced WAAF who introduced me to it.

This particular girl, a Scot, wasn't going to accept this nonsense. And many of the WAAFs knew that we weren't as primitive as we were made out to be – they saw how polite we were. I would never sit down until a lady had a seat. We all had pictures of home on the wall – I had all my graduation pictures, when I passed my senior Cambridge examination; pictures of my father and mother; and my home – and the girls loved seeing them, seeing what our lives were like before we came here, how lush and green everything was.

And by the time the girls got their instructions, relationships had already begun – maybe that is why the warnings had to be given. You mustn't forget that white men had gone off to fight the war so there was some frustration, although in those days there was a strong philosophy that you had to get married and hold off, but you were still kissing and cuddling.

Two of the girls became pregnant – one of them, a cook on the camp, was very much in love with the guy. When that happened they both had to leave the camp. She was told that if she put her child up for adoption, she could come back. But as soon as she found she was pregnant, she refused to get rid of it although there was so much pressure on her to do so. I think in spite of all the racism, they were women first, and women on the whole are more human. In fact when so many Black men were repatriated after the war some of these white women tried to protect them, to hide them and help them. Many of the relationships which started in the camps thrived. I know of many long and happy marriages between white women and Black men. Even before that the men who used to beg at St Giles Circus in London were called the Black Birds of St Giles, because they linked up with the Lascars, the Indian sailors, and white women helped them. They had a real affinity; it would be wrong to assume it was only because of sexuality.

We spent many holidays in the homes of WAAFs, too, and although it might be hard to imagine these days, we were very well received. I will never forget one particular family near Manchester. They were all tall – even their twelve-year-old son was six foot. We used to go Old Time dancing at the Manchester Belle Vue and they treated us as more than equals, they treated us like we in Guyana treat visitors – you get the best. I found the people of Lancashire very open and friendly.

I spent most of my early life in Soho. I was introduced to Soho by a Trinidadian seaman called Happy Blake who ran clubs in the Harrow Road and the East End, and I too ran clubs. In those days there were some clubs that wouldn't allow Black people in and there were also some public places that wouldn't allow us in. But I can't think of one club run by Black people which didn't allow whites in. It would have been stupid because the majority of us were men so we either had to be poofs or befriend white girls, so mostly it was white girls who came with us. White artists and people like that used to think it was very classy coming to the Black clubs. If you were a young Black woman, you were a pearl. You couldn't get near a Black woman, everyone would flock round her like bees to a honeypot – and most of those women married white boys.

Many Englishmen have asked me: 'How come you got all the girls?' Well, we were a meagre minority among a vast array of women whose husbands and lovers were killed during the war. Many of them were married and they used their superior skills in love to attract us, and I learned a lot. When two people decided to be close, the one who is more advanced helps the other on. Now in spite of all the sexual stories about Black men, I was shown sex by a white woman from Nottingham.

Everything was rationed – clothes, food and all that – and those women used all manner of encouragement to attract us. If someone uses their clothing coupon to buy you a kerchief or some socks, you understand what that person is giving up.

I have never felt rejected in this place, never – maybe because I am fortunate and can look at a problem and be analytical about it, and I could do that even when I was pretty young. Of course I felt hostility, a lot of it, but it washed over me. If you allow these things to affect you . . . I had been to the United States and seen what can happen. I think I was more hurt in the USA. The Englishman's sophistication means he can carry off the hypocrisy in a very suave way. When we were with white girls, we never got any remarks – they were scared of us, I think – although the girls did, they were seen as fast and cheap. Of course there was racism. It increased when the Americans came, but it reached a crescendo when the men who had fought with the East African forces came back – they brought the worst forms of racism.

I have been married twice. My first marriage was in 1951, to a girl I met in 1946 when I was working here escorting West Indians back to the Caribbean. She was from Harrow-on-the-Hill, from a good family. Her father was a war veteran, a war hero. He didn't object to the marriage, but her mother, who had come to London in service, thought I wasn't good enough. She stayed away completely until the first boy was born. I still maintain that it was because of those attitudes that we divorced. I bought a house too near my mother-in-law, and that's where the problems began and ended. We separated in about 1954 and then divorced in 1960. When I married my next wife, my first wife cut all ties.

Because my second wife, Betty, was a working-class girl, and I met her in a club, she was a prostitute according to my first wife. In those days any white girl seen with a Black man could be nothing else but a prostitute. If you meet any white girl married to a Black man in the forties or fifties, they will tell you that. After all, we were only capable of attracting prostitutes.

When Black women began to arrive here in the sixties, some of them found that their husbands had not only white girlfriends but another family. I don't know if they knew before they came. I would not have sent for my wife from the West Indies without telling her what had been going on – that wouldn't have been fair, and most women wouldn't have taken it. I know of one woman who actually thanked the white woman, an Irish girl, for looking after her man when she came here, and they are friendly up to today.

After the mid fifties, Black women really started coming up. Some women – adventurous types, individuals – came up by themselves before that, but those who were sent for did not really come until the mid fifties. The men had to work for the money to send for them. There were ships available and people were encouraged to come here and do the dirty jobs.

I am very religious and believe in the spiritual life, but the churches turned their backs on Black people. Whenever I went it was difficult to get used to the stares. The older white people and the church leaders have good intentions but don't respect you as a Black person, they speak down to you.

I had problems with my family over marrying Betty – not from my parents but from two particular sisters who gave me hell. They wrote me all manner of letters saying, 'Why are you with a white woman and what do you think you are doing?'

I long ago gave up thinking in those terms. I don't think I would have seen the world during my travels the way I did if I had thought just 'Black'. I don't think I would have made friends with the people I did if I had thought like that and seen myself as being Black in a European society. I had a good relationship with the elders from the community who had been here long before any of us came – they had no consciousness of Black and white. Now both sides are more conscious because the media have made them so.

Wherever imperialism has been, these attitudes survive – white skin, light skin, is better than black in India, in Guyana – between Indians, between the descendants of the slaves in Guyana. But the attacks on us were orchestrated. The Blacks who were here had got themselves rented property, thanks to Rachman. You know he wasn't a bad man. They hated him because he used to let rooms to us Blacks. He got on fine with Blacks – he drank with them, gambled with them and would give rooms, particularly to Black women. In 1957–8 the National Front started holding meetings in this area, saying Blacks had taken the jobs at a cheaper rate and were putting whites out of work. This was Mosley's message. Now many of us at that time were ex-servicemen. We were proud and had learnt to take no nonsense. The Southern Irish stood by us and there were some whites who supported us, physically and morally. The police – their attitudes were as they are now. I remember when all this was going on I was arrested and questioned eleven times in one night.

Betty

When I met Andrew I didn't particularly want a Black man for a boyfriend, and he wasn't looking for a white woman. It was just the attraction of two human beings – we never thought about colour. But it did affect me. I was working in an office in Praed Street. Everybody used to talk about their boyfriend – I'm ashamed of it now, but I never told them. I told them I had a boyfriend, but I never said he was Black. It bothered me a lot at the time, but you couldn't just say 'My boyfriend is Black' – you just didn't say that sort of thing.

Then one time a couple of guys came into the office. They had all gone out and they told me the place was full of niggers, and I said, 'So what?' One thing led to another and I said, 'You don't know any Black people, that's why you are being rude.' Then I added, 'Did I tell you that my boyfriend is Black?' – well, 'coloured', that's what you said in those days. They all gasped.

I think another reason why I didn't say anything was because the men in the office used to try it on and be fresh, touch you on the bottom, things like that. It used to worry me that if they knew I was going with a Black man they might think that I was a loose kind of girl. That was a thing in those days – if you went with Black men you were thought to be rubbish and trash – only trash, or a white girl who couldn't get a decent white fellow, would go with them.

There were problems with my family at first. Actually I could understand my parents, there were such pressures around, and I felt sorry – not that I had fallen in love with a Black man, but that they didn't get what they wanted. They felt that I had let them down, but after a while it was all right. Now my mother adores him, she defends him and says I would never find another husband who was so good.

People would come up to us when we first started going out – I remember one elderly woman, she was very pleasant, not rude or anything, and she said, 'I hope you don't mind but I really just wanted to ask, does the Black come off?' She was genuinely asking me that question! I couldn't really be cross with her because she truly wanted to know. That kind of thing happened a lot, especially when I had children. The man at the market called me a whore because I had mixed race children. It was quite common here, you can look around and see many mixed race children of my children's age, but it still wasn't accepted. In fact, it seemed the more children there were, the more unacceptable it became. Remember at that time there were hardly any Black women here – maybe that had something to do with it.

When they were young, Simon, the eldest, was always 'Black' in his interests, and Michael was 'white'. All Simon's friends were Black, all his girlfriends were Black, he listened to Black music. Michael was the opposite. He liked white music, like the Osmonds, that kind of thing. He liked English food, whereas Simon preferred West Indian food. All the friends he brought home were white.

As they got older I think Simon went through life happy with what he was, but Michael had more problems. I always knew that Michael would marry a white woman, although the majority of his friends are now Black and he has had Black girlfriends. When he married Catherine, who is white, many of his Black friends, especially his Rasta friends, decided that he had done wrong and didn't want to know him any more.

When Simon was six or seven, he called the Black girl next door a wog. Her mother came in and complained to me and I said I would sort it out. I spoke to Simon and he said angrily, 'But she *is* a wog.' So I said, 'In that case your daddy is a wog.' He said, 'No he is not', and I said, 'Yes he is, your daddy is Black and Jane is Black, so if she is a wog, so is he.'

He thought about it and we went to apologise to Jane. We talked about it afterwards – it had clearly never dawned on him that she was the same colour as his daddy. His daddy was his daddy and I was his mummy and it never meant anything that we were Black and white. The wog thing didn't really mean anything to him. I am glad it happened because otherwise he would have gone on to think these things and we would not have dealt with it.

Then things would happen like he would hold up his hand against mine and say, 'I'm white, Mummy, just like you' – his hand was the same colour as mine. And I would say, 'Yes, but I am white and your daddy is Black and you have both, you are a mixture because you come from both of us.' We would say, 'Look at your hair, see how you have a bit of both of us', and try to be very positive about it. We would explain that some people would call him half-caste, that it wasn't a term we like very much and 'what we say is that you are mixed race'.

Some Black women used to feel that women like us had stolen their men and they said so, but I wasn't intimidated by it. I think we should understand that when they started coming over to join their men, they probably got an awful shock to find that their boyfriends and husbands were living with or associating with white women. I now have a lot of Black women friends.

I remember as a kid, when I was six or seven, the first Black person I ever saw. He bought a house in the street where I lived. The first time I saw him there were a lot of us sitting out on the doorstep and this man passed by and I rushed into the house and told my mum I'd just seen a Black man. She said, 'Yes, they are sunshine people, because they come from places where the sun shines all the time, and that's why they are Black.' So every time that poor man passed by, we would yell, 'Ooh, Sunshine Man!' But he was very amiable and would smile and wave to us. I think my mother probably really thought that – she wasn't very educated.

But you do hear some strange things. When I was working at an advice centre, an Indian man came in. He was having problems with his flat and his neighbours – and he started saying, 'They are niggers and they smell' – I couldn't believe it! I said to him, 'But you are Black, to a white person you are Black' – his skin was darker than Andrew's. Because to us white people he was Black. He was saying some terrible things, and I really felt it.

Ayesha and Ian Gordon

Ayesha Gordon is a senior television news producer for an international television news agency. Trained on local newspapers, she has been a journalist for ten years. She was born in India and came to Britain in the 1970s.

Ian Gordon is Head of Upper School and Head of Science for an international school in Ealing which has an intake from – amongst other countries – Japan, Kuwait, Lebanon, France, Sweden, Iraq, India and Germany.

Ayesha

I was in a terrible state when I met Ian. It was 1979 and I had left my husband, which just wasn't the done thing in my background. I remember sitting on the floor of my flat crying. Then there was a knock on the door and this tall man came in and said, 'Excuse me, would you like to join the residents' association?' It was ridiculous. My life was falling apart, I had no job, no husband, no money. But in a strange way I felt as though a bit of sanity arrived when this Englishman walked in. It was real physical attraction from the beginning. I really fancied him, lusted after him. I had always liked that stereotype, the tall, handsome, dark-haired, blue-eyed man. In the end, though, he ran after me. I did not come from a background where women did the running.

If there have been problems about our backgrounds, they come from the fact that Ian is from a very working-class background whereas I am from a middle-class, colonial background. Not pro the Raj – in fact half my family fought against the Raj – but they were all educated in Britain, were in the army and air force – all my uncles were brigadiers and colonels. The independence movement was a middle-class thing, there were many shared values between them and the rulers. I also had the language, I had grown up speaking English, so fitting into this country was not a problem in that sense, although physically it is very difficult. The cold, grey climate is still very difficult for me to get used to, and the coldness of the people, their lack of warmth. But I think the real difference between us comes from our class backgrounds.

I realised this in the week before the wedding, when my mother arrived. My mother is a snob – God knows why, because she is not particularly highly educated, or rich. But she is a snob. The first thing she said was, 'You could have had anybody, you could have had a rich industrialist, you could have had a houseful of servants and played cards all day. Instead, you marry a teacher.' My first husband came from a very uppity middle-class family and had been to public school.

Then, by complete contrast, Ian's mother turned up. She is very working-class, very northern and solid. They just didn't get on because my mother looked down on her so much. I remember it was Princess Diana's wedding just before ours. Ian's family are typically royalist and as we were watching the wedding, my mother yelled out, 'Oh my God, that dress is all crumpled and crushed!' To his mother this was an unforgivable insult. Then my mother added more insults, saying, 'In India, we hate the British; we threw them out. My father went to jail because of them.' She talked as if she was blaming his mother personally for all this, which left her shell-shocked.

It got to an impossible point. My mother retired to bed at eight o'clock while his mother cleaned the house, did the back garden and sorted everything out. When I asked my mother how she could lie in bed while Ian's mother was slaving away she replied, 'My dear, these people are made from peasant stock, not like you and me. They are used to physical work.'

I do have problems with Ian's family. The first time I met his mother, he'd said as a joke to her, 'I met this starving waif from Calcutta.' I was the first girlfriend he had brought home since his marriage broke up, so they knew it was serious. I guess they were expecting a little person in a sari with a dot on her forehead, and of course I came in, in a shirt and trousers. His mother, who has all sorts of complexes about her lack of education, didn't know how to take me. One of the first things she said to me was, 'Your English is good, dear, isn't it?' It's a cliché but it's quite true. I replied by telling her that I had a degree in English.

I found his father difficult to cope with too. He was one of these hail-fellow-well-met working-class men – not traditionally working-class because he had worked in Ghana and Pakistan and travelled, so he was aware of other parts of the world. In some ways, perhaps, this had heightened his prejudices. He would talk about 'these wogs', not thinking that I was in the room. I found that unbelievable. Ian says he was doing it to bait me, but if that was the case it makes it even more upsetting. Ian wouldn't react because it was his father. He would make excuses for him, and say that he didn't mean it in that way. But I remember feeling absolutely choked up about it at the beginning. Then I thought: this has got to be stopped, and it did stop after Ian talked it through with him.

I saw their reaction to me as a racial one. Ian chose not to, he wanted to duck out of it. But I felt a complete lack of welcome for the first four years into our marriage. It changed when his parents had a big ruby wedding party and all the uncles and aunts really liked me. I remember I was wearing a red skirt and they all said, 'Ian's wife looks like a Hungarian.' I feel that was the first time my mother-in-law came round in terms of accepting me, when other people in the family had bestowed their approval. A lot of them didn't even know I was foreign, because I am quite pale-skinned. I suppose she is the kind of woman who, because of a lack of education, is always worried about what other people think. She always studiously avoided the subject of race. Ian's father would make all these comments to get me to rise, but his mother would actually avoid the subject, she chose not to confront it. But there was a lack of concern and something quite revealing about the avoidance. It really hasn't changed all that much except that we have learnt to give each other more scope and we deal with each other as women now.

But on the other hand, when you strip away the financial, economic, cultural and class factors, there are many similarities between his mother and many of my aunts, for example. My mother said to me once, 'Ian's family is very Indian.' It is a very emotional family. They all have rows, and air their feelings in public, and are always having little spats and going off into the sunset.

I carried the history and the scars of my first marriage for at least two years. It took that long really to see Ian as he is and realise that this man was not what my first husband had been at all. He was a Parsee, a Zoroastrian. For eight years I had fought being put down in private and in public. My first husband's view was that his wife should sit there with her pretty smile and there was no need to take her seriously – it is that macho thing which is deep-rooted in all men, but especially affects Asian men. But Ian is not competitive towards me, he is not jealous of my success, he is not trying to put me down. That is an attitude that is often very difficult to find in Asian men.

Ian and I are also very compatible in living-together terms, which I wasn't with my first husband. Although he was Indian and from the same background and education, there was deep, deep incompatibility. Everything upset him: if I blew my nose too much, if I held my wine glass in a certain way. There was a mixture of snobbery and a need to control and mould me. Most Asian men are pretty sexist; they are spoilt, and want to own you as their possession. In this marriage, Ian and I give each other a lot of space. I can do my own thing and I don't need continuous attention.

But there *are* differences in the way we carry on. He sulks until he is really mad and then he shouts and threatens to break doors down. But in terms of positive showing of emotions, outpourings of love, he can't do that, he is very English. Married to an Asian man, I was much more apologetic and compliant than I am now. But at a deeper level those influences remain, and maybe that is no bad thing.

Asian women have an almost subliminal desire to look after men, however badly they treat them. It is that softness, that femininity – now in disrepute – which is coming back. It is not a good thing to say, but however successful I have been in career terms, I have always looked after my men. When I used to go to Birmingham for my job, I would cook for Ian for the week. Much of that must come from my Indian background: I can't stop myself. Not because he is not capable of doing it – it is subliminal, part of my duty as an Indian woman, to feed him properly and see that he is physically comfortable. It is part of my conditioning which I cannot exorcise. And many white men love it – maybe a bit too much! But at work I wouldn't dream of it. And many of the white women I work with – they wouldn't either.

There is also the question of sex. Ian and I turn each other on. There is something about Asian women that turns white men on. There was an article in a men's magazine where white men were shockingly open about this. They talked about wanting a certain type of skin which 'doesn't have bulbous bits and freckles'. They talked about a supple quality of the body and small compact bodies and passivity, which is a part of it.

In my teens I felt so constricted by India that I couldn't wait to leave, although I knew that I was leaving a phenomenal lifestyle. Besides the physical inconveniences, the main reasons were that I felt hemmed in by the system, the people telling you what to do, telling me what my role was as a woman. I could never live there. I find the society highly oppressive. The women I went to school with haven't changed at all, or if they have, they have become like my mother – they live in the same boring social world with bridge parties and the talk of servants.

I guess that I see myself as urban, metropolitan British now, and I have no angst about who I am. I did have some longings before about my identity and India. When I first came here I suffered from horrific bouts of almost physical nostalgia. And every time I went back to India, and saw the horrors of life there, I would come back and be purged until the next time something brought it up. But this is less important now. The last time I was there, I couldn't wait to get back. This was a shock, because I actually see London and England as home now. In India I feel completely foreign and they know I am a foreigner and treat me as one.

Ian

I think our first marriages are much more significant in our relationship than either class or race. I don't know if I even realised that Ayesha was Indian when I met her, although I knew she wasn't English. And although it was obvious from her accent that she was very proper, I didn't appreciate her class background until we went to India, two years after we married.

Ayesha had come from an unhappy marriage in which she had allowed herself to become totally dominated and had obviously decided that it wasn't going to happen again. I had come from a marriage where I had totally humiliated my wife for most of our marriage and I was determined I was never going to do that again. What I did was terrible and I had decided that I would not go through that again with Ayesha, although of course she wouldn't have let me. So when we met I was wanting and needing to be as nice as possible to make up for the shit I had doled up in the past and there was Ayesha, a strong Asian woman, with clear parameters, looking out for any sign of me being a shit.

I never saw my parents' reaction to Ayesha as being racially based at all. When my father made comments to her I knew that basically he just likes to annoy people, and it's not purely about racist things. I do remember things they said when I was a kid. There was one discussion with some of their friends about marrying foreigners. They couldn't see the point of doing something like that with all these English people to go round. My parents said then that they would be upset if I married a foreigner, but I think when I actually did they had changed a lot. When my father was working in Ghana I had dated girls there, so the mould was broken anyway. I had no qualms about that and nor did my parents, although they were horrified that my sister dated a Lebanese guy. My first wife was foreign, American, and by the time I married Ayesha they were surprised about other things – that she was so strong-willed, perhaps a bit too much like my first wife had seemed.

The funny thing was that Ayesha's mum may have seen herself as upper-class but my mother did not see her that way. To her, because she had grown up with racist stereotypes, she was just another little Indian woman.

I think that because Ayesha has lived largely in London, she doesn't appreciate the homogeneous world my parents live in. We were brought up in Cheshire, and people in Cheshire hate change. When I was growing up, everyone came from the Wirral. They thought they were better than Liverpudlians with their Scouse accents, and that *they* were foreigners. There was a Cockney who lived in the same street as my grandmother, and he was a curiosity.

Things changed after I left home at eighteen and went to Manchester and discovered Indian restaurants – I knew the difference between a Madras and a Vindaloo within two weeks. I also widened my interests in other ways. I estranged one of my first girlfriends by confessing to her that my dream for the future was to experience sex with every race in the world.

Rifat Wahhab and Derek Perry

Rifat Wahhab was born in Bangladesh and came to Britain in 1964. Derek Perry was born in Birmingham. They met at college and married in 1980. They live in North London and have no children.

Rifat

When I met Derek I was not worried about what my family might feel because I think I had decided that college was *my* territory. I had been brought up by my parents' rules and followed my parents' instructions, but at college my thought was: I am an adult now. I needed to sort some things out for myself, although I knew the dangers that was likely to present. Or maybe, like a lot of Asian youngsters, I thought college was a kind of holiday from the responsibilities that had been drilled into me.

But then, as our friendship grew, the question of 'What if it isn't a holiday, a passing romance?' grew in my mind. Of course at college Asians are allowed to have a 'romance', and then you are expected to come back to the so-called fold and everything is forgiven, but there came a point when I knew I couldn't go back to that – it would have been living a lie.

But in between all that there was the guilt: what am I doing to my family, what am I doing to my parents, what am I doing to myself? In the end these things are not predictable, however much you worry. The person who reacted in the most hurt and hostile way was my father, which was surprising because he was the person I was closest to in the family and the one I thought would understand.

He wasn't in the country when all this was happening. He was teaching in Bangladesh and used to come back regularly to visit the family. So when he came, I prepared myself to talk to him. I was taken aback to see his shock and anger – something I had expected from my mother who, though difficult, turned out to be surprisingly accessible, at least in the early days. It must have struck a raw nerve in my father, probably because we had such a good relationship. I think if we hadn't been so close, he wouldn't have had such a strong reaction. So Derek didn't get to meet my father for quite a long time.

I don't think I will ever forget the day when I had to go to Derek and ask him to convert to Islam. His first words to me were 'I can't believe that you are saying this to me.' We had built a really honest relationship and were politically quite close. We had both questioned the existence of God and there I was telling him that our marriage would be in great danger if he couldn't convert. For me it was the worst thing that happened – it is still painful. If there is one thing I could choose not to do, it would be to do that again. I don't think I had the right, I don't think anybody has the right to change a man's beliefs. His belief was atheism – a real belief – and I respected that.

At the time I gave in to it because it was important to follow what the family said. I could see my parents' vulnerability and I did it for them, it was something they needed to make this thing legitimate for their family and friends and I had to balance between them. It was very painful, because hearing what Derek felt really cut me up and hearing it from my parents also cut me up. I think the reason I finally went to Derek was that I was hoping he could just go through the motions, but I don't think he believed that I really thought it was good enough. So we paid a price for it. I'll always respect myself for taking care of my parents' vulnerability, but I think I did not have the right to ask Derek to convert.

There are two types of reaction to you as a couple. There are the remarks that you have an opportunity to respond to, and then there are the unspoken gestures and actions that hurt the most. One incident sticks in my mind. We got up on a Saturday morning, we were going to shop for food, what every other couple does on a Saturday morning. We were walking down the road and a car stopped and out stepped an elderly Asian woman, old enough to be my grandmother. As she was walking towards us, I was wondering if I knew her, because she was looking at us so intensely. Then she stopped. I don't think I have seen so much hatred in anyone's eyes before. She wasn't looking at Derek, she was looking at me – all the condemnation was for me, and I couldn't even respond to it, because she didn't say anything. It was the unspoken words which got to me. And it affected my parents, even during the actual wedding. Some members of the community were making 'coded' remarks of disapproval among themselves, and sometimes to family friends. If people had the guts, they would have come to me and Derek and said, 'We think what you have done is absolutely disgusting.' But instead the silence affected my parents and they were just bystanders, I did not want them to be held responsible for the choice I had made. My parents never talked about it, their dignity stopped them, but you knew what was going on.

Some people were genuinely distressed, their feelings were based on real concerns, like racism. In the other camp were the real bigots who exist in every society as far as I can see. They were gutless, they did things surreptitiously, and that was what made me angry.

In our first few years together, I had mixed feelings about whether I should have married Derek. When the pressure is really on you, you do start thinking: Have I done the right thing? Have I let my people down? Could I have been better off like they tell me, with a Bengali man? But now I wouldn't change it for the world. Maybe I would have been more socially accepted and maybe I would have been happy – I would never say that I wouldn't have been happy with a Bangladeshi man – but now I wouldn't have it any other way.

I actually think that our marriage is quite a landmark. People expected us to fail, and used to say so. But now, eleven years on, we are not only proving them wrong, we have gone beyond that. We have made something of it ourselves and are deeply happy with it.

To be frank, we nearly did give up at one point. There was so much pressure from outside that it was affecting our married life. I come from a very Bengali family, rooted in a very Bengali community. I felt I was being scrutinised by the community and there were some who were especially looking out for things to criticise us for. All this very much restricted my movements. Once I had a haircut and my friends who had invited some people over started discussing it as though I had committed a crime. They said, 'This is what we expected of her – she is turning English.' My friend was so angry, she said, 'If I had married an Englishman, I would have stood in a bikini in front of you.'

These sorts of things mattered a lot, because I take my community very seriously. I am loyal to them, I care about what they say, right or wrong, so their feelings were important to me, even their bad feelings. If an English person makes a racist comment, even if it hurts, it doesn't really matter to me, I can deal with it because I don't feel that close to them. It is when you care about somebody and they say these things that it affects you.

In the early days it made me feel guilty, I felt I had done something wrong. What really got to me was the number of young people with nationalistic ideas, and there were feminist friends who made my life miserable. I expected to be guilt-tripped by the elders, but to be seriously guilt-tripped by Black feminists and white feminists – that was awful! When I think back to those days, I feel it is amazing that we survived it.

Looking back, I understand the Black feminists' reaction up to a point, because they have been through some very bitter experiences with white people and white men. But it was the hatred within the white women that shocked me. I would get condemnation for marrying a white man – 'couldn't I have done better for myself and married one of those wonderful Black men?' It was unbelievable. These women couldn't see that these reactions were patronising.

Ultimately, nobody was respecting an Asian woman's choice in determining her own affairs.

I had to rethink my views with regard to some feminist beliefs. So much about the way I feel about Derek, or how I love my brothers and my father, is alien to feminists. It's really difficult for some feminists to accept that it is possible to love a man – especially in non-sexual terms. I was on a bus with a Jewish feminist. It was brilliant until she realised that I was getting married to a white man. She then turned to me and said, 'We haven't finished with you yet.' I was OK up to that point, but not after I told her about Derek.

I think we are trying to aim for a balance in everybody's mind – the feminine psyche in the man's mind as well as the male drive in a woman's mind. I think it is very sad that we tried to kill femininity – by becoming more like men. That is where I think Asian women have in a way succeeded, because the femininity has been maintained as well as the intellect and the spirit.

These kinds of marriages are growing in our community but are still very unusual, especially for Bengali women. Most who have got married to white men come from very similar backgrounds to mine: middle-class. It is really only the middle classes who can afford to take such a step – the working classes have much less control over their lives.

There is sexism at play too. All across the Asian community it is OK for Asian men to have as many relationships as they like and to marry English women. Although it is frowned upon, it is nothing like the reaction if Asian women do it. But we have to be careful. Many Asian women who marry white men argue that it is because Asian men are patronising and sexist – I believe that *all* men are like that. Sometimes you realise how wrong certain assumptions are. When I look at my father's generation, they are amongst the least patronising men I know; I find young Englishmen much more patronising. My father and my uncles actually like women, they are friends with their wives, whereas Englishmen are still brought up to view women in a very strange way.

After ten years of marriage we have been able to differentiate between vulnerable people who raise genuine concerns and those who are real bigots. The one thing I do look forward to is talking to other mixed marriage couples – because nobody else understands as perfectly as they do. It is important to find your own strength instead of becoming a victim of every comment. It makes you grow, you can take nothing for granted, it enriches your life.

Being married to an Englishman is never going to stop me being Black, Asian and Bangladeshi. If you look at our house it looks like a Bengali house, I haven't made any compromise and nor has Derek. Furthermore I feel I am so rich – not for having married an Englishman, but for having maintained my culture. I have taken the benefits of his culture, and vice versa. It can all happen and the world really is your oyster if you can reach beyond the victim stage.

Many Black people lack the confidence to do that because of the way they have had to suffer in this society. It is a fantastic situation to be able to be in: to be able to wear saris one moment and European clothes the next – it is a privileged position. I am bicultural and I am thoroughly enjoying it.

Derek

There was no problem whatsoever when I announced at home that the woman I was interested in was from Bangladesh. I had left home ten years previously and had a second career and to my family my life had been a bit strange, and unsettled, so compared to the crazy things in the past, this was no problem. From the beginning, Rifat was accepted as somebody who came along with me. The only person who showed any prejudice was my niece who, at the time, was quite young and associating with skinheads. I told her a few things and we haven't had a word since.

Even when I decided to convert to Islam I didn't discuss it with them – I don't even remember mentioning it. Religion was not an important thing in the home anyway. I converted because it was put to me that unless I did, we couldn't get married in the mosque and unless we married in the mosque, it wasn't going to be acceptable. I treated it like a tourist. In a way it was quite interesting, coming from a Christian background. I could sit and discuss the difference between Islam and Christianity with the Imam. I didn't feel false at the time, because it was a test. Could I do it? Could I really stand in the middle of Regent's Park Mosque and pray like a Muslim? Well, I did. Can you overcome the fear, can you face the challenge, can you do it? So I did it.

But in the end it became a farce, because I was asked not to explain the real reasons for wanting to convert and to say that I was this intellectual free spirit who had finally found the right way. So I couldn't be honest with the Imam whom I was seeing once a week at the mosque about why I was doing it. And when we went to get married the man who actually married us was the same Imam. He had my certificate, confirming that I was a 'Muslim', which he has still got. He didn't give it back to me after the wedding. Now I resent having been put through that, and I resent myself for going through it. Whatever nice tourism it was, it was against my principles, as I am an atheist. The rest of it, the ceremony and so on, I don't mind. That didn't cost very much intellectually or emotionally.

When Rifat and I first married, it was a fairly unusual occurrence and I was very conscious of the fact that we had married across race and culture. I did notice responses from other people – more from other Asians than anyone else, as my friends are quite cosmopolitan – but there was never as much as I expected. Now I can see that maybe I didn't really notice the responses because I wasn't fully aware of them. Looking back on it, I can see the difference. Now that I am completely accepted, I can see what it was like when we got married – it was quite a strain.

Our relationship was accepted by one or two people who weren't really central to the family, one or two people who did more than just accept me – they almost adopted me. One man called me his son – I knew what that meant to him to do that – and he helped us a lot. He found us somewhere to live and did far more than was expected. In a way that made up for the nastiness that we had experienced. It was simply human concern, bringing someone into the family.

I'd like to think that I have been open enough too. My family – a standard working-class family from Birmingham – could be called racist with a small r, it is what would have been expected of them. My father would have made racist comments about Black people on television, comments which were unkind but not violent. He was a milkman, he died twenty years ago, a long time before we met. But other things about the way I was brought up perhaps made it easier. It was a very fair-minded family. We were very democratic. We were all treated equally except in terms of gender: the girls had to be in by half-past ten! But apart from that, everybody had to contribute to the chores equally. Our pocket money and everything we got was shared absolutely fairly. We weren't very well off, and all the sweets would be laid out so that they were absolutely equal.

I developed my own feelings, and political and philosophical reasons for treating things as I do. I don't identify with racists. Racists might be white, but that's the only thing we've got in common. Those people are my enemies, as a socialist. My politics predates everything with Rifat. My anti-racism grew a long time before my socialism and goes back to my teens, when I grew up in a place where there were no Black people. I don't know where it came from, it just grew as I grew up and became aware. I started when I was a Christian, as a liberal, feeling sorry for Black people. I would wonder why people were in that situation, what had happened to them to make this difference. Then it changed because I grew up and became aware that Black people in Britain had problems. Then I got to university and, for the first time, met a lot of Black people – not Black people from Britain, because they didn't go to university then – extremely interesting people who were involved in liberation struggles. There were Marxists from Calcutta, I met Bengalis, people from the Zimbabwe war of liberation. I didn't understand about colonialism but I knew something was sinking in. I don't know why, but this awareness developed almost without me noticing it.

The first time I got really angry about racism was in the early seventies. There was this man David Oluwale, a Nigerian tramp, who was arrested. He was picked up by the police and he died in a police cell. I think that was the first time I felt directly angry about racism and realised so directly and powerfully that it really was violent. It is really important to see how racism has changed over the years – from slavery to imperialist racism and then to what became the racism of immigration. And the subtle changes and the way it was used by the ruling class.

As time went on I realised Rifat was having a hard time. I had been away from my family for ten years, so I didn't have to suffer the sort of things she did. For her it was a complete readjustment, and it was very hard to watch. I knew lots was going on but in some ways I couldn't understand it, so I would react in various ways which were not entirely helpful.

We went to Bangladesh for six weeks, and we were very well looked after by some influential relatives who could get us taken to places. I saw most of the country, in very pleasant circumstances. It was fantastic. What was so great was the very strong sense of history and tradition, especially as the fight for independence was so recent. There is a very strong identity in being Bangladeshi. It is a respected tradition as well – its art and culture are very apparent.

3. Love is Colour-blind

❛ *I think what matters most is that with a white man I have been able to find safety and security in being me, as an Asian woman, as a radical Black writer, in a way that I could never have done with my ex-husband, who was Asian but who just couldn't wait to get into his green wellies and his Land Rover.* ❜

– MAYA MEHTA

Trevor and Mary Watson

Trevor and Mary Watson met forty-six years ago when Trevor was with the RAF and based in Britain, as were many Black men from the Empire. They got married at a time when interracial marriages were still rare, particularly outside the main immigrant areas.

Trevor: I was in the RAF in Nottingham at a camp called Newton aerodrome and we really met through our love of dancing. I was fond of dancing and I decided to go to the

95

Greyfriars ballroom and that is where we met, because my wife is also a good dancer and we used to meet to do a little jitterbugging. She used to teach me ballroom dancing, which was quite unusual for me, coming from a rhythmic country, but eventually I did get into it and it was quite nice. Most of the people who attended these places were men from the army, the navy and the air force – very few civilians, you see.

Mary: And the girls went for a good time and of course when the West Indians came it was like a thrill to us, you know, to see other nationalities coming over. As a young girl, I'd always had a thing about Black people. They always intrigued me. When I went to the cinema and I saw these Arabs with their headdresses, I always thought they were great. But there were a lot of white Americans and Black Americans at the time and there was animosity between those two, almost like segregation. So the white Americans didn't like it because the white girls seemed to prefer the Black Americans. When I first saw Trevor walking down, it was a thrill because the Jamaicans used to press their uniforms differently to the Englishmen. They had their own style. We used to say they were really lairy, you know – that means they looked fancy and smart. The passes would come from both sides. They were good dancers – oh, they could dance! – and I was going for my ballroom dancing medals, but then Trevor came along and it became jitterbugging and all that. I was a lot slimmer then and he used to throw me up and swirl me around. You have to understand that what was so important in the past was the way the Black man treated the white girl. He was a gentleman. They knew how to talk to a girl. I find – and I shouldn't say this, I know – but Englishmen, they haven't got that thing about them that makes a woman feel good.

Trevor: What I experienced was that we had a certain gathering of girls and they seemed to want to meet the West Indians, you know. In the RAF, with many white men and WAAFs, there were problems. One time I was confined to barracks because a WAAF was my main dancing partner on the camp and we used to dance together. And this white corporal, he was so jealous that every time he saw me he wanted to put me on the charge. I didn't take any notice of him, and then eventually he got me confined to barracks for a week. We talked about some of these girls we wanted to meet for our enjoyment and pleasure. There was nothing immoral or corrupt in the West Indian approach or anything like that. We just liked being together, having fun.

Mary: When I first saw Trevor, I said to my sister, 'That's the man I am going to marry.' Honestly. And my sister laughed. There was just something about him. There *is* something about you – I don't know, you were such a gentleman to me, and that's the way you are now. You are still the same Trevor to me as you were forty-six years ago. It's the way my husband has treated me. I would never let anyone else say anything to him. It is that deep exceptional feeling that you can sometimes have for a person, and then when it has been difficult because of other people, that feeling gets deeper and no one can shake it off. I came from a big working-class family, you see, and these things are important. It doesn't seem like forty-six years. I have never regretted any of it. If I had, I wouldn't be here today. But I felt it when I first saw him.

Trevor: I didn't know she felt that way, but I know that I had the opportunity of meeting other girls, more girls, but we always looked forward to meeting each other. There was something like a magnet between us. We would always dance with each other for the whole night.

Mary: We'd known each other for only about eleven months when we got married. We had to do it quick, otherwise we couldn't have done it because my parents didn't agree and his parents didn't agree – I mean, it works both ways, you know.

Trevor: If we had stopped to consider their decisions, we might not be together today. I wrote to the family and the only person who sent me congratulations was my grandmother.

I think they were worried about the objections that would have been there from the white community and the Black community which would make our lives difficult. You know, things like socialising and that – we would not be accepted in either community, and that was a thing which at the time was very strong.

Mary: It was very hard at that time, you know. Ours was just about the first intermarriage in Nottingham. And it was terrible, we went through hell, didn't we, love? But we stuck it out. My parents said, 'If you do that, don't come back home.' But when we had our first child, it was my mother's first grandson. And when she heard, she sent my sister down and told her to say: 'Tell Mary to come down and bring my grandson with her.' And from then on we never looked back and she got to know Trevor and eventually she said, 'I think you have made the best marriage out of the family.' You can't take things at face value, can you?

Trevor: My father-in-law would visit us and have philosophical conversations regarding colour and attitudes, and this was so different from his older sons, some of whom felt – what shall I say? – a sense of disdain for me and for what we had done. And my father-in-law had a talk with them about these attitudes in front of me.

Mary: My brothers had travelled to certain parts of the world where they had seen Black people living in terrible conditions, you see, and they visualised that my husband had come from that sort of background and drew their own conclusions. But these things didn't really worry me much. We were younger, and we were too busy with our own lives, I was in love. But of course, nothing stays the same. In time we realised that when we wanted to go out, we would look to see if there would be any other mixed couples there – you felt more secure if there were. White people in those days were inclined to stare and it was terrible, but we just had to put up with that. But I was rather cheeky in those days and I would say, 'Would you like a photograph?'

Trevor: You just had to try and not be too sensitive about what was going on, with the white people. They would not say anything, but they didn't encourage you to be amongst them. You have to just keep aloof, keep a certain distance, to avoid being insulted. Although I must say that there was no direct arrogance, never.

Mary: You see the white people didn't appreciate me marrying a Black man and the Black people didn't appreciate him marrying a white woman. And we had worse times when the West Indians started coming over in large numbers and then the Black women began to arrive. And then I had another thing to go through, you see. That was hard, being made to feel you had taken a Black man away, stolen him. I understood, but it was terrible. Because Black women didn't really appreciate me at all. Gradually they came round as well. I remember my very first visit to Jamaica – I was glad to get back home, I can tell you. I felt I was cut out of everything as a white woman. I was the only white face among these Black faces, and I felt it. I used to wonder: What do they think of me? I was very sceptical, but I kept a low profile.

Trevor: We have always tried to keep away from a certain category of person. It was only people of low thinking who used to molest us more than anything else, so we never frequented pubs and places like that where these people would get a chance to infuriate you.

Mary: We moved to London which was different from Nottingham. It was more mixed up and it is even more so now, with so many people of different nationalities. I thought that was just lovely. You were free. I loved it. You didn't feel that you were pushed into the background. But there were problems here too. Even the white friends who were different and used to invite us – I used to worry that it was maybe as a curiosity. The hardest thing was getting somewhere to live. The signs saying 'No Blacks' and the fact that I was white made it worse. Obstacles are put there for you to get over, you know what I mean. We got through all that unscathed.

The reward is that after all these years, we are still together. Some people just couldn't take it and they were destroyed. It is other people who have caused the split-ups in these marriages. You've got to be very strong.

Trevor: There were other mixed marriages in Nottingham before we moved here, and after we came down here a number of organisations began to build up, like the West Indian Ex-Servicemen's Club, and so there was no isolation any more. Looking back, I feel I was in love and colour didn't mean that much to me. What was important was that kind of telepathy we had, to live and work together in harmony. We were part of so many changes, between men and women and Black and white. I think we were foreseeing something. We were ahead of our time. We were breaking many traditions. We were setting a standard. We didn't let other people deter us from our thinking. We get letters thanking us for the example and courage we have given them in a small way. We have been like an advisory service on this.

Mary: The world was changing so fast then. Before the war, a woman got married, got into the kitchen and brought kids up. When we got married, it was different. I worked for munitions and we were getting our independence from the men. We didn't want to be like our mothers. And I took that change further with my marriage.

Maya Mehta

Maya Mehta came to Britain from East Africa in the early 1970s with her husband as a postgraduate student. She went on to teach and lecture, and is also a writer. She has one son aged fifteen.

Maya

I came to this country with my husband when we both went to university to continue our studies. Like me, he was an

100

East African Asian, a professional man, and as far as I was concerned we had a very equal marriage. Ours had not been a so-called arranged marriage. We had met at school, fallen in love and married with the blessing of both families.

Coming here was a double shock – firstly because it was a time of great anti-immigrant hysteria. I remember within days of arriving reading these awful reports of how Asians were being put up in expensive hotels by the local council and feeling embarrassed by these people and worried that I would be recognised as one of them. The other shock was that it was a time of great industrial upheaval and political unrest in this country – the three-day week and all that. I think I should explain that when you grew up, as I did, in the colonies, what was rammed down your throat was how super-efficient the British were, and how the rest of us around the world needed looking after because we couldn't build our own roads or lavatories. So to find a country so dishevelled and incapable of looking after itself was a bit like finding that your mother was a drunkard. The other shock of not wanting to be identified with the other Asians in this country because they were a 'problem' was a deeper shock, I suppose, because before that I had always been very proud of who I was, and of my community.

I think that shock affected my ex-husband even more deeply than me, and he seems to have spent the next twenty years on a kind of bizarre project of disappearing, of becoming white, but a nicely tanned white. And it all culminated, I suppose, in his going away with your archetypal blonde bimbo. These things have a deep effect on you, and living with my ex-husband in the years before he left involved lots of strange contradictions. My response to the disillusionment with this country was to discover a political identity within Black Britain and, parallel to that, almost vehemently reasserting my Asianness. I started listening to old Hindi songs which my mother used to listen to in the forties and fifties. I became much more comfortable about my Asian background and relished and valued my new relationships with people from Afro-Caribbean and Asian communities. I also became very publicly involved in fighting white racism and didn't feel any gratitude, only anger at what had been done to us historically and in Britain today.

My ex-husband, meanwhile, was going the other way. He couldn't stand what he saw as my political rantings. He became frightfully middle-class: discovered skiing, the English countryside, wine bars and wildlife safaris, which is a bit ironic considering we came from East Africa. I know it sounds like a small thing, but one day we were in Southall and I remember feeling a real sense of security and belonging. I was very shocked when he turned round to me and said, 'God, look at these people, when are they ever going to change?' I knew then that we were developing in opposite directions, but there was enough compatibility between us and so much happiness in our marriage that it didn't really create problems.

It was hard with my child, though, and looking back, a lot of mistakes were made. His father was so keen that he should assimilate that he was adamant that my son shouldn't be taught our language. I regret letting that happen, but I also realise that in spite of the cosmetic changes that my ex-husband was going through, underneath it all the basic assumptions of his rights and power as a man over a woman – which are much more pronounced in Asian men – and my inner belief that this was what should happen, lay intact. So whereas I would now resist such dictates with a passion, then I just let it happen.

Then he left, saying that this sort of thing 'happens all the time, couples get divorced all the time and it's just stupid to imagine that people should be together for ever'. I suppose his leaving me for a white English upper-class woman was just following a time-honoured tradition. After all, a white wife is a considerable social asset – you just have to look at prominent Asians, from one of the first Asian MPs to leading Asian authors and media men today; they all have white partners.

Besides the terrible shock of him leaving, of discovering that he had deceived me for years, of him breaking up the family, other things began to emerge in my own head. I realised just how differently we now thought, and how this country had been responsible for the creation of this very angry woman and this 'mimic man', as Naipaul describes them – those from the colonies who become white. My ex-husband's view of marriage, of fatherhood, of responsibility, was now entirely based on the Western view of individual freedom and choice. Mine was rooted somewhere back in my cultural heritage, where there is a balance between an individual life and the needs of family and community.

I met a white man a year after he had left. I had never been with anybody white before. We fell in love and got married recently. There are several ironies that are coming through now. With my political views, and the way I felt about myself, I was terrified of being with somebody so utterly English. I thought this was maybe God's punishment for my going on at white men for so many years! And I *was* worried that all I had learnt about being Black in a white society, all my commitment and, I suppose, my background, which was hybrid but with very strong Asian elements, would be squeezed out or end up as a kind of museum piece once I had married John. That I would wear my saris at cocktail parties and everybody would squeal and say, 'Oh, how lovely!'

In fact the very opposite has happened. I remember my son saying, the day John moved in, 'Isn't it nice, we can eat Indian food with our hands now that Dad's gone.' John is so secure as a man and so self-critical as part of a society which has done so much damage around the world – a view he had arrived at long before he knew me, so it's not something he uses to impress me with. It makes it much less of a struggle for me, being Asian and politically uncompromising. He gives me the confidence and the support to be myself and encourages those sides that have been suppressed. And so, at the end of the day, there are fewer battles except about why I don't wear shalvar khameez more often, or why I neglect my mother.

My mother, I guess, put her finger on it. She said, 'Coming

to your house with your first husband was a nightmare, he looked down on me and made me feel like a peasant. The love and respect John shows me is wonderful, I think he must have been an Indian in his previous life.'

He has also been profoundly important in making my son see himself for what he is and be proud of his background. Recently, for the first time ever, my son came home from school with an essay he had written on just this issue – a complete contrast to when his father was here, when he would for ever deny that he was Asian and even lie in school about what his favourite food was. I knew, and he knew, it was tandoori chicken. His school thought it was hamburgers.

If all this sounds too idyllic to be true, I have to say that I deeply wish my marriage had not broken up and that, particularly as we were refugees, my son could have had input from both of us, firsthand and in an organic way throughout his life, about his background. I regret the corruption of my ex-husband by this country. I remember what it was like in the early days – the ease, the language we both shared, the idioms, the memories of where we had come from and our families. That is a real loss. And relationships within my present husband's family seem sterile by comparison, although I get on very well with his mother. But I think what matters most is that with a white man I have been able to find safety and security in being me, as an Asian woman, as a radical Black writer, in a way that I could never have done with my ex-husband, who was Asian but who just couldn't wait to get into his green wellies and his Land Rover.

Elizabeth and Nasir Ahmed

Elizabeth Ahmed was born and brought up in Scotland. Her father, who was Scottish, was considered unusual because he married an Englishwoman. Elizabeth had a 'good' Christian upbringing. She worked as a social worker in the international field. She married Nasir Ahmed in her late thirties.

Nasir grew up in Calcutta and East Pakistan – now Bangladesh. Politically active since early days, he has lived in Europe all his life. Born into a Muslim family, he has firsthand experience of other religions and believes that a sense of personal moral spirituality is essential. He works in the field of mental health.

They have a son and a daughter.

Elizabeth: My family thought it was very adventurous to marry someone from the other end of the United Kingdom, let alone the other end of the world! We met at a party and Nasir had a slight Austrian accent because he had been there for a few years. I remember thinking he was Czechoslovakian – why I don't know, because I knew a lot of Indians; he just seemed different, perhaps he was already an international person.

I was a social worker, and one of the things I had to do was to run an advisory service for those marrying foreigners. They would give you information if you were marrying someone of a different nationality or religion. It would cover things like the nationality rights of children in such marriages. I was doing that quite happily, never thinking that I could get involved myself.

Nasir: When I first came here I met this man at a party who thought I would do very well teaching disturbed children. So I walked into a job, just like that, at the first school for maladjusted children in London. Then I got into working with refugees, which had been my passion when I left India. I had done some work during the terrible days of the partition when I saw scenes that were beyond imagination. That was a time of great political change, the anti-British movements, the nationalism – I was passionately involved in that. It is important to remember that we were anti-imperialist, not anti-British. We didn't hate people; our quarrel was with the system of oppression. I have always had a deep commitment to the universality of human beings, and I still do. Maybe that is why I see these things in a different way.

Elizabeth: That was what was so extraordinary about Nasir. From the age of twelve, he was politically involved. People here go on marches and that sort of thing, but not to the extent that Nasir described to me. He can still get quite passionately angry with the British and with other injustices. I had been to India in the sixties before I met Nasir, which was a very different scene. One of my sisters was out there as a missionary, which I really rather shudder about now. I went by boat. That was a fantastic experience because there was a boatload of Indians who had been here for five years, returning home with great expectations. I found them fascinating – their traditions and the way they thought about themselves, their commitment to their families and their country: quite intense feelings.

I didn't have that imperial arrogance because of the missionary influence, I think; the people I was with were very much for abrogating and moving out. They weren't like the tea planters and the army.

Nasir: When we met and after we decided to go out together – even when at one time we were seeing each other every day, and we bought a house together – we kept on saying, 'We aren't going to get married, no promises.'

Elizabeth: This went on for about eighteen months. Both my parents had died before I met Nasir – that was where you might have got the quite strong reaction. I come from a solid Scottish professional Church family; my father was a theologian and one of my mother's sisters was a doctor and a missionary in Jordan who had spent her life trying to convert the Muslims. I don't think she wanted to meet Nasir, but my sisters were very welcoming. I don't know if there were underlying things, but there was nothing I saw or felt. But that is my close family. I have cousins who tend to be quite narrow-minded and we've been discriminated against from time to time by them; they have not invited us to weddings and things like that. On the other side, Nasir has a lovely relationship with his mother. So we really had quite an easy ride.

When we got married, I remember someone saying I should be more worried that he was a psychotherapist than that he is an Indian. I see their point. But there was nothing else. And it is quite interesting, I had had some disastrous relationships and had decided to get on with my life without a man when I met him. He had had lots of women, from all parts of the world.

Nasir: When I wanted to register our marriage, the marriage superintendent, a very nice man, had a long chat with me and said, 'Do you understand the complications of such a marriage? Go and see the lady who runs the foreign marriage advisory service!'

When we met, my mother was alive, but my father had died a long time before. I think she was very pleased because at least I was settling down. My two nephews were here because there was trouble in Bangladesh. So my close family were fine. I don't know how my extended family felt about it. I am almost certain that they must have made comments and felt uneasy about what I was doing, but I have a reputation for being absolutely straight and I don't believe that I should listen to somebody because they happen to be an elder uncle or whatever.

A question I do ask myself is: have I made any transition at all in cultural terms by moving here or getting married to Elizabeth? I can tell you when I made the physical transition to come here, I was really disappointed, because London was so much like bloody Calcutta. I began to think in more cosmopolitan terms long before I came here.

And I had changed culturally a long time before. I had converted to Hinduism when I was at home, and that was the biggest shock to my mother. But she reacted typically. When my father died I became the eldest male in the family so I could do no wrong. Friends had got used to the idea that I was somewhat different and when they told her about my conversion, her reaction was 'Well, everybody goes mad in their own way.' She was so remarkable; although I knew she was upset, she didn't say a word. Once I had this argument with my mother and I said to her, 'Don't blackmail me emotionally. If I'm convinced that what I am doing is right, and you threaten that if I do it you will commit suicide, I will still do it.' She looked at me and said, 'I am glad you said that.' So she was very unusual and we were very lucky in that.

Elizabeth: I was lucky to have met her the year before she died in 1973. We went via Delhi and met Nasir's family, it was a real gathering of the whole Ahmed clan in Dhaka. Meeting his mother was exciting, but it was difficult because I had only learnt a bit of Bengali and she didn't speak any English, but we were able to communicate.

The extended family is quite overwhelming when you are not used to it. One of the things I find most difficult is that you are never alone. I would find it very difficult to live there for that reason. We went later with the children, when they were eight and twelve, when they were old enough to remember it, and they found it quite difficult too. I think they see themselves as a quarter subcontinental. Because they have been brought up here and they don't speak the language – although they will proudly say, 'I am half Indian' – they don't know very much about the tradition; I don't think they are particularly interested, not yet.

When I married Nasir, I felt as if his two nephews came with the package. That was something I sometimes resented because I felt that we never had any time on our own. I remember thinking at one stage: we have never spent a night on our own in this house. We used to have to go away to be alone. If he had been an Englishman we wouldn't have had that, he would have made time for us to be on our own.

Nasir: I never felt it in that way. I have a very different concept of privacy; maybe that comes from life in India, where there really isn't a notion of privacy, so you learn to be private inside yourself. I can do that, not only in marriage but when I'm with other people. I remember on one occasion we met this girl and I asked her out and we did go out, but with three of my friends! I can be very private in a crowd, sit very quietly and be inside myself. So if someone is staying at my house I don't feel they are invading my space or my privacy.

There are probably certain culture-bound expectations in our relationship at a deeper level; I am sure they are there, but I don't know what they would be any more. From the word go, my life has been so mixed up that I don't think I am located in any culture in that narrow sense. I would not fulfil those cultural norms even if I had married within my community, because of my life history. I suppose I have been a kind of rebel all my life. Perhaps it says something about me that I will always link up with the opposite group to the one I am expected to belong to. During the Hindu–Muslim riots I joined the Hindu relief centre, with my Muslim name. Everyone used to say, 'You must be bloody crazy, they will kill you.' I am still alive.

Elizabeth: Because he is the eldest male in the family, they have certain expectations of him. All his brothers died, so he is the chief and holds a certain place for his nephews and nieces.

Nasir: I honestly don't think that is true. Maybe they are following a tradition, but I don't think deep in their hearts it is like that. I don't think they give a damn what I think.

As for identity, how does one define one's personal identity? My identity is when I feel harmony within myself and my environment. I have found that in many strange places. In Austria I felt in harmony, although I didn't speak one word of German. That identity, that harmony you carry within yourself – it isn't determined by external features in a simple way.

Elizabeth: I think Nasir really is a citizen of the world. I am not nearly so cosmopolitan as he is. I am much more British, or perhaps European. Not Scottish – I quite like my Scottish roots, but I wouldn't describe myself as having a Scottish identity. I chose to move away; I would never want to live there now.

Maybe that is what has happened – we have dissolved away a very tight sense of belonging to one part of the world, and that gives us many more options in terms of an identity. Perhaps it works better if people with these international outlooks, people not too culture-bound, marry across. That doesn't mean you think alike all the time. You are constantly surprised about the alliances you feel. The Gulf War brought out strong feelings in Nasir and in me. Nasir has become quite strongly anti-American and anti-British, and takes up positions which are very firm, but which you can't put in a box. I often don't know how he is going to react. That is the difference between marrying the boy next door and marrying Nasir Ahmed. On a whole range of issues, I just never know. That can be very exciting in a way. The children are like that too, very open about every issue and not tied to certain predictable positions because of who they are. They feel like Londoners. Not British, not Indian, not white, not Black – New Londoners.

Nasir: Living the way we live and being the person I have become, there have been many gains; I don't know if there are also losses. You can define losses only at a very deep level. You have got to feel it in your guts. I may have lost a tradition, but I honestly can't say that it has troubled me. I have felt it when I have been in India, where I can feel very left out. Now if I go back I might feel more dislocated and less in harmony than I did last time. I started to feel dislocated when the partition happened. That was traumatic because there was then a great emphasis on your religious identity. Before that I used to pray in a church, a Hindu temple and a mosque, but suddenly you were told you could not go to these places. I felt the loss like a child.

With growth and experience, our perception of our identity and culture changes. It is not static, thank God. I remember saying to Elizabeth, 'I don't want you to wait for me to eat', because that would be the normal expectation in an Indian household. That was probably a reaction to what happened in my family – all the women waiting for their menfolk. I didn't want that for her or for me. I wanted to have that sense of freedom.

Elizabeth: But there are some things that are still there – I mean, you give orders. Instead of the British thing of 'Do you mind?' he will tend to say 'Will you get me this' and not the usual 'please' and 'thank you'. It's something I have found difficult, I have thought he is often very brusque with people. I had to be a spokesperson for him sometimes because he wasn't being 'nice' enough. That, I think, is cultural.

That surprises Nasir about me – that I am too nice to everyone. I am a bit Calvinist in my ways, I think. Deep down, that is quite hard for him.

Nasir: I don't mind Elizabeth being nice to people, but I sometimes feel she does it in a servile way and does not assert herself. You ask which group do we two belong to? It is a very important question. I think we belong in bits to different groups in different situations, bits of various groups that we feel comfortable with. We don't swallow any group identity lock, stock and barrel. And that probably reflects how I cope with various relationships, a little bit at a time, and they do the same, otherwise we would go crazy. We are very fond of each other, but within certain limits. So we pick the bits that we can tune in to, and it works very well.

Elizabeth: I don't think we do belong to any group, and we aren't like many other couples who have close friendships with other couples. When the family, whom we are very close to, come over from Bangladesh, they are in and out of the house, but we don't live in each other's pockets all the time.

Nasir: One of the things that is very important to me is to be myself. I have never become culturally bound because of the family pressure, nor have I broken away into some other kind of culture because of some other pressure. The biggest compliment my friends have given me is that over the years I have not changed, I have behaved exactly the same whether I was living in Bangladesh, Pakistan or here, within or outside marriage.

And I have no sense of guilt about how I have lived my life. We haven't forced our children to go any particular way, ever.

Elizabeth: Perhaps not enough. Perhaps I feel the guilt. We haven't, for instance, brought them up with any religious background. I mean we celebrate Christmas, but not in a religious way at all. I feel guilty that they don't know enough about the religions, but then that is how most children in London are brought up these days.

Nasir: Our children are very aware of racism and what that means, and perhaps they are very idealistic. They are anti anything unfair or cruel. They do not tolerate discrimination even against the whites.

Elizabeth: They haven't suffered any racism directly that we know of – perhaps because they don't look particularly Asian, they could be Mediterranean. I am pleased that we live in an inner-city area rather than suburbia, partly because I feel that people are less prejudiced and more enlightened in these areas. We don't deliberately put ourselves in a position where we would find prejudice, like certain pubs – you just don't go to places like that. But we are living in a good age. I really think it is easier now. If we had been living like this twenty years ago, it might have been quite different.

Shyama Perera and David Rose

Shyama Perera is a freelance journalist who has worked on national newspapers and television for fifteen years. She was on the staff of the *Guardian* and has been a presenter for

BBC2. She was born in Russia of Sri Lankan parents, and came to Britain when she was five.

David Rose was born to a Jewish family, though he himself is not a practising Jew. He is also a journalist, and worked for the *Guardian* for several years before joining the *Observer* as Home Affairs Correspondent. Shyama and David have been married for two years and were expecting their first child when they were interviewed.

Shyama: My parents split up within four weeks of arriving in Britain – my father went off with another woman and I have had little contact with him since. I have been back to Sri Lanka only once.

Because the Sri Lankan community is scattered and because my parents were divorced my mother had to work and I didn't have a traditional upbringing, I didn't have a strong sense of cultural identity. I was a latchkey kid from the age of six. My mum, who is a devout Buddhist, went to work before I went to school and came home at six or seven at night. All her friends were and are Sri Lankan, but they didn't all live round the corner, so there was no question of someone keeping an eye on you. I didn't have Sri Lankan friends and I don't have Sri Lankan friends now, apart from family.

I was very aware of my mother being Sri Lankan and my not being Sri Lankan. Everything I identified with was here and white, and my mum really hadn't tried to stop that happening until it got to adolescence, when she started to regret the fact that I'd been allowed so much freedom – and by then it was too late. I could break away and do what I wanted. Looking back now, I see she wasn't at all restrictive, but at that time it felt as if she was and I put that down entirely to the fact that she was Sri Lankan and didn't understand the way things happened here. I felt culturally restrained, but I think now it was more that she expressed herself in a culturally different way, not that all the restrictions were culturally dictated. I didn't see the difference at

113

that time. I left home at sixteen and went to live with my boyfriend and barely spoke to her until I was twenty.

Looking back, it was terrible for her, it was a terrible shame; the Sri Lankan community is very decorous and I was blowing all the codes. For a long time she spun out stories about what I was doing, to cover for me. Only now do I realise how much she suffered. I knew she was having a hard time but I felt she deserved it; I had no understanding of the cultural problem.

My mother had a relationship with the white community that was based on mistrust and fear. I didn't, which was another reason why I was unsympathetic to her. I thought she wasn't making an effort. We lived in one room until I was thirteen and then got a flat on an all-white council estate. I was blossoming, an adolescent, I had nice clothes, the boys would pay attention. You dressed the same, had the same hairstyle, so they identified with you even though you were Black. I knew I was Sri Lankan, but I didn't feel that it made me different. Whereas my mother dressed in a sari, and if she walked across a group of skinheads they'd shout out 'Paki', if I walked past they would whistle at me – the opposite reaction.

So from that early age I had very strong views about how you integrated. I was very critical of my mother for not having English friends, I felt that as long as she thought of herself as different, she would always *be* different. There was always that division between us, and there still is to some extent. The breakthrough came when I was about twenty. We went on holiday to Sri Lanka together, which was fantastic and really gave me a sense of identity. I felt like I was at home. I couldn't live there, but I loved the country. I suddenly understood how my mum felt. That was the beginning of us starting to make it up.

Racial prejudice? I've thought harder about it as I've got older. I don't think you notice racism and its associated problems so much when you're with middle-class people, and although we were poor my mother came very much from a middle-class background. You don't start to notice until you reach the glass ceiling professionally, but even then it's very hard to say whether you've reached that point because you're Black or non-Oxbridge. There are so many different criteria people use to judge suitability. I think racism is near the bottom of the pile.

I didn't really start noticing it until I joined the *Guardian*. It's the way people look at you! There was this absolute delight that I was not only showing them a bit of street culture, but that it was a little brown person doing it. I was seen as exotic. It's a kind of liberal racism. A lot of people genuinely believe they're colour-blind and that's the most dangerous thing of all.

All my boyfriends were white, apart from one Asian and one Nigerian, but it was never an issue. I never met any Sri Lankans, I wasn't averse to meeting Sri Lankans or Asian men but there really weren't Asian men around who were on the right kind of wavelength for me. Since I was seventeen I always said I would marry a man called David with brown hair and blue eyes whose star sign was Cancer. And I married the first one I met, but that wasn't until I was twenty-nine. I always knew I would marry a white man, although I never thought about it in those terms. I knew when I started going out with him that would be it, he was *the* David.

By that stage my mum was very grateful to get me married; I was getting beyond a marriageable age in her eyes. At first she was worried because he's Jewish and from a very orthodox family but he's not religious. She'd thought we'd never marry because of that. It didn't bother me – I didn't even know he was Jewish until we'd been going out for a while. It's a cliché, but all my best friends are Jewish, and so I was more Jewish than David in a strange way. I asked him whether he wanted me to convert to Judaism if he wanted the child brought up Jewish, but he categorically does not. His family are brilliant. They had given up any hope of him marrying a Jewish girl – only one of their children has married in.

Race wasn't really something that came into it, although it slightly did with me because David had an obsession with

India and all things Indian and at first I was quite suspicious of his interest in me. I suspected it was an extension of his love of things Indian – Wouldn't it be nice to have a little brown girl on his arm? So I was very careful in checking out his motives for wanting to go out with me. Then I realised that I didn't fit the picture of a traditional Asian woman and it wasn't anything to do with that!

We went on honeymoon to India. What a nightmare! I hated India, hated the way of life, and that's when I decided that I most definitely was British and applied for my British passport. I'd never been to India before and I had a complete culture shock. I loved the country and at the same time I loathed it. Even though I don't come from India, I felt as if I did because everyone was physically like me, and so my feelings intensified. I couldn't detach myself from it in the way that visitors normally can. While I enjoyed the sights and the history, I loathed the way of life, the overcrowding, the poverty, the restrictions on people, the heat, the dust. I found that I was very British in the way I looked at India. Above all, I hated the lack of order.

David loved it. All the British people I know love it, but that's because they know they can leave it behind. Interestingly, we went to San Francisco and in the centre there were all these homeless people and David was horrified; he said, 'It's terrible, a disgrace.' At the end of the day I said, 'You have seen twenty white beggars and you are outraged, yet in India when I was outraged at thousands of Indian beggars you were saying this is just the way of life here – that's racism.' I was outraged in India because those people are my stock somewhere along the line. I didn't like seeing people who were like myself living such awful lives. At the same time I felt they were nothing to do with me. Their lifestyle was completely alien and alienating. That's when I realised that although my mother had an absolute claim or right to the subcontinent, I didn't, and what's more, I didn't want one because I was a different type of Asian, I was a British Asian, so I could say this is not where I come from, I come from a different country, with different rules and regulations, which is equally valid. I suddenly saw that they might all be brown, and the reason I was feeling so upset was because I was identifying with them, but at the same time they were nothing to do with me, they were a different type of Asian. I had no more in common with them than an Australian has with a Serbian.

In a strange way David was quite shocked. He's very left-wing, very liberal, into race issues. He saw it as my reaction *against* India rather than *to* Britain. I've had a strong conviction about it ever since I came back. Now I want British Asians to sit up and see who they are; we have to be able to stand up and say 'We're British', not 'We're Asian' – 'We're British Asians'. It made me very sure of my own identity as a British Asian. A lot of Asians I meet are highly politicised and think I'm abandoning some kind of political ideal. It's not a popular view. On the other hand, young Asians know what I'm saying and in the right company would say it too.

As Sivanandan at the Institute of Race Relations says: What is culture? It's a nebulous concept, something that changes wherever you are. I think what's happened here is that white people have a perception of our culture as rigid, but Asians are trying to maintain that rigid culture as well. And what is it we're so preciously guarding – a few dances and a bit of tabla music? So who's trying to deny our culture and take it away from us?

To me, for the child we are expecting, religion is very important, because I think every child learns good and bad through that. I'm not religious but I went to a Church of England school and had right and wrong told me through Jesus and then went home and had it told to me through Buddha. So religion as a spiritual concept was important. The only religion I would not bring up a child in is Islam: its views on women are not only medieval but dangerous as currently practised in Islamic States. David is adamant that we ignore all religion, he had very bad memories of orthodox Jewry as a child. However, if, as a result of contact with its grandparents, the child wanted to be a Jew, neither of us would stand in its way. So if we have a boy he will be circumcised, just in case. I have no views about Buddhism, but David feels that if we have to espouse anything then Buddhism would be better because it's easygoing and doesn't stick a God down the child's throat.

The second consideration was the name. We thought about it long and hard. Somebody in David's office had come back from India and said to him, 'Oh I so envy you all those lovely little Indian babies, how lovely to have one!' I hit the roof and said, 'It's not going to be an Indian baby, it's going to be a British baby.' These liberals look at us and see Indians; they don't see us as British at all. That's our novelty value.

I thought about it for a long time and said to David that I thought it ought to have an Eastern name, because with a name like Freda Rose, people are always going to be looking at it and trying to work out where it comes from. It would be better called Nimisha Rose or whatever. I thought it was important for the child to acknowledge from day one that it came from a mixed race family, and the easiest way to do that is to give it a name that reflects that.

There was also a fear in me that if the child was very fair it would be very easy to pretend that it didn't have an Asian background – just to say 'My name is Freda Rose', and not think about being of mixed race. It's important that the child is aware of and acknowledges its origins because it won't hit it until it's eighteen or twenty. One hopes that in an ideal world there won't be people saying 'Where do you come from?', but I think there will on both sides. I think a lot of Asian kids grow up and are almost embarrassed about being different, because they're Asian. I want our child to be proud of this strange first name, its history and its context.

We're not deliberately going out of our way to tell the child about its cultural background. We felt the grandparents should take over that part because we live a fairly standard British life. We have the usual Eastern prints and Chinese rugs and lots of Ravi Shankar records. We eat curry and bagels and go to our parents' on Holy days – is that culture? While our backgrounds have made us what we are, they're not something we're conscious of. But we definitely want to take the child to Sri Lanka to meet its cousins. The fact that it's British doesn't mean it doesn't have roots in Sri Lanka, it just means it's not Sri Lankan.

Class makes a difference, so I don't think the child will have serious problems. I think I might worry more if it was going to the local school on the corner. I think the middle classes here of all races have quite a different life because they have economic independence and can do what they like. I think class is a greater consideration when you're marrying across the boundaries. And the middle classes are educated enough to keep their prejudices to themselves, which doesn't necessarily make them better people but means you have a better life. Because they're not going to let you know their prejudices and make your life difficult. They control them where possible. Maybe they're not going to invite you to certain dinner parties, but they won't cut you dead in the street, or call you names, or abuse your children.

I don't think the child should be 'politicised' in the sense of seeing life as 'them and us'. My feeling is that you start to create problems when you see yourself as different first or Black first, or anything first. The problem is that when you become politicised you need an enemy, so you look for it outside and completely ignore the enemy within. I think that's one of the reasons why you still have very poor and disadvantaged Asians. We're so busy educating everybody else about our problems that we're not actually educating our own people to get themselves out of the situation. You bring children up to have one foot in each culture, and instead of getting bilingual children you get semilingual children; instead of getting well-educated children you get semi-educated children. You're constantly splitting up what little they have.

I would hope my child would be socialist and want everyone to have equal rights, not because it feels disadvantaged but because it feels strong enough to stand up and fight for those people who are. I want it to see the cultural thing as a richness – not something static that has to be put away in the corner, but something that it can mould and change and delve into if it wants to, but as no more relevant to its life in many ways than Morris dancing or fish and chips. Go into an English or Asian middle-class home – they're not going to be much different, apart from the food they eat.

I think colonialism left enormous scars on the countries involved. I think it made a difference in my parents' generation. I don't think it should make a difference in my child's generation because time has moved on. A lot of people are still trying to get their own back for the things that were done to us by the British. So they say, 'When we come here why can't we do the same as the British? They came to India, lived their own lives, kept their own culture and here they are; when we do it to them they don't like it.' However, the difference is that the British owned India and Sri Lanka, they were top dog and that was what gave them the power and freedom to do exactly what they liked, whereas we are at the bottom of the pile and the longer we continue this grudge-bearing we keep ourselves down. The children we produce are home-grown British Asians, that makes them part of the oppressive not the oppressed. It's a conundrum that we must apply to ourselves.

My mother sits in her bought council house, and will still go on about colonialism. I say, 'What has that got to do with getting on in Britain? You're not going to right the wrong by feeling this way. You just make yourself feel bitter and then you want to put that bitterness on to me, and then you'll want me to put that bitterness on to my child. I'm not willing to do that.' I don't see what relevance it all has to my day-to-day life.

David: I saw Shyama on the 'Six o'Clock Show', soon after I started at the *Guardian*, and I don't know if it was anything like love at first sight, but I had this sense that I had to get to know this woman, that it was extremely important that I should meet her, and see what she was like. I tried to get this mutual friend to set up meetings two or three times and these fell through. She had meanwhile heard bad reports about me from her friends on the *Guardian* and so she would avoid meeting me, until she couldn't! I don't think her being brown had anything to do with it at all. It was just her. She is a very untypical brown person anyway.

I have had a long interest in the Indian subcontinent, especially its history, and I've always liked Asians, to put it absolutely bluntly. But the fact is that Shyama is so un-Asian in her attitudes and her general outlook on life that frankly I found myself far more knowledgeable and culturally aware than her. And it was funny when we went to India – she was appalled by the exploitation, the squalor and the poverty and I was going around cooing, 'Oh, isn't this great?'

So you can see in marrying Shyama as an Asian woman I wasn't trying to raise my credibility. I had never been out with anyone Asian before and although I have a lot of friends and contacts who are Asian, that is not what this was about at all.

My parents were all for it. They had been wanting me to get married for a long time. I had a long relationship which was going nowhere and it was clear that it all needed some sorting out. They were also very anxious to have grand-children. In fact, as soon as Shyama's byline started appearing in the *Guardian*, my mother said to me, quite spontaneously, 'Why don't you ask that nice Shyama Perera out?' She had watched her on the telly and she had thought she was just the sort of girl for me. But you know when I first told my mother that I was going out with Shyama, she said, 'Oh, little brown babies, how nice!'

Neither of us is particularly religious. It seems to me that when people have very clear ideas, a set path on these things, then it becomes much more of an issue and since quite frankly, if I am anything, I am an atheist, it really is not a problem.

Shyama: I actually think the cultural thing has been a problem for my side. When David's parents, for instance, were introduced to my family, I felt the Sri Lankans had great difficulty talking to them. And they in turn had difficulties welcoming them and actually making them feel as much a part of their grouping as they did with me and my mum. I think the truth is that I was very Westernised, so it was easy for them to take me in, but with my relatives I think they did find it very difficult. It took about four or five meetings for them to relax with each other. In some ways, too, it took a lot longer for the Sri Lankans to accept David than it did for his family to accept me. And his parents still feel quite awkward when they are stuck with all my aunties and uncles.

David: With the baby – if it is a boy we will have him circumcised, just in case he decides one day he wants to rediscover his roots. And we will make sure that it goes to temple and all that. We will teach it about both its families. We were thinking about doing a giant family tree.

Shyama: I think that is important – to tell the child: This is what you are. Because I do think that what we are turning out is a hybrid. And it is very important to me that it sees itself first as British, before the colour, and not as 'British but . . .', because that way it will see itself as disadvantaged. It has to see itself as of this country. And I think for a mixture such as ours, we have to understand that for that child, one half of its history is white. The heritage is half oppressor, half victim.

David: What I think is so incredible is those people who try and create chips on people's shoulders about colonial history – now I love history, but to try and create the feeling that people should feel personally aggrieved because of what happened two hundred years ago is ridiculous. And it is always complicated. My grandfather was stationed in India for twenty years as a soldier, and my family history is very complicated. There is an East European side, but my mother is a very sort of straightforward English country type who converted to Judaism after she met my father. And you know, when she was pregnant again soon after I was born, her mother said to my father, 'I want you to remember she is not of East European stock, you know – all these babies one after another.'

Shyama: You can't bring a child up to hate what its father's side did a long time ago to its mother's side. You will put more conflict into the child – and why? We want the child to be aware of where it comes from but to see that as something that makes it better rather than something which diminishes it. I feel that I was sent out into the world from an Asian home feeling that I was not as good as everyone else, and that was why I was discriminated against. It is very important to us that the child doesn't first of all see itself in terms of colour, because then it will feel that it is inferior.

David: I think it is tragic that so many of the young Black and Asian kids are already so set in their ways that they feel they could not have mixed marriages. That is because they have been loaded with this old colonial history and the fact of the matter is that we haven't been a colonial power for nearly fifty years. So much has changed in the communities who now live here. So much has been achieved, in so many different ways.

Shyama: If our child was abused, I would always teach it to retaliate and not to do what my mother always said I should do, which was to turn the other cheek. These are my child's peers and my child has as much right to sock that kid in the jaw or to retaliate. That is the way these other children learn.

David: This thing about having a group identity as opposed to a family identity is something that I don't feel is that important. It so easily leads to problems – an appalling fundamentalism or that sort of belief in culture which is frozen in time and space, and really I rejected all that in my own life. I was brought up in a kosher household which didn't have electricity on Saturdays. It was ridiculous. I was chosen to play in the rugby team – you can imagine how proud I was, and I couldn't play because my dad would not give way. I couldn't believe that I was expected to give that up and go to the synagogue and listen to this bloody chanting in this foreign language. I gave it all up and didn't step into a synagogue after my bar mitzvah, which initially was a huge disappointment. And it all came to a head when Shyama asked me if I wanted her to convert to Judaism when we had a child, and all the horror came back to me. I said no way did I want my child to go through that. Only one out of four of us married in. One is married to a nominal Catholic, another – of all things! – to a German Lutheran, which was harder for my family to accept than Shyama.

Shyama: I think spirituality does matter to me and after thinking long and hard about it I offered to convert to Judaism because it has ritual and tokens and things which meant my child would have something – because it is better suited to a child, perhaps. But David feels so strongly about not bringing the child up in that tradition that I have bowed to the pressure.

David: I would like the child to learn about Judaism and I hope that my parents will take it to the synagogue to participate in the ritual – but not ram it down its throat. And although I can see the need for spirituality, it is not through Judaism, which is all just ritual.

Shyama: I am keeping an open mind about this. I think when our child goes to school and is taught about Christianity and Islam and other religions, David will suddenly rediscover Judaism.

David: On the other hand, if I feel that Jews are under attack, I am very militant in their defence. I would like my kid to have that kind of identity on both sides. If the child wanted to take up religion – either one – that would be fine. I would be much more depressed if it became a Christian.

Shyama: I think the child has to define what it is. I don't think we have the right to put all this upon it. We will give it the stability and the support it needs to see that through. I don't think that is too idealistic. I don't want my child to feel that it is a victim of life. The Jewish community in this country have a sound economic basis and power, so they are equipped to fight the discrimination they face. (This is not to diminish their problems.) Whereas the Asian community are a new community and are still finding themselves.

This is controversial, but I feel that our parents have failed us very badly – it is very easy to blame the white racist in the street, and certainly they take the blame for many many things, but our parents have to take a large percentage of the responsibility for sending us all out ill equipped. I think they are so steeped in traditions, rituals and superstitions, they express themselves in terms that are irrational and stupid, ignorant, and their children then follow them on the tread-mill of ignorance. I think it is the people who have broken away from this who then make it, those who say 'Ya Boo Sucks' to their roots, and pull away. So I suppose if my child comes home and does Kathakali dancing or Morris dancing it will be out on its ear.

Kojo Annoh and Claire Evans

Kojo Annoh is forty-two, the sixth of seven children. He was born in Accra, Ghana, but left the country in his early twenties to further his education in Britain. He trained as a psychiatric nurse and currently works with adolescents and their families.

Claire Evans is thirty-four, the eldest of four children. She was born and brought up in Surrey. After qualifying as a doctor in 1981 she travelled and worked in various branches of medicine before deciding to specialise in psychiatry. In 1990 she became a consultant in geriatric psychiatry. Since this interview Kojo and Claire have married and are now expecting their first child.

Claire: We got to know each other about five years ago when I went to work on the ward where Kojo was the charge nurse, a ward for disturbed patients, a strange place. I found this environment quite hard to cope with and Kojo protected me – or I felt he did.

At first it was just friendship. I remember spending hours talking to him. He was a very popular person at work and had a circle of young women who told him their problems. They felt pushed out – especially as I was a doctor, which was high-status as they saw it.

Kojo: The status didn't bother me. I was just fascinated by this person, she was so vulnerable. I was very conscious of her difficulties. I liked her and thought I must get close to her. I arranged to play tennis and then cried off. I was married at the time and I wasn't sure what I really wanted, what I was getting into. But it didn't take me long to make my mind up.

Claire: More was going on than I really faced up to. I certainly didn't ever see us having a long-term relationship. I think I thought I was going into a short, enjoyable fling. I moved into a new flat and Kojo came round, and that was the start of it. Then I became ill, I had an ovarian cyst. I'm a hypochondriac, like a lot of doctors, and I became convinced that I was going to die under the anaesthetic. I was awful until after the operation, but in a way it pushed us together faster than would otherwise have happened. He was very supportive and helped me through it.

When I was convalescing I went back to my parents, so Kojo met them much earlier than he otherwise would have done. Although I'd been living away from home for some time, it was difficult with my parents – but I only sensed this. As a family we cover up our feelings, so I never really knew – and still don't know – what their reactions were. I think my mother found it hard to get used to the idea that I was going out with somebody Black – and that he was married. *And* he was a nurse! They would expect him to be a doctor, at least. My mother said something, just a comment, but not until a while afterwards, partly because I didn't give her a chance, I didn't want to hear it. Our family is a great one for avoiding confrontations and any messages come in circuitous ways, so

I might find out about my mother's thinking by asking my brother. That's how my family protects itself.

Kojo: On my first visit, Claire's parents, as far as I'm concerned, were nonjudgemental about our relationship. I felt that we'd known each other for a long time. I didn't feel nervous and it didn't bother me much what they thought, but I never got any impression that I wasn't welcome.

Claire: My brother and sister have been very supportive. They are very close to Kojo and protect him. Kojo did gradually get to know my parents and they're very fond of him now. I don't know if they have any reservations – perhaps I should ask them because I think they may have, but they would say that it doesn't matter because I'm happy with him.

We had a traumatic few years mainly because Kojo was married and we were having an illicit relationship. He had told his wife about our relationship, but it was still very painful for everyone. I felt guilty, especially because of the children, who were only three and five. Kojo had come to the conclusion that he didn't want to spend the rest of his life in that relationship long before he met me. We finally decided to live together and Kojo moved into my flat, leaving everything behind.

Everybody was terribly unhappy, but at the same time we both felt we were happier than we'd ever been – if that doesn't sound silly. It was the first time I'd felt that I could have a long-term relationship with anyone. We talked a lot about splitting up, but I felt that if I let him go this would never happen again. I think all the splitting-up talk was about testing out how the other person felt, reassuring ourselves that we should be together.

Kojo: What kept me going was the fact that I knew I was doing the right thing. The race thing was not an issue for me, although my ex-wife was also Ghanaian. I am conscious that Claire is white and different, but in the same way as I would see another Black person who looks different, but

Black. I don't think I'm that colour-conscious. What I worried about was the comments other people would make. I wondered what my family would say to me, my brothers and sisters in Accra, how they would take it.

Claire: They do have quite a lot of anxieties about Kojo marrying an English woman. In a way it's quite parallel to what my family went through with their prejudice – not wanting to prohibit it, just feeling concerned about whether it's the right thing.

Kojo: Two things were said to me: if I married a white person, then that would confirm that I would never ever go to Accra again; and if I did, I would bring this white person, and would they be able to deal with a white person? That white person would be too different. They were worried about losing me, as *they* knew me and knew that I would never be the same after being with this white woman. It was a feeling of almost being sucked in by the Empire – you know: 'How could you have done that? You know that a long time ago, when our fathers were sitting down under the trees smoking their pipes, these white people came up and started to say we've discovered you. Now look at you, you're going after them, marrying them.' That, I guess, was going through their minds. At the same time my family know that I am a man in my own right and I will do what I want.

I went back to Accra on my own to talk to them about it. One of my brothers had come here four months before I went back, because I had written a letter talking about Claire. He came to see whether he could mend things with my wife, but he realised that I was very fair in what I was saying. He didn't meet Claire, he was staying at the other house with my wife.

I think my family were worried about the children; they didn't want to lose them and I needed to reassure them that I was not going to lose contact with them. The family back home meets monthly to discuss family issues, so when I went they had to call a meeting. I was trying to say, 'She is just like us.' Then they asked, 'What does she do?' and I said

128

she was a doctor. My elder brother said, 'Well, if Kojo says so, then that's it.' I had to reassure them that Claire was not the kind of white person they imagined – someone who is loose, cheap, a tart.

Claire: I was shocked when I heard it. I thought: how could Kojo's family feel like that about me? I'm a respectable person, but now they think I'm not good enough for them. It is a shock, but it's a good shock to have, because it makes you think. Once I'd got over the initial feeling of being insulted by it, I found it quite reassuring.

Kojo: I was quite happy for everyone to think what they wanted to think about me, because in the end nothing would change the way I feel about myself. If they hadn't supported me I would have gone ahead anyway; I would have been happy to isolate myself.

Claire: But it's important for me that they supported you, important for me to know you have roots and family. I haven't met the family yet, although I hope I will sometime. None of them will come to the wedding, it's too expensive.

No one in my family would have expected me to end up with somebody Black. In my year off between school and university I went and taught in East Africa. When I left, my grandmother and great-aunt used to say to me repeatedly, 'Whatever you do, dear, don't come back with a Black man.' I do often wonder why it is that I'm with somebody who my family would never have imagined I'd end up with. I sometimes feel that for me it's a late rebellion. I've always been a quiet and conscientious person. The fact that we are getting married is very important – to say that we are committed to each other, this is something permanent, not just a fling – to my family, and friends as well.

Kojo: I remember talking to an aunt whom I saw before I came to this country many years ago. She said, 'When you come back, make sure you don't marry a white woman. We've got lots of women here!'

When I was twelve I went to a boarding school in Ghana

129

which was very much like a British public school with British graduates who came to teach, so I was very familiar with white people and I came to terms with my prejudices at an early age. I was prejudiced against white people. There was an English boy in my house at school and we used to call him imperialist; Impy. He had a really bad time. He wasn't imperialist, just unfortunate enough to be a white boy in a school full of Black people.

Claire: In a way Kojo had more of a conventional British education than me: houses and prefects, and fagging and Latin. We always argue about class. I maintain that because we come from a similar kind of background it influences our relationship because a lot of our values are similar. But Kojo insists that he's not middle-class, he thinks he does not belong to any class, although I think he is middle-class. But Kojo is not in any way a snob, he doesn't try and judge people or even pigeonhole them by their class.

Kojo: I look at people and see their humanity, not where they came from. I came to England twenty years ago and although I haven't experienced racism directly, I've known people who have. Some of it surprised and shocked me – especially when it came from adults and people in high positions. When it came from my peer group it didn't shock me because we had done it when we were young, it was just happening the other way. And you have to see things the way they are – I mean about feeling superior to Black people. These same people have feelings of superiority to white people too. There is an inability to perceive and value other people's cultures.

Claire: Since our relationship started, I've become much more aware of racism and the legacy of colonialism. It makes perfect sense to me now when I hear things on television about the unfairness, but I would never have thought about it before – now it makes me feel angry. I had some Black friends, had been to Africa twice and I'd been really interested in Africa. That meant I was always well disposed to Africans. I'm very tolerant of other people's views and values, I've always found it easy to get on with people of other cultures – my snobbery is intellectual.

When I see photographs of us together I get a shock because I think he's so Black and I'm so white, but I don't think about it from day to day. I'm so familiar with what Kojo looks like that I don't think about it any more. I don't see the colour. I think we both defend ourselves against racism by laughing at people's ignorance. We've never had any horrid comments, but sometimes I expect racism – that one day we'll turn up at a hotel and people will say 'Sorry, every room's taken.' I fear it. It's something that's quite difficult to prepare yourself for, except by using your imagination. Undoubtedly my imagination is worse than the reality. I'm sure I will be able to cope with it.

Kojo: I don't worry about these things. I've dealt with the issue of racism. I don't get angry about it, I just feel sad and powerless.

Claire: I am aware that a Black man carrying a mixed race baby doesn't attract the same kind of comment as a white woman with a mixed race baby. It's something I think and agonise about – how will people react to me with a mixed race child, but also how will a mixed race child make out in the world, knowing the prejudice that is there? I look at mixed race children all the time, want to go up and talk to the parents, although I have never actually done so. Say, 'What's it like, how do you cope?' I think it's up to us to give the child a good upbringing so that the child is able to deal with those sorts of things. Because Kojo is very cool about colour and very self-confident about it, it helps me. And I realise that to some extent we are insulated against racism by our class and occupation. In the field of mental health there are a lot of mixed marriages and we go to lots of parties where lots of mixed race kids are running around. And in London the chances are that when children go to school there will be lots of other mixed race children. I just hope that our children will have the personal qualities to be able to overcome it.

Kojo: I don't worry about it – people are just human beings. My son came to me one day – he was the only Black boy in the school – and he said, 'They all call me the chocolate kid.' I said, 'How does that make you feel?' and he said, 'It makes me feel very important.' That seemed a good attitude. Of course he is different, that's special, and if he can see it as positive, that's great. We do need to give children the mental equipment to deal with the problems. You do it by setting the right example. If you are not sorted out yourself, then you are going to have children with problems. Especially at the early ages, you have to set the right example. We have to make sure that they value the differences rather than seeing them as problems. We can't stamp out prejudice. In many ways things have changed, though the older people are still a problem. The attitudes of fifty-to-seventy-year-olds here and in Accra are very similar.

If you're confident about yourself, you value yourself and you know your roots, even when you experience racism, you have something to fall back on. I will always know where my roots are, and that will stay with me.

Claire: We are very similar in many ways – background, class, etc. – but undoubtedly Kojo is very African. We used to argue a lot and I would get so annoyed because he argues and thinks in completely different ways to me. His thinking is all over the place. It's very complicated. I would get very cross but go away and think about it and then see his point of view. But in an odd way that has been helpful to me. I think Kojo is largely responsible for my success over the last few years. I was very lacking in confidence and had a very low opinion of myself; I would never have made it so far if he hadn't helped me to improve my self-esteem. In my family we tend to run ourselves down, whereas Kojo helped me see I couldn't survive like that. He has chosen not to scramble up the ladder, partly because he likes the nursing work and partly because he didn't want to expose himself to the possibility that he might be humiliated. He is so proud, it is sometimes hard for me to get used to that.

Kojo: But I too have become more ambitious because of Claire. I'm embarking on all sorts of things that I wouldn't have done without her encouragement, although I'm not doing it just for her. Claire thinks it's about both of our psychologies; we complement each other. Colour is not the primary thing as far as I'm concerned. You have to go beyond colour to find the qualities that make a relationship. And other people – family, friends, the general public – as time goes on, look beyond the barrier and see a human being. There's an attitude among some Blacks that if you go out with a white person and marry one, it's a bad thing. They don't want to mix the two, dilute the race. But it is also true that everyone wants to find someone different. I want to be with someone special and different – that's what concerns me.

Terry and Dee

Terry – Afro-Caribbean, twenty-five – is a sports instructor. He lives with Dee who is white and British, twenty-three and an office worker. Since they have moved in together Dee has not seen her family.

Terry

I know I will be killed for saying this, but I would not go with a Black woman. They always give me the impression that they can do without us. They are too defensive and demanding. There is nothing soft or feminine about them. It's like my dad – my mum always gave him a hard time when he came home. She would be waiting for him and as soon as the key was turned her shouting would begin. He was a quiet man, a good man, but she hassled him till he died; he was no good, he didn't earn enough money, he drank. When he wasn't there I was the one she picked on. I was going to be no good, just like my father. She never tried to understand that he had come here with his qualifications, and nobody had given him what he deserved. I saw him crumble. But she didn't care. So what did he do? He found a lover – a white woman who lived near his factory and used to make the tea there. She was not a clever woman, not a good-looking woman, but she gave him love. He used to take me with him sometimes and she gave me those pink almond sweets. She spoke quietly, and that was her best quality.

Dee works in an office. My Black men friends say she is a typical blonde beauty, but that's not it. She does exactly what I need, and I mean so much to her. She makes me feel like a real man. If I am angry at her, she cries. That is special to me. I don't make her cry, but she cries when she is disappointed in me and I just warm to her. I never saw my mother crying once. My dad yes, never her. My sister is just like her, too. She has just got divorced, and it is terrible.

Dee values me. She gave up her family to move in with me. That is sacrifice, proof of love. And all the white girls I have been with have really liked me, made me feel special. They go through hell with their friends and families, but they stick with you. They feel for you. You know in the early days, many Black men had white wives in this country and those women stood by them and suffered terribly. This Black Muslim woman in America has written a book telling Black women to behave like white women if they want to keep their men. Our women should read those books. I work with one other Black woman in the gym. She is nice and soft when the white supervisor is talking to her. But if I am standing in for him, she treats me like I am nothing.

There is something fine and delicate about European women, something that turns me on. I like the slim look – most Black women don't have that. I hate that bright-red lipstick on a Black face, and those tight dresses. Dee is really modest and has a really pure look, with no make-up, like an angel. It isn't inverse racism or anything. Perhaps it is because we Black men and women have had such a hard history that we can't make it together. There is too much pain and reality, not enough escapism and romance. And maybe I treat Dee in a special way because I think she is more special than a Black woman. We all have things deep inside us – you know like those South African Black nannies who believe that their white babies are better than their own Black children . . . I don't know.

Dee

We just don't think in terms of Black and white, but everyone around does, so you are forced to remember all the time. And you feel hemmed in. My parents were awful about this – not when I first told them, before they met him. I think they thought it was quite trendy, fitted in with their Bob Marley records and anti-South African feelings. And I think they expected somebody who looked like Harry Belafonte. So when Terry turned up – and he is really Black, with beautiful dreadlocks and wild clothes, and he can't sit still – they were paralysed. Like *Guess Who's Coming to Dinner?* I think they were more shocked at themselves than at Terry. I remember when he hugged me on the sofa, my mother was watching me with this terror in her eyes. They were very nice, of course, being English, and they said as we left, 'Do come back again sometime', like you would to someone you would expect to see once every two years.

I had told my mother we were living together, that this was the big love affair. And you know they were sixties people, they were both teachers with the Inner London Education Authority and did all their anti-racist teaching about Black heroes. I was more disappointed in that lie than that they didn't like Terry, so it wasn't hard leaving them behind. But the reactions of Terry's Black friends are something else. I feel frightened at the strength of that anger with me because I am white, and typically white I suppose – blonde, and so on. If things don't work out with Terry, I don't think I would have the guts to go with another Black man – not because of my friends and family but because of the way Black people have made me feel about it. We all grow up together, and nothing changes.

4. Tears and Fears

❝ George left because he was a man, like any other man, not because he was Black. The way my friends responded, it was all because he was Black. It was really difficult – I had to defend this man, even at times when I hated him, because it isn't fair to blame his colour. You don't have to be a certain colour to leave a woman and kids. ❞

– SUE NORRIS

Sue Norris

Sue Norris is a white single mother, living on a housing estate in East London. Her partner, George, was born in Ghana, but moved to Britain as a child. They split up three years ago. They have three children, the eldest nine and the youngest four. Sue is now back at college trying to acquire skills so that she can find work. She was adopted as a child and traced her birth mother only six years ago.

Sue

I got together with George twelve years ago when I went to a club with a Black girlfriend. I was the only white woman there and felt really self-conscious; there was no doubt that some of the lads didn't like me being there. But no one said anything to me. No one asked me to dance either. I was turning red when this very smooth guy came up. He didn't ask, just took my arm and swung me round, really tough like, and started dancing with me, cigarette still in his mouth and no kind of interest in me, although he had obviously noticed my embarrassment. He danced with me for about an hour and then just walked away. I fell in love with him there and then.

That was the way the rest of our time was going to be. He was tough and cool, cared about me, but wanted to do what he wanted to do. He had a lovely voice and although he wasn't handsome, he was really strong, big and masculine. My boyfriend, who was white and in the army, really seemed a weakling. I went to the bar and bought him a drink. He came home with me that night, laughed at the picture of Len on the coffee table, made love to me all night whether I wanted to or not – I could hardly walk the next day – and made me breakfast in bed, which no one had ever done. I was completely overtaken with passion for this man, yet I always knew he would be no good for me.

Then, after about a month, I started feeling terrible, went to the doctor and found – like in a bad film – that I was pregnant. I had stopped the Pill when Len joined the army and George just laughed when I told him to use Durex. As a Catholic I couldn't kill the baby, so I went to the club to see if anyone knew where George lived. I found him and he was wonderful. He was so happy, he hugged me and said I brought him luck. Then he gave me £20, took me for a drink and moved in. I was in heaven. I wrote to Len, who never wrote back, but his mother rang me and told me I was a bitch.

So we lived together and the twins were born. He was

great with them for the first few months. I found it difficult to be a mother, but he was fine – I didn't know then that he had done it twice before. What I couldn't cope with was his sexual appetite – he made love all the time and wanted to even when I came back from the hospital. Then little Esme came along and I thought I would die, I was so tired and weak. She was lovely and he adored her because she was a girl, but the sex went on. He was getting more and more demanding. If I was breastfeeding her, he would wait till I had finished and want me to make love immediately. I began to hate him for the very thing I loved him for.

He started saying to me that, sexually, white women were nothing compared to Black women. Then he grew more aggressive and threatened to find someone else. I remember one day when he made love to me, I just cried and wanted to be alone, asleep and not with him always inside me. He saw this and he was so hurt he just got up, got dressed and left.

He came back after a few weeks to get his clothes and to tell me that he would send money – which he has always done – and see the kids when he could. I begged him to stay, but he wouldn't. I had called him a Black bastard when we fought and told him he was an animal, things like that; I wish I hadn't. But he shouldn't have left me with three children, should he? He knew I loved him. I would do anything to have sex with him now, funnily enough, though sometimes I am so angry I want to kill him.

I've tried to sort things out in my own head. George left because he was a man, like any other man, not because he was Black. The way my friends responded, it was all because he was Black. It was really difficult – I had to defend this man, even at times when I hated him, because it isn't fair to blame his colour. You don't have to be a certain colour to leave a woman and kids, the estate is full of mothers like me. I hate being put into a position where I am trying to explain that it was just two people who couldn't work it out. And I hate it when people look and say, 'Huh, he's left her, that is just typical, Black men only use white women for what they can get.' My best friend then – but not any more – said to me, 'I hope you won't go running after a Black man again after this.' I even had a letter, unsigned, saying this was revenge for slavery, that Black men needed to take revenge on us because of what white men had done.

You're looked down on as if you have degraded yourself and made to feel as if you have done something impure, something immoral. White men stare at me, and once or twice I have been spat at and called a whore. Black women think you are taking their men away. My neighbour used to say that to me: 'You white women' – never 'Sue' – 'You white women have fantasies about our men and they will go for you because they know you won't give them a hard time.' Some of them are really pleased that George now has a Ghanaian woman.

And it starts to affect you. However much you believe that what you were doing was right, you do doubt your own instincts. I feel guilty about everything – about the fact that Black women feel that way, that whites feel I did something wrong, that somehow it was wrong. And – especially as it has gone wrong – I do sometimes feel that maybe I deserved it because I was naughty.

Edgar Thompson

Edgar Thompson was born in the 1930s. After a spell in the RAF, he trained as an architect. While a student in Edinburgh, where he still lives and works as a consultant, he met Pratima, another student, who had come over from India to study. Pratima now also lives in Edinburgh.

Edgar

I was brought up in a very loving home, but certainly one where there was an aura of racial prejudice, there's no doubt about that. Not overtly, but I remember my mother, who is a white South African, absolutely refusing to go to a Black doctor. I think I had always had that feeling at the back of my mind that Black people were in some way inferior. After school I was a pilot in the RAF, then, in the late fifties, I was invalided out and went through a sudden very traumatic shift of interest. I had been a well-brought-up young fascist, carefully trained to kill people, and I suddenly rebelled and decided to become an arty architect – I think it was a reaction to being slung out of the RAF; somehow it made me think: What do I really want to do?

The day I started at college in Edinburgh was a Sunday. I arrived and got off the train and this unbelievably beautiful woman got out of the next carriage. Physically she was just amazing. She had the most amazing skin and this enormously huge sensuous mouth, but at the same time she looked very innocent. She had a big red Hindu tilak mark and she was wearing a yellow sari. It was the most incredible image and I stared open-mouthed at this apparition, I followed it down the platform and waited while it got into a taxi. It wasn't even a person, it was like a kind of icon. I pulled myself together and thought: I'll never see her again, but what an amazing woman!

I went off and unpacked and installed myself in the first-year architects' studio. Suddenly that same woman came into the room, this time in a blue sari. She looked at me and walked across – it was as if it took three hours for her to walk across the room – and she said, 'Hello, my name's Pratima, can I sit here?' – which, it later turned out, was a very uncharacteristic thing for her to do, because she was a very self-contained and shy sort of person. She said afterwards that I was staring at her so intensely – she wasn't used to blue eyes, having come straight from India – and it was as though the sky was shining out from my head through holes in my skull, radiating towards her. She was very attracted to me in the same way that I was to her; it was the most extraordinary coincidence really.

But there were a lot of tensions to start with; it was a sort of love–hate relationship. We started off as friends and all my ideas about the inferiority of non-white people were totally bulldozed out of the way by the actual person, who wasn't in a category at all, she was unique. There were certainly ideas of prejudice hanging around *her*. She was a very high-caste Hindu from a very aristocratic family; her family were the traditional rulers in what is now Pakistan and got thrown out of there, and although they still had money, they did not have so much status in India. She was therefore very ardently Hindu and quite anti people who weren't Hindu.

I knew I wanted to spend the rest of my life with this woman – I felt that within a tenth of a second of meeting her. It sounds ridiculous, I know, but it was love at first sight. But I was actually fairly rational about it. I thought: she's only nineteen and she's disorientated and in a different culture and the first relationship she has with anyone isn't going to last for sure. So I cast myself in the role of amazing friend while she had a relationship – not a physical relationship, but a romantic relationship – with another man. When that finished, I thought: now's my chance. I let her get it out of her system, which isn't like me, and I took a lot of trouble to make this work. I found out a lot about Hinduism, about Hindu culture, and learned some of the language.

Although we were both very physically involved with each other, it was two years before we went to bed together, and even then it was very tense. She was a virgin and before she came to England she had never even kissed anybody. She had enormous social conditioning about how you don't go to bed with anyone unless he's your husband. She had been engaged to someone when she was fourteen but didn't go ahead with it. It had been a struggle to persuade her family to let her come to England. But in a funny kind of way she was a feminist; she was an independent woman and wanted to develop herself as far as possible.

I wouldn't say we ever had a satisfactory physical relationship, and that was quite difficult for both of us. We wanted to, we both desired it, but she felt enormous guilt. I remember the first time we made love, she was half drunk and I'd been making up to her for about a year. She drank a lot and

I said jokingly, 'One day I'll get you into bed', and she said, 'Right now, you bastard'. There was a lot of hostility, as well as a lot of desire, I think because she was rationalising it as something she shouldn't be doing, and which I was forcing her to. I think that was easier for her to live with – not to think she was doing it because she wanted to. This gradually went, but it was always an unrelaxed kind of thing. And I kept saying to her, 'Look, it's obvious that you don't think you should be going to bed with someone you're not married to, and I want to marry you. So let's get married.' I was ready to become a Hindu, I would have done anything – in fact I went through a phase when I really, really wished I was Indian because it would get rid of all these problems. I had no doubt at all in my mind that this was the woman for me.

This went on for about three years. Eventually we ended up living together, although we weren't supposed to be – we had adjoining rooms in a house and as far as everybody else was concerned we weren't. I don't think there was ever any prejudice against us as a couple from any of our contemporaries, I think the main feeling towards me was probably one of envy because she was such a shatteringly beautiful woman, and very intelligent, very nice. This was in the early sixties, the melting-pot time; it was the thing to go to bed with Eastern or African women, and I think there was also that element – that Pratima wondered whether she was a fashion accessory. Although it wasn't something that affected me, I was certainly aware that she was aware of it.

I learnt a fantastic amount from her. She had an incredible shaping effect on my whole character. Her attitude to life was of accepting the situation she was in and trying to achieve as much as possible of her own potential. I had a more Western idea of wanting to change the world and being in favour of organising everything for the maximum happiness. She felt that there were seeds in your character that you have to go along with and get as far as possible with, accept the way you are and develop it, which influenced me an enormous amount.

We were incredibly close friends, that was the thing, but

although the hostility went, although eventually we both physically enjoyed making love, there was always this sense of guilt. I suppose I felt mad that she was guilty and kept trying to persuade her that to get over the guilt we had to formalise the situation and get married.

At one stage she almost agreed that we should get married, but she was very insecure. She was brought up by her guardian, who was much older, and her mother, who was very traditional and hated the idea of her marrying a Western man. She had written to them early on saying she had met me, and that I wanted to marry her. They both said to her, 'You can marry any Indian you like, but who is this man?' He's just any Westerner, he's nothing. What is he, what are his parents – a bank clerk, are you mad?' After a while she stopped telling them and I think as far as they were concerned she had stopped seeing me.

Then her mother was very ill and she went home. While she was there I wrote to her every day. Unfortunately her mother found and opened some of my letters and a great row ensued. So there were a lot of pressures – social pressures on her from home not to marry me, pressures from me to marry her. Pressure from my parents, too. They thought she was a terrific person, but said awful things like 'Well, you're very much in love, but what about the children?' which made me very angry with them. Funnily, she was upset when I was angry with my parents because she thought that was a dreadful sin.

Looking back, I can see that she was terribly torn and very upset for the last six months we were together. She knew that she couldn't possibly abandon her family – in that kind of society, family relationships are incredibly strong. I don't think I understood at the time how important that was; if I had, I would have been altogether softer and more sympathetic. I was of that sixties generation, and my whole upbringing and my training in the RAF was that if you wanted something, you went for it. I was the worst sort of person to be in that kind of situation. I even said, '*I* don't care what my parents think – why are you such a wimp? Tell the old cow to get lost' – which of course was deeply offensive to her.

I think part of the problem was that I had set up a world that contained only two people – who the hell cared what anybody else thought? She hadn't done that.

So she obviously came to the conclusion that she had to get out of it. She couldn't think how the hell to do it, there was no way she could get herself to say to me, 'Look I've got to go back to India.' So she pretended to me that she had had an affair with someone else. And I, like an idiot, believed it. I was distraught, I said lots of unforgettable things, and that made it very easy for her to go. So she went back to India, went on a social whirl.

I wrote to her all the time, but she never answered any of my letters, although I know she kept them because she still has them now. They seemed rational letters at the time, but now they sound as though they were written by someone who was insane – blood-and-guts romantic, quite scary. She never answered. Finally I wrote and told her to piss off and then, tremendously on the rebound, I married my wife, basically because she needed me. And we have a successful marriage about 90 per cent of the time, it's a good solid marriage.

Then, by a terrible irony, Pratima started writing to me again. I remember the day I got the letter – it was the worst day of my life. It was as though an awful hole had opened up – if I had got this letter just three months earlier . . . I had this loving, eighteen-year-old child bride, she was someone I was very, very fond of and couldn't possibly abandon.

So I wrote back and said, 'I love you, but I've married someone else.' So she did a really stupid thing: she married someone on the rebound too, and tried, with him, to do all the things we had planned for our life together. But it was a disaster from start to finish. There was never any real rapport between them, and they split up.

I didn't hear from her for eight or nine years. Then one snowy evening in Edinburgh I got a telephone call. Pratima has an unmistakable voice, she didn't say hello, she just said,

'I've been thinking about another snowy evening a long time ago', I knew instantly who it was. We arranged to have lunch – I felt terrified but compelled to do it – there hadn't been a day in that eight or nine years, there still isn't, that I haven't thought about her; she's like a part of me, and vice versa.

So she came to live in Edinburgh and we started sleeping together again. It got very heavy and I seriously considered leaving my wife and kids. I had thought so much about what it would have been like to marry Pratima and have children with her. In the end I didn't. You know through all this she has never said, 'I want more, you must leave your wife.' There were points where I wanted to but she never made any demands – in fact she discouraged it, she would have regarded it as a great sin to have broken up the family.

It has all been very hard for her because she broke all the rules, all the taboos, and she was an Indian woman on her own, with her children from her first marriage, although she *is* very strong and has developed a tremendous ability to look after herself. I think on one level she still regards it all as something she shouldn't be doing and shouldn't ever have done. It's not a happy situation and she's not happy about it, but as she gets older she copes with it more easily. It helped a lot when her mother came over here to live with her. I don't know what her mother thinks, she's very inscrutable, but I think she has probably just given up; she's very aloof with me. I know that it's much easier for me than for her. I have tremendous feelings of guilt about the situation and have often felt I should get out of the picture altogether, although until relatively recently I couldn't have brought myself to do that.

Now, twenty-two years on, we see each other two or three times a week, we are incredibly good friends, and we still go to bed together. It's turned into a different kind of relationship – a more Platonic thing, but very important, like the later years of a marriage. Now I don't think I would mind if she fell in love with someone else, but she has never had a physical relationship with another man in that time – she regards me as her husband. But one of the things I do believe in from her is the idea of continual rebirth, and we have this fantasy that it will all sort itself out in some future life, which has helped to make it more bearable than it would otherwise be.

Elaine Rose Singh

Elaine Rose Singh is Black, British and has lived in Britain for most of her life. She has been involved in education for a number of years, lectures in further education and is also an author in her own right. She has two grown-up children. She separated from her partner, a Sikh, after more than twenty years of marriage and shortly before this interview.

Elaine

I remember the night I met Narinder. I was a student nurse in Kent and he was at the local RAF camp. They put on a function for overseas students and Narinder walked in, wearing his white turban. He looked very nice, but strange and fascinating. I'd seen Sikhs from afar, but never so close up. Later that evening I got talking to him; we were friendly and we exchanged phone numbers. Then about four weeks later I started to think of him. It was like telepathy, because within a few days he rang and invited me out.

For the first two months we were going out I was very cagey. To put it bluntly I thought he was after a free lay, but I wouldn't have sex with him because I was brainwashed into the idea that you have sex only with the person who will ultimately be your husband. I didn't see him as a potential husband because I felt he wouldn't have me as a wife because of his Sikh background. But at the same time he was extremely loving towards me, so I had mixed feelings, I couldn't work out what he wanted from me.

Maybe for him there was a fascination with the fact that I was a Black woman, because he came from Kenya and his family had met Africans and had Africans as servants but he had never really interacted with them. But I think it was my personality more than anything. At the time I was a very bubbly, extrovert Jamaican, I didn't fall into any stereotypes and I think he just really liked me.

Three months after we started going out, he got posted to Germany. Within a couple of weeks the letters started arriving. They got more and more intense and I realised that I was really missing him, I really cared about him.

A year later, we decided to get married. I didn't want to live with him, it had to be marriage. I hadn't met his parents, just his brother who was going out with a West Indian girl, but he explained that they would be up in arms. They said that all the brothers were setting a bad example. It was all very traumatic – his sisters used to ring and pretend I wasn't there, and then say nasty things down the phone.

We had a registry office wedding with twelve very close friends. My mother was against it, simply because I was here and she wanted me back in Jamaica – end of story. She did accept it, but for a couple of years she was really angry.

We had a lot of problems in the first eight years, mainly with his family. We were terribly happy together, but his family refused to accept it. They kept trying to pair him off with other Asians. Every time he went to see them – I didn't go with him – they would say, 'We have a doctor who is interested in you.' He used to come back and tell me that they were fixing him up. What I didn't realise at the time, and only recently learned, was that he didn't tell them we were married until 1980 – by then we had been married for nearly twelve years! They thought we were living together.

So he kept going, and they kept having a go at him, and he didn't have the courage to say 'I'm married'. Then in 1983 we moved to London, to a new job. We had just moved into a new place when the doorbell rang. I opened the door and there were his mum and dad, come to see us for the very first time. They must have known about the marriage only a year or two before and learnt we were there in London. Since then we have always been friends – when I was working and very busy, his mother even offered to come and help me in the house. The main reason for not telling them was the fact that I was Black. As he kept saying, they had Black servants in Africa, they didn't fraternise with Blacks. They couldn't accept a Black person within the family.

There *is* an inbuilt racism within the Asian community that they don't talk about. There is this thing about fairness – the fairer you are, the better. It happens in many colonised countries. If you have something imposed on you, in order to get on and be part of it you have to ape it in some measure. You will see an Indian person with a white person, not with a Black person, because a white person is subconsciously seen as an ideal to be aspired to. Even some Black men do it – if I get a white woman to carry me off, my children will be fair, they won't have curly hair, etc.

But in a way the anti-Black feelings of the Asian community didn't affect me. They have never really said – even though it was openly known – that they were against me because I was a Black West Indian. They never said the dreaded words 'Black woman', they just said 'Your wife is not suitable or acceptable.' In the beginning I had nothing to do with them. I thought: if they don't like me for what I am, that's their loss, and I said to Narinder, 'You go and visit them with the children.' At first he used to go by himself, that's how they didn't know we were married. Then he started taking the children and had to admit that they were my kids and we were married. Then I followed. I never went there until I knew I was accepted.

There was no resistance to my marriage from the Black community. They were bemused and interested by it, but I've never had any animosity. In the Black community, if you've chosen your partner you've chosen your partner. I might have had more reaction if the person was white.

Being in the air force shielded us because we always had to move around, we always ended up living mainly among white people, we were just another RAF couple. So other people were not our problem. Whenever we socialised, I was just accepted.

So I have a network of friends, some Black, but we moved around a lot in mainly white areas – that's why we were so close to each other. I do see it as a loss that I wasn't able to have more Black friends, because you need to reach out to people and reinforce who you are. But we both lost that – he lost the Indian part of him, I lost my West Indian part. I didn't give it up, it gave me up; circumstances made sure that I couldn't pursue it. The shops around me sold no West Indian food, there were no Black people for fifty miles. I don't miss it now, because I've adjusted. I have all sorts of friends: West Indian, white, Asian.

And our children don't see themselves as Indian, or West Indian, or white, they just see themselves as mixed race kids. They have two cultures they can draw on, they see it as an absolutely positive way of life, and they appreciate my background and their father's. My daughter went through a stage where they used to tease her at school and call her a 'Paki'. It got to the point where she rejected her father because she began to see herself as white – she had the long hair, she had the features – and she couldn't cope with her father having a turban. I had to talk her through that because she was almost the only Black girl in that school. His family treat them as equals to the other children, once they got used to us over the past eight or nine years.

We made a very unusual couple. Everywhere we went, mouths dropped open, especially Asians'. A man wearing a turban and a Black woman cause quite a stir, especially when I wear saris. I remember when I was a teacher: every time I took assemblies, and would sweep in in my sari, it stopped the place. It lowers barriers immediately; people find it really amazing.

But I've never worn a sari to his parents'. That is deliberate. I wear one when I want to wear one and not to fulfil an expectation that I'm now part of the family, so if I wear a sari I'll be more acceptable. I could see as they got to know me they wanted me to become more and more Indian, and I was determined that shouldn't happen. I don't want to be an Indian. I feel if I wore a sari to his parents' I would be saying,

'I want to be accepted, so I'm going to deny my identity.' I am a Jamaican person first and foremost.

The most enriching thing about the last twenty-five years was him as a husband, because he has been a very warm, family man, he worshipped me, there was nothing he wouldn't do for me and he has a strong sense of duty and caring for us. He was very warm, very kind, he cared about his kids tremendously. On the other hand he has got hang-ups about himself – his job, his identity – and it's as if he has had to prove things to himself throughout his life.

And now just this week, he decided to leave after all this time to go off with another woman, an Asian. There are several reasons why things went wrong. I think we have changed – we are two different people now from when we met. And there were different expectations because of the background – deep down he wanted to see me as a typical Indian woman, if there is such a thing.

When we first met I was a little naive, having come from my sheltered background, and he loved the way I was. I went to church, I was a wife he could protect, a wife he felt comfortable with. But as we got on and I decided that I wanted other things and started working towards them and intellectually and educationally left him behind, he couldn't cope. He saw a new person emerging, and it started to damage his confidence because he didn't know how to deal with it.

From about 1980 we started drifting apart – I think he was afraid of losing the person he had married twelve years before. Originally he loved me – I was bubbly, I was an extrovert, I was ambitious, but he saw it as containable. He would go on with his work and achieve great things; I would be the wife beside him to carry him, but not excel him.

As my qualifications improved, I got a degree to post-graduate level and a diploma, and he was still where he had been twenty-four years ago. He started feeling very insecure and resentful, and the more I saw that, the more I resented it.

I think the fact that I am a strong Jamaican woman is a big

part of it. Jamaica is a matriarchal society, and I just didn't fit the picture. In the early days he felt almost heroic, my knight in shining armour, and in some respects probably thought he was doing me a favour. But as I lived with him and my personality emerged, he realised that he wasn't doing me a favour at all because I didn't see him in the way he wanted me to see him. I just saw him as a man I loved, whereas he wanted me to see him as an Asian man who had lifted up this Black woman.

It's fascinating that the woman he has gone off with now is an Indian. She is probably exactly – or almost exactly – like I was twenty-four years ago. Working, yes, independent, not subservient, but looking up to him, agreeing with him, bowing to him in certain respects.

He's a man of conflicting expectations. On the one hand he wants someone who looks good – it doesn't matter how sexy she looks – yet when he's ready he wants someone who conforms to an Indian type of behaviour, whatever that is – a docile type who doesn't attract too much attention, isn't too loud, too upfront. That's what I think he hasn't been able to cope with. Men see Black women as being more available, more outward, whereas there's something very exciting about an Indian woman who is forbidden fruit and isn't even supposed to enjoy sex.

There must be a lot of going back to the role model – what his mother was, what his sisters are. He has suppressed it over the years – that was the British, the white way of doing things. He accuses me of not being a proper mother. All the time, I hear how I don't look after the house. I think he sees a good wife and mother as someone who will more or less do what he says – have a little thought of her own, but more or less bow to him and what he's doing. A quietish person, one to whom he can come in and say, 'Here I am, big he-man, I've been at work today, I'm looking after you.'

We had horrible rows about who he was. I saw myself as a Black woman and I was very proud, but he thought not in Indian or Asian, but in white terms – he didn't face who he really was. He still wears a turban, but he hasn't come to terms with his own identity – if he had, he wouldn't wear a turban. If I had to put it bluntly I would say that to him a white person is more acceptable and more a boost for him than an Asian or a Black person. If you ask my husband where he comes from, the first thing he says is 'I'm British, why do you ask me that? I could have been born here.' Well, he could, but he wasn't. If he wears a turban he is giving a specific message about his origins, and he doesn't see or accept that. There were times when he honestly saw himself as white.

Does it surprise me that he's gone off with someone Indian rather than white? Well, the girl before this one was white, and all the women before that were white too. I think one of the things which propelled him in an Indian direction was that I accused him of being racist and he couldn't cope with it. I said, 'For God's sake look at me. I am a Black woman, I have all the features of a Black woman. If you're only going out with white women, you're giving me a big signal, you're saying I lack the outward features that you want in a mate. It's pointless trying to pretend there's no racism in it, a blonde woman, a woman with thin lips and white features who is totally different from your wife. You're actually rejecting me, just like your parents did.' So I think he got to a stage where he had to question it.

And he is gravitating towards type. As we get older we revert to type, especially if we are in a void – he lost his roots many years ago when he joined the RAF. If we have people around us to reinforce who we are it doesn't matter, but there is this feeling of 'I'm getting old now, where are my roots, what am I?' He's getting very Indian; before, he didn't want to be Indian, he rejected it. Now the prodigal has returned. His family matter a lot to him, and they are beginning to matter more and more to him as he gets older. It's fascinating to see now how he is inching back. How long that will be sustainable I don't know.

You come back again to the rejection of twenty-two years ago from his family because I am Black. That's what I keep saying to him: the colour bit might not bother you, but it bothers me. To some extent I wouldn't care if he went to a white woman, but to an Indian, when I know subconsciously that's what he's always wanted but tried to repress! Why wait twenty-two years to marry one, why not marry one in the first place? Why go through all that pain and isolation with your family when you could have married an Asian then?

I think all the time about what life would have been like with a Jamaican man. I know it would have been worse because, again, the sort of person I am would turn a lot of men off. I am too independent. And it would have to be a Jamaican person who sees eye to eye with me. A lot of Jamaican men also have preconceptions about women and what they should do. My husband is not unique – he might be an Indian, but he is basically a man with expectations of women and their roles. I know that a Jamaican man and I would have had problems, the only difference is that we wouldn't have this colour thing so that would have been one factor out of it. White men don't suffer less from that, all men do. All men are fearful of dynamic women who can hold their own, but some cope with it better than others who, because they have this ego trip about themselves and can't handle it, turn against the wife.

I've been surprised by the support Narinder's family have given me. They have lined up behind me. They now accept the marriage as it stands – there's still hedging about me, I'm still a Black woman to them, but they know me, they're used to me, so no matter what reservations they had, they are family. If anything this woman he's gone off with has made them worse, because she's a Muslim. You don't have a Sikh and a Muslim. She's not a young girl, that might have swayed it, she's a separated woman, with a child. So all taboos are broken. At first the family were on his side because he told them I was going to leave him, but when I told them I was leaving him because he was sleeping with another woman it changed. Now they treat him like a pariah.

The new man I've met doesn't see me as a Black woman,

he sees me as a woman. I see a white man, but I also see a man. I don't see people looking at us as mixed. I see his whiteness because he's different from me, but I don't see it in a negative or positive manner. He's just a man who's not like me, but one with whom I share a lot and who makes me happy.

The man I've met now may be the person for me in the future; my values have changed. And my husband may have actually found someone who is really for him now. He is already back in the system, back in the Indian enclave – but our future is based on our past and he can't cut his out with a Black person with two children, so it will always come up, it will always recur.

I still love my husband, and for a while I will continue to love him. I *would* find it hard to forgive him. However, if we reach a point where I feel he can see a different picture, where he can come to terms with his own self and come to recognise that he really loves me, then I would have him back. It's a very unusual marriage and that's why what happened is so sad, because it's broken up something unique.

Marcia Williams

Marcia Williams was born in 1960 in London, the only daughter of Jamaican parents. Her parents split up when she was three and she was brought up by her mother. She is now a clothes designer and still lives in London.

Marcia

I never really had a bad experience with race because I was always aware that I was Black, that was it. When I went to secondary school they used to pick on me because they thought I was mixed race – a lot of people do, there's a real thing about colour and shades of colour. I've got this theory that because so many people have their children very young, they don't develop any thinking about race identity until later. So by the time their parents develop their own awareness, the child is mucked up. And a lot of people aren't bothered, it's not a priority for them. They think you're going to be fine, irrespective of your colour.

At first I would go out with anyone. I went for the lust. I was in the Labour Party when I was very young and I was very political, so I believed everyone was OK. I started with socialism, fairness for everyone, I thought everyone should be free and live in a multicultural society. Then I realised I had been a victim myself and thought: Hey, hang on a sec, I am not sure if this works. I started to notice that we young socialists could never attract any young Blacks, and I wondered why. I was sixteen or seventeen and went round with these other young socialists, all white, except for one other Black woman. I went out with this white guy, David, and at first never really thought about it. Then I started to question things. We used to go on counter-demos to the National Front. Then I thought: What would they do if we got attacked by the National Front? They wouldn't defend us.

David and I went out for years. Then he went away to India and when he came back, he was only interested in owning me. And at that stage I really started to question things. I had a gut reaction about the Black–white thing. I stopped seeing all those people. I felt a lot of me being with them was to do with their trendy lefty 'Yes, we'll have a Black woman here', like a sort of badge for them. It had become good to know Black people, but one Black person was enough.

If I was a passive person I could choose to blank out the issues associated with being Black, but I don't choose to do that because the repercussions are so dangerous.

When I was with David people used to say to me, 'What are you doing with this white guy?' I think he did actually love me, but it was this exotic thing too. He wanted to possess me – I've had quite a lot of experience of that. It's always the same thing, always to do with possession, although maybe with a bit of pushing I could get them to recognise what's going on in their minds.

It's something that's happening more and more – for example, lots of Italian men want Black women. If you go into lots of European cities you see these fat dumpy white men with beautiful Black women. It's the sexual thing, they have this idea about Black women, they think you're going to be a rampant sex maniac. I think English men think that too. It's a lot to do with these stereotypical ideas about Black women – they look after you really well. People say to me when I go abroad, 'I really like Tina Turner' – well, what has she got to do with me? I've had lots of incidents where men have had these ideas about Black women. I met someone in Amsterdam who was saying to me, 'I bet you would like three in a bed.'

So now I'm really wary when I meet a white guy. I've developed this sort of sixth sense, wondering what they are after. I'm wary of Black men, too, because of their own internalised racism; they choose me because they think I'm lighter-skinned. I started becoming friends with this white guy and one day we were crossing the road and he said something to me like 'Are you a prostitute?' – I was so shocked I nearly got run over. It was because he had this idea of Black women and I realised that all he wanted to do was sleep with me.

But the thing that really finished it for me with white men was my experience with John. He was always around, in the background, but ten years older than the rest of us. A white friend of mine, Mary, used to go out with him. He came from the West Country, a working-class family; he was an artist. He had always fancied me, even when I was at school. When he was with Mary he used to take her down to the West Country to see his father, but when we got together he wouldn't take me; as far as he was concerned it was all right to go out with me while he was in London, but not to take me home. And quite honestly, I didn't want to go, I didn't want to be set up. I was annoyed rather than upset about it. I had always asked him questions about what going out with me, me being Black, meant to him. And as time went on I asked him more and more, and he would always say, 'Oh no, it's not a problem.' But I became really disturbed by his attitude.

At one stage I thought I was pregnant. That was the last thing in the world I wanted. I could never bring up a child knowing that its father was a man like that. I remember watching the television news, something was going on with Nelson Mandela, he was sick and I started crying about it. John turned to me and said, 'Why are you crying?' I said, 'It's because as a Black person, I know we're continually in this situation.' He just treated me as though I was pathetic. He could not understand in any way how I felt as a Black person – I tried to explain that it really hurts to know that hundreds of years on we're still fighting. He could never take any of that on board.

John sold his flat to me. He was moving out of London, and it became clear that he intended to keep his links with me so he could have somewhere to stay, even though he wouldn't have me down there. In the end we didn't even split up, I just never contacted him again, we never even said goodbye. As far as I was concerned that was the best thing to do, not to go into any dialogue with him because it was a waste of time. The trouble with not actually talking about it is that you feel really angry with yourself that you've let this man, who is basically racist, use you.

All that made me very wary of white men. I felt used, but I also felt in a way that I had colluded because I wasn't that keen on John. What was odd was that at a certain point I realised what he was like, I knew what was coming next, but it was as if I needed to experience it and see it for myself. Maybe it crystallised all the things I had thought before.

What about the power thing? I always have the upper hand, but yes, white men do see me as a challenge, they think: I'll tame you. It's as if they're going on a safari and they're going to tame this animal. I'm not interested. I don't want to be tamed.

At one point I thought maybe I look into things too deeply,

maybe I'm oversensitive. A lot of my friends are in mixed race relationships and when I see things that happen, I think, 'My God, I could never do that or put up with that.' There are lots of little things. I've got a friend who has a child by a white guy. We were talking about her son – he looks European, Spanish or something. She said to me that as far as she's concerned he's to be seen as white. And I said, 'No, you've got Black blood in you, you can't pass him off as white.' Then the white guy ran off with someone else and it suddenly clicked that maybe it was all about her being a Black woman. But they had been living together for two years and she had never even thought about it. I can't understand that. Those are my first questions: 'Why do you want to go out with me? What do you want out of me?' I don't want someone to sit down and say to me, 'I've never been out with a Black woman and I bet it's really fun!' I'd tell them to sling their hook.

I wouldn't go out with another white man unless he was someone who was really unique, very strong. All the stereotypical ideas that white men have about Black and Asian women are so colonial, plantation owners screwing slave women. Underneath everything there is this power thing, the idea of crossing the boundaries where no one else has gone. I have met some mixed couples who are exceptions, but now white men are seeing Black women as accessories, it's the latest thing to do.

A lot of men try to use these power games on Black women, I think you have to be very clued up and have experienced a lot of things to suss out exactly what they're doing, and question it. Most of them don't even realise it. It's like a hobby, a game to see if they can get a Black woman into bed – you know: 'I've had a Black woman, an Asian woman, etc.' I think because I don't let people push me too far, most of them don't even attempt anything now. A lot of white men say they're frightened of me. I don't know what I do to make people nervous – maybe people know you can suss them out. But one particular guy who told me that he was frightened of me was one of the white people I know who was reading a lot, trying to understand, really trying to do something about it. He came from a really strong political background, a working-class background; he recognised his own racism and the need to sort it out. He was frightened of me, yet he was a very strong person.

I've also been out with Black men who refer to me as 'a nice red-skinned girl like you'. You either go for one or the other, and for some of them it's more acceptable to be seen with someone who's lighter than them. Or if you go for Black, you're more politically aware. I feel that it's very difficult to win whatever I do.

I suppose a lot of things have to do with personality too, but I tend to look at things like the number of Black friends your partner's got. It's one thing saying you're living with a Black woman, but it's another when it comes down to how much you take on their culture – or are you just expecting them to slot into yours?

What about having a mixed race child? I would feel very wary about it. It would have to be spoon-fed information about Black culture, it's so fundamental to their psychological development. I've met so many mixed race kids who are screwed up: they tend to go towards the white side because it's so much more acceptable, and I think it's really sad. If you disregard where you're coming from, it says something fundamental about yourself, and if you don't think it's important, then that's quite a serious problem. And when you're mixed race you're also seen as 'privileged'. If you're going to go out with someone from a different race, you have to think about the consequences and the repercussions. And you have to take on board their culture to a certain extent, otherwise you're a passive observer.

5. All the Same in God's Eyes?

> ❛ *I'll never forget when my sister said she was going to get married, she had only been going out with this man for three weeks . . . All that concerned them was that he was Jewish. If he had two heads and came from Mars but was Jewish he would have been acceptable. My mother said, 'You're right'. That was all that concerned them – that he was Jewish.* ❜

– RUTH HARVEY

Selma Khan

Selma Khan met her husband, a doctor from Pakistan, when she was working as a nurse in a hospital in Yorkshire. In 1965 she converted from Christianity to become an Ahmadi Muslim, and married soon afterwards. Selma and her husband have been married for more than twenty years and have four children: three sons and a daughter.

Selma

My husband and I met in 1964 when I was a staff nurse on the ward where he was a Senior House Officer. He was different from the run-of-the-mill people I had met. We worked on an acute medical ward where patients were collapsing and we would resuscitate them – he was different from the others because he always seemed to be praising God when we had been successful rather than taking the credit for himself. I thought what a shame it was that he didn't know anything about Christianity. I'd asked him what religion he was because I was intrigued by this attitude, and he said he was a Muslim. I was a Methodist and wanted to work as a nurse in a mission hospital in the Zambezi valley, so I decided to try and convert him. He said, 'If you can convince me that something is true – if I can be persuaded to believe – then that's fine.' So I thought: great, this will be a cinch.

Then, of course, he knew far more about it than I did, despite the fact that I thought my feet were firmly planted inside Christianity. He started questioning all my basic beliefs and the more I thought about it, the less sure I felt. In Christianity you are asked to take a lot on trust. I hadn't questioned it and had certainly never looked outside it. I started to feel angry that I couldn't answer his questions. I belonged to a nurses' Christian association and would ask for answers to all the questions I was being asked. The more I asked, the more unsure I became.

I started to read about everything – Hinduism, Judaism, everything except Islam. Somehow I was antagonistic to it – angry with this young man for asking questions that I couldn't satisfy myself on . Then I read a book about Islam, written by an opponent of Islam, and found I could see through it, I didn't accept the point of view of the Christian author. I was intrigued and read more, prayed a lot and began to think: maybe I'm just a Christian in culture rather than in actual fact. I still went to church but felt hypocritical because I didn't accept the views I was meant to hold. You start to assess whether you're being honest to yourself or not.

It was a gradual process. Over a period of a year I realised that what I really believed in was the Islamic point of view as projected through the Ahmadi movement. This young doctor and I still talked to each other, but not on a regular basis. Then in early 1965 I became a Muslim. I realised that this was what I had to do about three months before I actually converted.

I had tried talking to people – friends, family, people at church – but without much effect. They all thought it was weird. Deep down, not many people are that interested in religion. They think you're a bit weird if you believe in religion anyway, but if you believe in a foreign religion, as they see it, you're one hundred per cent round the bend.

It was an enormous decision, but I have never felt for one minute that it was the wrong decision. I just regret that I didn't do it quicker. My family were not happy about it but they thought it was maybe something I would grow out of, a passing phase. It became much more of a threat afterwards when I married.

By the time I started seeing him again my anger had changed to love, and we got married. My family didn't come to the wedding. It's difficult to know whether the problem was religion or what. They probably felt that they had lost me, and were angry and hurt. They said things that are not good to dwell on but I have a good relationship with them now, so I don't want to start raking it up. It doesn't do any good. Families would always like you to remain in the faith they have brought you up in, regardless of whether it means anything to you or not. My family are quite OK now, but they would probably feel better, even now, if I had reverted to whatever it was they accept themselves.

I had always been brought up to believe there was no difference in mankind regarding race or religion and I firmly believed it, so the marriage wasn't such an enormous step. It was a natural evolution, a natural consequence, what I wanted to do.

But that wasn't the only difficulty. It's one thing to be convinced of something yourself, it's much more difficult to try and explain that to other people, particularly when you're still coping with these new beliefs and thoughts yourself. And twenty-five years ago it was a different kind of set-up; nowadays it doesn't create quite so many ripples. It created ripples among friends, too – only two of my friends came to the wedding. It was upsetting at the time, but there's no point brooding on things that could have been different or regretting people's attitudes. You have to be philosophical – people are like that, and maybe the friendship was not true enough. I never felt bitter about it. You have to be true to yourself and know that you're doing it for the right reasons. In my case I wanted to get closer to God and I felt that this was the way, the only way, the one that made sense to me. And because I believe in life after death and that I would be accountable for what I do, it had to add up – I can't proffer an excuse on Judgement Day.

I don't believe in artificial barriers. I don't believe there are such huge differences between people of different races, different cultures. They may have a different attitude to different problems, but I don't believe the people themselves are different. And if you are on the same wavelength as your partner, it doesn't matter two hoots what background he has come from, as long as your basic beliefs are the same. It's a unity of mind then. I could never have married someone who didn't think like my husband thinks. From my point of view it's been one hundred per cent perfect all the way through. I've never had any regrets and I would like to think he never has either.

And we don't have any problems with our children because they know what our views and values are and they're quite well balanced. They would not blindly support England or any other country, they would go on what they feel is right and just.

People from Pakistan and India call them English; English people call them Pakistanis. Each side pushes them to the other side. But in a way I think this makes them stronger

164

because they themselves know who they are and what their values are. I think it would be different for a child who didn't have a strong personality of its own, but all mine are pretty vocal, they can hold their own quite well. In one respect they don't belong anywhere, but I don't feel that in a negative sense; you carve your own niche.

To be an English Muslim is weird according to most people, but in Islam there is no barrier of race or colour, so I have not found any problem within the Ahmadi community, everyone is very welcoming and loving. In fact there are probably a lot more concessions made to me because I'm in the minority. Maybe people go out of their way to be even nicer.

My husband's family in Pakistan were very good about the marriage. There was always this thing in the back of everyone's head – beware British girls! – but my mother-in-law was delighted. I was a Muslim and that was all she wanted to know. She was delighted that her son had, of his own volition, selected the girl he wanted to marry. For her it didn't really come into it that I was English or otherwise, the fact that I was a good Muslim was sufficient. She died soon after, before we got married, and in a funny way it probably made my passage into the family much easier because it was almost like her last will and testament. I had her vote of confidence, and she was a very strong figure. When I first went to Pakistan and met my husband's father, he was very kind to me and later wrote a letter about how my husband should always be good to me and never upset me.

And once we were married and my family realised this was it, things got back on to an even keel – perhaps not one hundred per cent, as it had been, but good enough. But even if they hadn't come round eventually, I still knew I was doing the right thing. For some things, maybe there is a price to pay. I could not have lived with myself feeling a hypocrite for the rest of my life. I felt that Islam was the right thing and once I'd committed myself to that, then everything else was a natural progression. There is no way I could have married someone who was not a Muslim. There was no point in sitting and deliberating about prices to pay.

There are bits that my family don't approve of. They don't particularly like me covering my head when I'm outside. But now they accept things much more. My sister's youngest child, for example, will come and pray with us and do what we're doing, there's never been any friction. I think one sister was a bit dubious some years ago – her children didn't come and stay with us very often, and they only ever came with her. Maybe she thought we were going to try and indoctrinate them.

The race thing has never worried me in terms of my kids, I never really dwelt on it – maybe I was too blasé. There was awareness of racism, I'd come across it a few times through the comments people made when they realised who I was going to marry. If I had not been prayerful and religiously motivated, I think I might have found it very difficult.

But I've not had any really bad experiences personally, although when I was helping a friend to find a flat when we lived in Edinburgh I telephoned, we went round to see it and when the woman saw the couple I was with were Pakistani, she said it had gone. That attitude was there at that time – people didn't want people of another race, particularly Asians.

And when the children were very tiny, they would come in from school and ask questions about why they were called 'Pakis'. But they managed to cope with that. The first two were good at rugby and could hold their own. At one stage there was some bullying going on and they sorted that out themselves because the school didn't. Eventually I gave my children permission to thump back and there was no more trouble. We would talk to them and answer every question openly and honestly – I think it must have worked, because they are never sitting on the brink wondering which way to jump.

But there are some funny attitudes in teachers. I remember one headmaster at my son's school – the middle one – he's very good at debating and is going to be a lawyer. One day the headmaster was sitting with the boys in the sixth form saying what he thought each boy was going to do and when he got to my son, he said, 'I can imagine you being Prime Minister of Pakistan.' My son thought: why Pakistan? This is the attitude of the headteacher. The boy has only ever spent one month of his life in Pakistan, yet the head couldn't see my son, who is British, as a politician here. And this is meant to be a good public school! My son was put out, because if a child is born and brought up in a place, then he expects to be successful in that society. But schools obviously have a different attitude, and immediately the racial thing comes in.

When my eldest boy started playschool the lady running it was a very committed Christian. She told me after a few days that she couldn't have him there because he was so disruptive. Whenever anyone fell and hurt themselves and she picked them up saying she would pray to Jesus to make it better, my son, who was only four, would say, 'No, don't pray to false gods.' So from a very early age, they've known what it is we believe and they've been able to rationalise about it. She thought I should be angry with him, but I felt proud that he knew enough to be able to say this. The middle one had to attend assembly but didn't participate in hymn-singing because we would feel it was idolatry. One teacher told him to bow his head and show respect and he was cross and said, 'No, I don't bow to false gods.'

I don't think it's done them any harm, they know where they are. There are problems in the minds of other people and we will probably feel it even more as time goes on. One of the two eldest boys wants to be a lawyer, one wants to be a barrister, although all our family are medical. Law is a notoriously racist area and a name like theirs is not going to be an advantage in any way. The only thing you can do is try to be better than other people in the hope that your performance is going to get you there. I don't think it's fair, people should be taken on merit regardless, but it's a fact of life, we have to be philosophical about it. They're well aware of it, otherwise I'm sure my eldest son would not have done a master's degree. He's doing that so that he has something extra, because he knows the system is not on his side. He hasn't got a placement for his articles yet. Most people have been promised places, he hasn't – despite the fact that he will have a master's and most of the others won't. It will probably be even more difficult for the one who wants to be a barrister. Being the right colour with a European name is what seems to matter.

My daughter married an Ahmadi, from Pakistan. We arranged the marriage through the family. My son-in-law is a doctor and they're living in Blackpool at the moment. They seem very happy together. We knew the family very well and she knew him – not terribly well, but whenever we went to Pakistan we used to see them. There was no problem, no conflict, they both liked each other. I didn't suggest just picking someone out of a hat; I knew there was some interest. Their family had approached me some years beforehand and I had said she was far too young, they could ask again when she was older. We prayed about it a lot, we didn't just say yes, we deliberated long and hard. She knew she would have an arranged marriage, but she also knew that we weren't the kind of parents who would force any of their children into this. This is something they have to live with and you have to debate it and discuss it in a very democratic fashion. There's much more consultation goes on than people imagine, although I believe some people do arrange marriages like that. You have got to know your family, the person you're marrying, inside out, and you've also got to know the other side very well, otherwise you can't even contemplate it – it's for ever.

People have married for stupid reasons – convenience, passports – which I think is a recipe for disaster. This is a nice middle-of-the-road way where you have logic and common sense. Both of them were quite keen. My daughter was a trainee journalist and when she married she said she wasn't going to do two jobs, she didn't believe in the so-called emancipation of women, so she would give up work.

At first my mother was very upset about my daughter having an arranged marriage. But when she met her husband she liked him very much – he's a very gentle boy – and he totally won her over. Now she doesn't feel bad about it, she thinks he's right for her.

I hope we'll arrange the boys' marriages too. They are at university and obviously go to classes where there are people of the other sex, that is professional. They go on courses, but they don't go out for dinner or socialise as such with members of the opposite sex, they keep it on strict Islamic lines so far. They themselves opted out of living in university halls. After studying they go to the mosque, do things there. They've never said it's difficult and they are very open children. But they stopped mixing with members of the opposite sex at about the age of seven. My children have never been to discos, and they never went to mixed parties when they got bigger, but they never asked to. I never had to make decisions about that because it seemed a natural thing. It meant that my daughter decided for herself 'well, I don't do this', without coming back and asking permission. The boys never did it either. There was never any rebelling against it.

I'm delighted about it, it makes life a lot less stressful for everybody, because then there won't be any conflicts, I hope. When the time comes the boys will marry someone who thinks as they do, there's no recriminations later on, no problems. I think my children have enough integrity of their own to do what is right and proper. One thing is that there is no clash. Our children know they are Muslims, they believe in what they do – not just because we do, but quite sincerely in their own right.

I don't know what I would do if they did rebel. I meet things as they come. There's enough reason in Islam for doing things, and if you do things on that basis there's no conflict. To protect family and society there are one or two things that have to go – free intermixing is one of them, and to me that's a small price to pay for a good secure family set-up. I think when there is too much freedom you get rocky marriages, people looking in other directions. If you are fulfilled you don't have the urges to do those things that the rest of society is doing.

If one of them did leave the faith, I'd feel sad because I believe it's the true faith, but I wouldn't want them to be hypocrites and do things to please me. And one thing to remember is that they are used to being a different minority. They have been in the minority in the schools they've attended, they are still in the minority. In one way they've been cushioned because of that. It's probably much harder if you're a child living in an area which is predominantly Muslim. We have had prejudice against us because we are Ahmadis; many other Muslims don't accept us as followers of Islam.

Do I mix freely? It depends on the occasion. My husband and I never go to dances, we go to dinners together and we will sit together and I'll talk to whoever is around, but I wouldn't put myself in a position where it could be misconstrued. I wouldn't go to a mixed dinner on my own, and I don't think my husband would either. You can become vulnerable without being guilty of anything. I think my awareness of this developed over time. Previously – with workmen in the house, for example – I would have made a cup of tea and not thought about it. Now if I do, I would put it there and leave the room. And the children have picked all this up naturally.

Before I became a Muslim some things bugged me, like men having four wives, for example. It doesn't now. It would if I had a rival, but it depends how you look at it. If you consider, for example, *Jane Eyre*, when Rochester's wife was mad, it seems very unfair in such a situation that a man has to do without a wife, and it's unfair to divorce the wife who needs some kind of attention. Rochester could have married Jane while his wife was alive, and all three would have been fulfilled in their own way and have their needs met. If you look at it like that, then I think it is good there is a provision for all eventualities. It's far better than what happened here after the Second World War when there were so many mistresses and concubines and the fabric of society was undermined. The end result was a lot of illegitimate children who didn't have any rights and women who were left in no-man's-land. So, while it's always better that one man has one wife, I still believe that in some circumstances it's not always practical. You have to understand societies and not always judge them through our norms. For example, in Africa a family often isn't viable if there are not more women around. They don't have the same hang-ups about monogamy as we do. I would be upset if my husband took another wife, but then there have to be grounds for it in my view and as far as I am aware there are none.

I'm very aware of the prejudice against Muslims and the strange ideas people have about them – I'm astounded at most people's ignorance, and their views. I've discovered that talking about the Gulf War, for example, with my family. My views are so different to theirs. I don't know what I would have thought, what my ideas would be now, if I hadn't become a Muslim and married my husband. My opinions about so many things are different from my family's, but then again I was always a bit of an odd one out.

I don't have any truck with culture. I don't care whose culture it is, whether it's mine or an Asian one. I don't get involved in it at all. I think something should be done because there is a *reason* to do it. I don't celebrate Christmas, for example, which is part of my culture; it's not particularly a Christian thing any more. The children aren't particularly interested in the Pakistani cultural thing, but if it's an Islamic custom then I go along with it. But I don't get involved in things that are just customs. With Ramadan coming in a few days, I'll fast and at the end of it we'll have Eid. I participate in that because it's part of the faith. We may not have all the traditional food that other people have, but we will make it a special day and celebrate. But I don't participate in these other things that are really un-Islamic, like henna parties when people get married, and a lot of money is spent on pomp and ceremony. My own wedding was a very frugal affair: registry office, then the mosque, then a small feast the next day, no flowers or sweets – the whole thing cost only £10. It was partly the way it had to be because, for example, the sweets are given by the bride's parents and mine weren't there, and of course I didn't have an Islamic family, so some things were not done that would normally have been done.

As for the future, I think it's getting tougher. But it may be because I'm more aware of it now than I used to be, because previously I didn't have children at this age, trying to make inroads. My husband's career had progressed enough for him to achieve what he wanted to achieve, and we are cushioned a lot by the fact that because he is a doctor, when society comes to us they need help of some sort rather than us needing to seek help from other people. It might feel a lot different if I lived on a council estate and my children or husband had to cope with what happens on the factory floor. Then you see life from a different angle. I can appreciate what people in that situation must go through.

I don't get angry about it. What's the point? It's negative. You have to be constructive and deal with it in the best way you know how. What's the point of getting bothered about things you can't change? All you can do is be honest to yourself all the time and let people realise in their dealings with you that their preconceived notions of race or religion are probably not a uniform thing.

Catherine and Raju Abraham

Catherine and Raju Abraham, who are both committed Christians, met while they were both working in a hospital in Israel in 1972. Catherine is from the Highlands of Scotland; Raju is from South India. They were married five years later and live in West London with their four children aged thirteen, ten, eight and six. They are now planning to go and live in India for a few years.

Catherine

The last person I would have thought I would marry was an Indian doctor because when I worked with them in hospitals in Britain, they weren't my favourite people. Raju says I was racist, but I don't think I was. A lot of the doctors at that time couldn't speak very good English, and to work with them and with patients was very difficult.

When I was doing midwifery I met another nurse who had been at this hospital in Israel. I felt inspired by the idea of life in Israel because of its biblical history. My family were Christian and I had a strong faith in God, I don't remember ever not having it. I had made a commitment as a Christian. My background is very different from Raju's; our only similarity is that we have medical families. My father was a doctor, my mother was a nurse.

I remember we were on the same committee organising a Christmas party and Raju was coming out with all these brilliant ideas and being very helpful and I thought how nice he was. It was the qualities he showed as a doctor as well. If one phoned him in the night to come and see a patient, he didn't grumble.

I think one reason why it was possible for us to get to know each other and go out together was that we were both out of our own contexts – there weren't the same pressures as if we had been here or in India.

I used to write home to my family and friends telling them all about Raju – I was quite sure about the relationship early on – and then I discovered that he hadn't even mentioned me. Apparently he had jokingly said to his family before he left India that he would marry a Western woman. It was a big joke because they knew he wouldn't.

Then my mother came over to Israel to visit me. She'd been very positive about Raju in her letters and she wasn't at all surprised I was seeing him. I remember I kept telling her all the way from Tel Aviv to Nazareth how dark he was. In her mind I think she thought Indians were fair-skinned. I kept pointing to people, saying, 'He's darker than this and darker than this.' But when she actually met him, that was the thing she couldn't take. She just said, 'He's not for you.' She hadn't really met him or talked to him – he was too dark, she just couldn't swallow it. Yet she would never ever have called herself racist; she just couldn't see us together, and it was very hurtful for her. It was very hurtful for me, too. In the party on holiday with her there was an English guy – she didn't know him that well, but she was trying to get us together. It just struck me how ridiculous it was – she didn't know Raju at all, yet the colour was a complete barrier.

Then in 1973 I came back to England. At that point neither of us thought we were going to break up. In fact I would have happily married Raju over there, but at the time he was still going through the faith trauma, although he was very much living as a Christian. I had come from a very sheltered background as far as that was concerned, and I couldn't understand why all this fuss.

Eight or nine months later, Raju came over and I found it very difficult. He was in a very vulnerable position, coming here and not knowing the culture. So I was very aware of the differences, and my family, although they were welcoming to him, weren't really very encouraging. My sister and my mother thought we were too different. I think their judgement was based on both culture and personality. My sister's view was that we were two very different people; my mother's was probably more cultural. Raju thinks it wasn't really racial but that they thought we didn't have much of a chance because we came from different communities and we were very different people.

What is interesting is that both our families are from extremes of countries. I'm from the North of Scotland, so my parents had not been exposed to multicultural situations, and the same with Raju's mother. She came from the far South of India and hadn't really come across the British presence in the way northern Indians have. In these extremes in countries, there's far less racial mix. You don't see Black people in the North of Scotland and they haven't had to think through it and come across it as something personal.

And eventually I broke the relationship off, I went emotionally dead, I had had enough of the uncertainty. Looking back, I think it was a very good thing. Raju had to sort himself out faithwise – if he hadn't done that we couldn't have stayed together, especially with the two different cultures as well.

But then I went back to Israel and it rekindled all those feelings I had about the way our relationship was. At that point I really didn't want to marry Raju, but I had this awful niggly feeling that I would end up with him, although I didn't particularly like the idea. So when I got back here I sent him a postcard. He got in touch. And I think we decided at that point that we didn't want to drag it on, we were going to make a fairly quick decision, it was all or nothing.

The moment we decided and said we were going to get married, my family all came round. They didn't want it and there certainly hadn't been a lot of encouragement, but the moment we decided, my mother accepted it. In fact a while after we got married, she came to live with us. We'd been living in Kensal Green, which is a very West Indian area. It was funny, she would say things like 'There's so many Black people living around here.' She was completely unaware by this time that Raju was dark – she was calling other people 'darkies' to him! By that time she knew him as a person. Then my sister moved here to be closer to us, and it's not a problem for us at all now.

Getting married was completely different from what I'd ever imagined. I was quite detached and dispassionate. Initially we were attracted to each other, but because of all the traumas we had gone through the decision was a decision rather than being in love at that time. It was probably a leap of faith. Just before we got married, when Raju was in India, I remember him writing with a long list of things: 'would I be able to accept his mother living with us?', and so on. All of that was hard to cope with.

But there were plenty of other problems once we were married. The norm after a wedding is for the bride and groom to be on their own. In this case there was me and Raju, plus his mother, cousin, brother. I think my family thought it was funnier than I did. Then after two days of honeymoon we came back to London because his mother was having an operation. The really important thing in all

175

this was Raju's attitude to his mother. In Indian culture, as Raju was the youngest son, his mother would automatically have come to live with us. But ideally, after you get married it's just the husband and wife together. I think he was trying to please both of us, which didn't really work.

It was a difficult way to start. I was pregnant almost immediately and felt very sick and Raju's mother came to stay with us very soon after we were married. Raju was on call every second night. And although his mother was a lovely lady, and we increasingly got on, we were thrown together in rather odd circumstances. I was feeling sick and Raju's mum would cook Indian food every lunchtime and invite all the relatives round. In retrospect, Raju and I weren't prepared for it and hadn't talked it through properly. It was a matter of different expectations. Raju's mum was trying to look after him and make sure everything was all right for him. She very much expected an almost complete adaptation. So, for example, she wanted me to wear saris. After a while I thought: this is ridiculous, they're not practical and I'm not Indian, why pretend to be something that I'm not? Now I wear them for special occasions.

And it was difficult when we first went to India when Matthew was fifteen months old. Raju was going back there in a different situation. Before he had always been back as the youngest son; this time he had a wife, and not even an Indian wife. I was expected to go off with the women and Raju was nowhere to be seen, which I found very hurtful at the time.

So the first two years weren't easy. I never thought: this is wrong, but it was hard and you go through a lot of hurt and heartache, not understanding what it is all about, because it is not what you expect.

Our faith is definitely a big binding thing. We have a lot of differences, although in other ways we're very alike deep down – we believe fundamentally the same things, we're going in the same direction. But I don't think our relationship would have happened in the first place without our faith; without that we wouldn't have had the motivation to make it work. And I think we would have given up if it hadn't been for the fact that we are both Christians, which has helped us to accept and love each other for what we are. Because we are both very different people, and quite hard in our expectations of each other, we have had to work things out and, through our faith, learn to give to each other in love, to forgive and to listen to each other.

To me our children's faith is where their root is; at the same time I think it would be nice for them to be a part of the Indian culture. I think what's lovely about an interracial marriage is that they have two cultures to get to know.

Raju

We came from different ends. I was born in India and I went to medical school there. When I was out of school I had a very dramatic experience with God. Then I lost it and I became an atheist. I was part of the sixties generation, rebellious, and when I graduated from medical school in 1971 I travelled around India and worked in various hospitals. By then I was an agnostic. I tried for two years when I was in medical school to live as an atheist, but I couldn't, it always came down to the fact that I had to be moral, etc. Then I read a book by a man called Schaeffer who wrote *The God Who Is There* – he ran a residential centre in Switzerland where people who were searching for a meaning in life could study. So I travelled there and, while I was there, studied Western philosophy and art.

Slowly it made sense that there must be a God out there, but there were two things I hadn't studied thoroughly: Judaism and Islam. I wanted to study them in the environment where they were born. So I was looking for openings in the East and it was then that I applied to a hospital, which happened to be a Christian mission hospital, in Israel.

At that time I was very close to following Christ, but I despised Christians because of the Crusades. The cultural context of Christianity always grated, partly because of my nationalism. Nationalism was very rife at the time and I felt very strongly about it. Christianity seemed very Western, and the British had dominated India for so long, the two seemed to be so mixed. The cultural aspect grated because it was not Indian and there was no attempt to make it Indian. So becoming a Christian – well, Christians were so insipid.

But what I couldn't get away from was the terrific attraction of the person of Christ. I examined the life of Muhammad, Buddha, etc., and none of them was as attractive as Christ.

I don't remember how Catherine and I first started meeting together. I was very involved in meeting with Arabs, trying to find out what it was all about, taking my Bible, investigating all these places. This was just before the Yom Kippur War. Sometime during that time we met and started going out.

It was strange that we started going out together at all. We each represented something that the other person rejected or disliked. I think I was actually quite racist in the sense that I didn't really think that I would ever marry anyone but someone from my own community in India.

My brother had once had an infatuation with an English girl which made the whole family collapse in sheer horror, and I came out against him too. I think it was the fact that it was doing violence to our tradition, our community. We had heard of it happening, but we wouldn't get married outside South India, it wouldn't have occurred to us. The other incongruity was the cultural one. In our interests, for example, we were both completely different. There was no common ground. We just liked each other. We were everything you would call incompatible in every sense. We were just geographically together.

My difficulties with my faith created one tension between us, but the other tension was a racial one. I was so embarrassed about the whole thing that I refused to tell my family. I was too embarrassed to admit that, having just left home, within six to eight months all that I thought wouldn't happen had happened to me. I did write to my brother and best friend, who wrote back and said break it up. I didn't dare tell my mother. I thought it would break her heart. My sister's comment was: 'It may seem all right now, what will it be like later?'

I didn't feel I could cope with all the struggles I was going through inside; to have to cope with all the struggles I would have to go through in my community as well was just too much.

Eight months after Catherine came back to England I came over here too and we started going out again, but within three months of that everything fell apart. I refused to write home and I was still going through the struggle about my faith, so we broke up. I was a mixture of being unsure, lonely and lost here, so the break-up was much more difficult for me. We didn't actually meet again for two years.

I think the religious bond did get us over some of the cultural differences. What happened in the subsequent two years was that I came through and decided, despite all the baggage, that I had to respond to Christ. I was very attracted to Islam, but I felt it didn't have the content of Christianity. Finally I accepted Christ and became a Christian. Then in 1976 we met again.

When we did decide to get married, it was more like an arranged marriage. I felt that I had to decide whether I was committed or not, coming from a very monogamous type of background. I was committed to her, so I thought either you do it or you don't. So I thought: what are the reasons for not doing it and what are the reasons for doing it? So if it made sense, I thought the first thing I must do is talk to my family. So I flew home and spent six weeks with my family, my mother and my sister and brother, and talked through the whole thing. My mother cried the whole time. It turned out, though, that her problems were not racial; her problem was that Western marriages break up so easily and don't have a commitment to them. She said, 'I'm not worried about you marrying a person from a different community, I don't even mind you marrying someone outside, but the record of marriage in the West is not a good one. I don't want to see you divorced.' That's what she was really worried about.

And there were so many real fears on both sides. I went to my relatives and they thought I shouldn't be doing this. I asked them: 'Now if I go and get married to someone from another community, will you stop seeing me? If I come to see you with my wife, will you allow us in or not?' And of course they were at a disadvantage, I'm a professional person and my family is not that well off, so they said, 'Of course we'll allow you in.' So in the end they were saying they'd rather I didn't do it, but if I did then they would accept it.

As it turned out, that's exactly what happened – once I'd made the decision, they all came round. My mother and brother came for the wedding and after we were married we went there for six weeks and stayed with all the relatives. They just couldn't have enough of Catherine, and they're still like that. In retrospect, if my mother had said no I don't think I would have got married. I would have pulled out.

Catherine's mother's comment was classic. The engagement was decided and I was supposed to come and formally ask her for Catherine's hand. And there she was all dressed up waiting for me. I came in and said, 'You know we're going to get married.' She started off by looking me in the eye and said, 'You know we would have liked to get her married to one of her own kind.' And that was it. Having said her piece, she just got on with it and I couldn't have had a better mother-in-law. She now lives a few streets away.

If I had swung to atheism, I wouldn't have married a Christian, I don't think I could have in conscience. We feel that it's important for children to grow up in an environment where the parents are talking the same sort of ideological language, so they don't get mixed signals, thinking: my mother believes in God, my father doesn't. I think the big issues of life are religious, ideological, and if the two of you can't agree, then it won't work.

For us religion does ride over all these things. We did originally want to go to India once we were married because as Christians we are committed to helping people, but when we looked at the statistics we felt that if the spouse hadn't been to the country, particularly the wife, then the chances of the marriage breaking apart were higher than if both were in the same culture. So we knew the statistics were loaded against us and we decided that instead of rushing off to India, after we got married we would spend a few years here. I had never thought of living in the West and those first two or three years were a terrific problem. We were both trying to adjust – not only was it racially different, personality wise we were quite different; that was when our common faith overrode it, kept us together and started to help us to find commonalities even though we were what would be termed incompatible under ordinary circumstances. Our interests are different, our heritage is different, but our faith has overcome that.

I don't think I realised how difficult it would be. I just thought it was a commitment we had made and we would go through it. We got married and then we got around to falling in love with each other again. I couldn't dream of not being married to Catherine now, but in those first years it was very hard. For instance, the day we got married Catherine and I left with my brother, mother and cousin in the car. It didn't seem incongruous to me, but to Catherine it was a violation of all that she was brought up to expect. We went to a hotel in Ealing and dropped my mother, brother and cousin and then the next morning, just after our marriage, I took my cousin to the airport and saw him off. It was really hurtful to Catherine, but I didn't realise that.

Then we went on our honeymoon for a few days and came back to London because my mother had a throat problem. It wasn't incongruous to me to break up the honeymoon and then go back again, but to Catherine it was. Then my mother went off to the States for three weeks and then came back and stayed with us for six weeks. That would be normal behaviour in India.

But things that Catherine did were incongruous to me too, mainly because our interests were so different. We didn't have a proper holiday until five years after we were married – you don't go on holiday in India, you go to relatives. Now we do take time off.

The first few years were very hard, and religion really did pull us through. The first and most important thing was that a break-up was unthinkable. So when you start with that base there is no marriage that is incompatible, each of us has to be flexible.

Now we're planning to go back to India for a few years. In the last few years our relationship has gelled deeper and deeper and we're much more relaxed about outside tensions coming in. For example, in the early years I would go only to South India, where I come from, because the tensions of us having a different relationship in North India, which is unfamiliar, would be a little too much. Now we can go anywhere without feeling hassled.

Last July we both went to an international school in a hill station in India and felt that it would be fantastic for our children to have that time in India. It's important that they know about it, they would have a chance to get a feel for their Indian side. Here they have that in the superficial sense that they eat Indian food and like hot stuff and they know they're Indian and we talk about it. They each have an English and an Indian name. Their first names are biblical, their others are Indian. But I think it's important for them to have a feel for their Indian heritage.

I think that India has educationally a lot more to offer than Britain. It is far richer in culture, language, experiences. It will be better for them all round, whether they come back here or not, although I expect that they'll come back because they see themselves as English. I feel it would be the best way of them widening their horizons.

Ruth and Robert Harvey

Ruth and Robert Harvey were married in 1983 and have two children: Matthew, five, and Julie, three. Robert was born in Cheshire into a widely travelled Church of England RAF family; his parents are from the Welsh valleys. Ruth, an identical twin, was born in London into a Jewish family whose origins are in Eastern Europe.

Ruth

I was brought up Jewish and I went to synagogue, though we were never very staunch. We always observed all the holidays and it was a Jewish household. I feel very Jewish and always have done, it's inbred in me, I don't know anything else. It's difficult to explain what that means to me, it's a very private thing. I don't keep a kosher home, I don't follow all the set rules but I do feel that it's my birthright – not that I'm a chosen person, but that I believe very, very strongly in my God, I feel part of something. That is something I would like the kids to have. Robert doesn't follow any religion – although he was born a Christian, C of E – but he also believes that they should have some sort of religious upbringing – Judaism is all I know and it's their right. If Robert were Jewish and I weren't, my children would not be accepted. But because I am a Jewish mother I feel that they are entitled to that. Judaism is not something that you can suddenly choose at fifteen: 'I'd like to be Jewish now.' You have to be brought up with it and understand it because it's a way of life, not just a religion.

Robert and I met at work. We became friends very quickly, but I had to chase him. I finally wore him down and he asked me out. About eighteen months later we got married. I always knew it would be a problem with the family. I explained everything to Robert very carefully; he knew where he stood. I don't know whether he felt that it was a shock, even though I had warned him.

I had been very ill since I was sixteen and had spent a lot of time in and out of hospital. I was also the last of four children to get married. I remember quite vividly that when I started going out with Robert, my father was obviously very upset by it, but I think at the time, when I was permitted to go out with him, they didn't believe I would ever marry him or marry out of the religion. I had been out with boys who weren't Jewish, and my father knew about that. I don't think anybody believed it was serious.

Both my sister and my mother supported me and Robert. The only thing my mother ever said was 'I wish he had been Jewish' – that was the only thing. Both my mother and sister love Robert because of the sort of person he is, they adore him.

My own belief is that because I was the last one and all the others had married Jewish, in a way it was almost as if it didn't matter that much – almost: we've got three out of four and one falls by the wayside, which is bad, but not as bad as it might have been. I didn't consider that it wouldn't work. I didn't go into it with my eyes closed and I didn't do it to get back at anybody. I fell in love with him, end of story – it was never an issue with me.

We had a registry office wedding. Robert and I discussed it and I asked him – or he asked me, I can't remember which – whether he was going to convert to Judaism. There was no question of me converting to Christianity. He said that if I wanted him to, he would – but I didn't. It didn't matter to me and still doesn't. I don't think there's anything in my life that would change if he were Jewish. So it had to be a registry office. My sister had had a Jewish wedding two years before and it was very splendid, very big, very proper. We didn't want anything big or fancy, although my mother felt that she wanted to do the same for me as she had done for my sister, but it wasn't to be because the numbers were so much smaller. A lot of people didn't attend because it was a mixed marriage. And it was segregated – there were Robert's family on one side, and my family on the other, and the two never met. My parents knew Robert's parents, but there was no intermingling of relations at all.

I still feel very sorry that so many of my relatives feel the way they do, although I have nothing to reproach myself for. I'm sorry I hurt my father – and I did hurt him terribly. He made it very difficult for us: he wouldn't talk to Robert, there was an awful atmosphere in the house, he's not smiling in any of our wedding photos. I feel that he went through it with gritted teeth.

And although Robert now gets on very well with him, I think he would still have the same attitude. Perhaps he wouldn't be as antagonistic as he was, but it's still the Jewish thing. However much he likes Robert, if you asked him now, he'd still rather I'd married someone Jewish. I'll never forget when my sister said that she was going to get married, she had only been going out with this man for three weeks. I was lying upstairs in the bath and I could hear how happy everyone was. My mother and father were cock-a-hoop and my mother ran up the stairs saying 'Have you heard?' And I said, 'What do you know about him? You don't know whether he is going to beat her, let her down or anything.' All that concerned them was that he was Jewish. If he had two heads and came from Mars but was Jewish he would have been acceptable. My mother said, 'You're right'. That was all that concerned them – that he was Jewish.

If you marry out and you are going to follow a religion, then I think your relationship has got to be strong for so many things, particularly with Judaism. For example, next year Matthew will be starting Sunday classes so he will be going there until he is thirteen every Sunday apart from the holidays. We as a family are going to be affected by that and Robert has got to back me – it's as simple as that, it cannot work with one person doing it.

But you have to strike a balance. At the moment I'm doing a course to teach religious education in a Hebrew school, and some of the teachers who are teaching five-to-six-year-olds were encouraging the children to find out what Jewish artefacts were in their home and giving them a Jewish identity. I was alarmed at this, I don't want Matthew coming home – he will start this year – saying, 'But you haven't got this'. I'm not prepared to change my way of life because my son suddenly gets religious indignation. I don't feel that I want to overload my home with things that typify a Jewish house. I have done certain things, like lighting the Hanukkah candles, so the children get some sort of Jewish identity, but they have to realise that it's Robert's home too.

The relationship between our children and the two sets of grandparents is poles apart. They don't have a relationship to speak of with Robert's parents. We haven't seen Robert's parents for nearly a year. They live in Norfolk anyway, which is quite a long way away. My children are their only grand-children. I always feel that they are cold people; they were never warm to me and they are not to my children. I dislike them intensely.

My mother always has a lot of problems with my sisters-in-law, my brothers' wives, and I always swore that I was going to be a good daughter-in-law, and I was and I am. It's them that are awful. I bent over backwards to be nice to them and right from our engagement I thought: that's it, you will like me the way I am, I'm not going to be the way you want me to be. I honestly believe that they do resent me, the Jewish part of me. They were very anti Matthew's circumci-sion and they wouldn't come to Julie's naming ceremony. When a boy is circumcised he gets a Hebrew name at that circumcision, it's a religious ceremony, and there's nothing like that for girls, so in the Reform community you are invited to come along to what is to all intents and purposes a christening, where the child is accepted into the Jewish faith and given her Hebrew name. I believe to this day that if I had not been Jewish and my daughter had been christened, they would have been there.

They were here when I was due to give birth to Matthew, Robert's mother was coming down to look after him while I was in hospital. I came out on the fifth day and Matthew was going to be circumcised on the eighth. So there was very little they could do about it, it was going to happen and it was happening in my home. But my mother-in-law wouldn't go into the room, Robert's father wouldn't wear a kappah on his head, they just wouldn't partake in any of it.

One of the things in my life that has hurt me deeply is an incident with Robert's youngest brother, George. We had asked him to be Julie's godfather. Now you do nothing, it's a title, that's all. I don't care who you are and what religion you are, if you're asked to be somebody's godfather, it's an honour. And I wanted to give him that honour, we were close to him, I liked him. Ten days before the ceremony he took Robert aside and told him that he had a problem going into a synagogue. When Robert told me that I was devastated and hurt beyond belief, because I suddenly thought: Has he got a problem with me that he has never voiced? Does the fact that I am Jewish actually bother him? It was never spoken about. I won't have anything to do with him any more – because he wasn't honest with me rather than because of anything he might have said. Why can't people just accept you for what you are? Yes, I'm Jewish, I'm proud to be Jewish, I don't flaunt it, I don't stand on top of steeples and shout it out, it's a private matter.

It makes me angry because I want them to thump me with it – I want to be able to stand up and talk to these people and argue for myself. It's awful the way nobody's faced me with it and it's all hidden. I've made it a point that whoever I'm likely to get close to knows from the beginning that I am Jewish. I introduce it into the conversation and make sure they know, because if they have a problem with it, they either don't have to have anything to do with me or they can bring it out there and then. When I was at school the things that happened were mostly name-calling – Jews have more money, that sort of thing. I find that even now, and I deeply want to protect my children from it, I hate any kind of anti-Semitism written anywhere; when I hear that they're desecrating cemeteries, it upsets me deeply. Our friends, of course, are friends and accept it and are very interested by it. It was more family that were against us.

I think I'm more fervent about my Jewishness now, because I am older and, more than anything else, for my children. I haven't changed, I've just become protective of it.

I have said to Matthew that I'm prepared to answer any questions he has. I don't intend to bring things about anti-Semitism up with him out of the blue, to give him thoughts, but if he's got problems, he can ask me. At the moment it is very innocent. Matthew has realised that I am Jewish and he and Julie are too but Hugo is not. He said to me the other day, 'Mummy, Daddy isn't Jewish but we still love him, don't we?'

I would like them to marry Jewish. I honestly don't believe in the right to say you must or mustn't, but I'd like them to marry Jewish. To some degree it's made me realise what my mother and father must have felt like. Isn't that strange?

Robert

I've probably become more aware of the value of religion since we got married, and the fact that we are from two different religions heightens that awareness. If two Christians were getting married it probably wouldn't be brought to a point where you are consciously thinking about it to this extent. It was with us, because we had to make some choices before the children were born. We really were of one mind about that, I could see that them having a religion was going to be important and that Judaism made most sense. I don't really want to get involved in any kind of religion at the moment, I don't feel I need it right now, although that doesn't mean to say I won't in the future. So as Ruth was particularly interested in finding out and understanding more about Judaism, that is what the children got.

I think religion is important because it teaches moral standards that you don't get from society as a whole. It was more my school than my home life that instilled that in me. I went to a traditional British boys' grammar school, and every other morning we had to attend church and we had to do RE right the way through school. There was a set of moral values that came along with the religion which I think are ultimately the making of a person – religion provides that service, if you like. Any religion that I know of has a set of moral standards, and by and large there's not a great deal of difference.

People thought the marriage would flounder around the religious aspect. My dad said to me, 'What happens if you

188

get into an argument and start calling her a Jew?' I said, 'What if we get into an argument and she starts calling me a filthy Englishman?' He wanted to see only one side of it, the side of the vulnerability of being a Jew, and as soon as I started arguing back, it fizzled out, he didn't have much to say.

I have felt incredibly let down by my entire family. My father was in the RAF for years and my mother is really quite timid. I think my father thinks Ruth has too many opinions for a woman anyway, but there is the Jewish thing they react against. First the way they reacted to Matthew's circumcision. It was as if they were making a stand – their son might be getting swept along in this tide of Judaism, but they weren't going to be, and it had nothing to do with respect for anyone else's religion, they weren't going to do it because they weren't Jewish.

Then my dad phoned up about a week before Julie's naming ceremony. He had never, ever, on any occasion picked up the phone to us. He said, 'I don't think we can come down, your mother's ill.' 'Might she not get better by Thursday?' 'No, I don't think we can come down.' They weren't coming because it was in a synagogue, there was no way they were going to take part in it. My elder brother had a more genuine reason for not making it. Interestingly, though, he is the only one who really maintained any kind of contact with us and he's the one with whom the relationship was worst at one point. His personal relationship with Ruth was always very aggressive – he would pick on her, supposedly in fun, and she'd give back as good as she got. And George, the youngest, refused to be the godfather.

I felt very let down by all this. I didn't expect it because nobody ever voiced any opinions so there was never any indication as to how they were going to react. It was only when circumstances forced a reaction that we found out. They are still bothered now, I believe, but nothing's ever said.

My mum did try to get closer to us, she used to read novels which had a Jewish theme and things like that, although she doesn't do that any more. They don't come down. My brother actually travels from Norfolk to Gatwick every Monday and goes back on Friday; they could come down with him, but they never do.

As for Ruth's family – thinking back, I didn't come away from the time before we were married thinking: God, how terrible! She obviously tried to shield me a lot. Her dad didn't speak to me anyway, so it's not as if at first he talked to me, and then he didn't when we were going to get married. He just didn't talk to me at all. I understand that it was because I wasn't Jewish, but it didn't give me a lot of heartache. Nothing changed, it was a stable situation – he's her dad, he doesn't talk to me. Fine.

There's a total contrast in the kind of activities my family do around religion compared to Ruth's. It's a marked difference between the two. My family basically has the classic English Christmas, sitting in front of the telly. There is no family gathering as such, even around Christmas there isn't the kind of magnetism. There's more of a pull together around Christmas in Ruth's family than there is in mine.

I don't find the Judaism threatening. I think I'm going through a bit of a learning process myself in all this because there is a certain amount of rebellion in me. I think I tend to suffer from middle-child syndrome, and a lot of my life experience and maybe this marriage – I don't know – there's a little bit of rebellion against it. Although I'm not saying I want to know everything about Judaism, when we do the festivals and things I'm the one who is studying the books more closely than anybody else.

There have been lots of occasions when we have felt like protecting each other from racist comments. As soon as you mention to any group of people who don't know you that well, things begin to happen, and often not the very obvious things. The classic example is the guys I play golf with. Since they heard that Ruth is Jewish they are on their guard for other people making racist jokes and everyone is walking around on eggshells. To start with I was defensive about it, but after a while I began to realise that she can stand up for herself far better than I can. And she used to protect me against those in the Jewish society, me being an outsider. But I can also stand up for myself.

We're starting to be aware of comments from both sides – externally, from Anglo-Saxon people, and also from within the family. Innocent little comments that we're concerned the children will hear. The other day we were at Passover with Ruth's family and she was teasing her nephew, saying she had a girlfriend for him and would get them together. Then his mum said, 'Is she Jewish?' and Ruth said yes she was, and Suzanne said, 'That's all right, then.' I wasn't offended that they say these things in front of me because they obviously feel comfortable, it was more that the kids were sitting there and could have been listening and said, 'Hang on a minute, they're saying that to be Jewish is OK, therefore not to be Jewish isn't OK, and my dad's sitting here and he's not Jewish and I am.' Children pick up all sorts of things, and we can only do so much.

Nicola and Mabroor Bhatty

Nicola converted to Islam two years ago, some time after she met Mabroor Bhatty. She was working as a medical secretary at the hospital where he was a junior doctor; he had come to Britain from Pakistan only a few years earlier. Nicola and Mabroor got married in the summer of 1990 and Nicola is now expecting their first child. Nicola's Muslim friends know her as Naila.

Nicola

Mabroor and I used to work in the same hospital and I used to socialise with him and play badminton after work. He was trying to convert two of his Pakistani friends to Ahmadiyat and I would sit with them. I was not religious at all and he never tried to convert me. I used to listen to him talking to his friends and say things like I didn't believe in God. But I had one of his Islamic books and started to read it. Something in it really appealed to me and I started to ask him for other books. I became very enthusiastic about it.

It was because I'd found something so new. I'd gone to Sunday school and it had sounded like fairy tales to me, there was always something missing. This clicked into place. It's a down-to-earth religion, no miracles and things, and that is what really appealed to me. I was interested but really confused. So Mabroor got in touch with the mosque and asked if there was anyone I could talk to. I went to see a man in Birmingham, an English white Muslim, married to an Asian girl. It was difficult and frightening, but talking to him helped. I started to go to the mosque in Birmingham and to learn how to read Arabic so I could read the Koran.

I went to the mosque for seven months before I decided to convert to Islam. At first I thought I was having to let go of important things – I was worried about silly things, like not being able to wear a swimming costume or go swimming, not drinking, and giving up my bacon butty in the morning. It sounds silly now, but at one stage I was almost crying, thinking: can I make that decision? Once I made the decision I couldn't go back on it. I got to a point where I thought: this is really scary what I'm getting into, but I don't want to go back either. Now those things don't mean a thing. You just adapt. I don't wear all black or completely cover myself up all the time when I go out. I've got scarves and things that I wear. I feel much more decent, I have more respect for myself.

People have such strange ideas about the position of women in Islam. Women run the home, family, husband, money, etc.; they are treated very well. And people think Muslim women look dowdy, but they're not. Everything is really nice but it's saved for their husband and family, instead of putting it all on show for everyone to see. I used to wear smart clothes and make-up, look a bit flashy, because in our society you have to try and impress other people.

I used to want to be liked and did things to make people like me. I feel much more comfortable with myself now, I feel as if I'm me. Before I was trying to be something I wasn't. You tend to think if you become a Muslim you're going to become an Asian person and have to cover up, but you just have to be discreet and cover up in certain ways. It's just that thing in your head that you associate being a Muslim with being a Pakistani.

When I was at school everyone used to go out 'Paki-bashing', that was the thing to do. It's a terrible term. It's become a term of abuse. I don't like to say my husband's Pakistani – I say he comes from Pakistan, because of all the connotations. It sounds vicious to me. Some of the things we say are so wicked. I think my attitudes have changed since I was at school, I never thought I'd marry an Asian. I think I did have racist attitudes – even now I think I sometimes say things.

Mum has always been open about life and we always had a few Black friends. Mostly it was working at the hospital, there were a lot of Indian, Pakistani, Chinese people. I think class does make a difference. Some areas in Sutton Coldfield and Four Oaks – the Asians there are doctors, solicitors, etc., and you seem to look at them in a different light to others. I still *do* look at them differently, and I'm married to an Asian. Then on the other hand Asians look at us in the same way. They resent mixed marriages as much as we do. I tried to explain to my grandad, for example, that Asians are as much against mixed marriages as we are. We tend to think ours is a special view; we used to own land all over the world and therefore people should be grateful to us, which they're not – most of them think that we spoiled their countries. Grandad was quite surprised that Mabroor's equivalent grandfather would think just the same as he did about their grandson marrying an English girl. They think English women are loose.

Mabroor had to get the permission of the spiritual leader of the Ahmadi community – if he hadn't agreed to it, we wouldn't have got married; similarly if his parents hadn't agreed. There's such a lot of respect for them, he wouldn't have gone against them.

They were shocked initially, and in the beginning his mother was upset. I can't blame them for thinking awful things, they didn't know me, although they had talked to the people in Birmingham about me. I first met Mabroor's mum and dad when they came here for a religious festival and they liked me. They came to meet Mum and discussed it and thought that we could get married within a year or so.

I knew that if his family didn't agree, that would be it. I didn't find that easy to accept. It's hard to say what would have happened if they had said no, but I used to pray and say, 'Help me to be strong, if it comes to that I don't know what I'm going to do.' I couldn't have married him as I was before the conversion. I never went out a lot but I was interested in material things, spent a lot of money on clothes.

Mabroor's sister-in-law is half German, so there's quite a lot of mixes around. That's the way to make things spread. If I hadn't met him and learnt what I've learnt, my family wouldn't have learnt. What did my friends think? Most of them are oriental or Asian anyway. They thought it was nice, I got encouragement and support.

There were several marriage ceremonies. First of all we had the Nikah. (That's like a registry office wedding – from that day on you are husband and wife but don't live together.) Then, two weeks later, the registry office wedding in Birmingham. Then we went to Pakistan for three and a half weeks for the groom's ceremony. It was very tiring. After you're married, everybody invites you to their house for dinner and lunch. Everyone was really friendly, but I was very nervous and apprehensive, I was on show and didn't know how I was meant to behave.

I haven't noticed any adverse reactions from people, but I wonder whether they are there. For example, I wonder whether Mabroor's bosses think: What's a white girl doing married to an Asian man? although they've been very nice to him – especially as here in Banbury there are so few Asians. I don't really feel isolated because of his race and culture, it's more because he's a doctor and moving around on short contracts, he's studying and taking exams and I'm expecting a baby. I don't know where we're going to live in the long term – maybe Canada or America or Pakistan.

I don't know my mother-in-law very well, we don't live in the same country, but I get on very well with the family Mabroor has here, his cousin and his family. They're looking for someone for their son at the moment and even asked me: 'Don't you know any other nice white Ahmadi girls like you?'

You have the two extremes, arranged marriages and the way English people do things. Now I'm really stuck in the middle of it, I don't know how I'm going to bring my child up. He or she will be brought up with a Muslim background, but depending on where we live, it will be quite hard. It is still quite restrictive in some Asian communities.

Mabroor

It was difficult telling my parents about Naila. It's difficult for them, living in a completely different society. My father was working in Liberia for eleven years and my mother went back and forth to Pakistan. I felt apprehensive about it because when I left Pakistan in 1985 my thinking was exactly like theirs. I would never even have considered the idea of marrying a white woman. I would have thought there would be no way that the two cultures can mix together. I still feel that with the true culture back home and the true culture here, it is difficult. We've had to meet in the middle and form a compromise.

I have learnt good things from here and I think I have improved myself. But it is very difficult for people back home who are middle or lower social class to mix with people here, because of background and the thinking.

I was a bit shocked at the low level of understanding people had of Islam and other cultures – considering the media here are so strong. Islam is never presented in a positive way. For example, men taking more than one wife. It's often just practical – if there is a war and all the men are killed, what's going to happen to the women left behind? It makes sense for men to take more than one wife, giving them a respectable status within society.

My brother and my sister-in-law were encouraging. They had met Naila and liked her, I knew her and liked her, but to begin with I wasn't prepared for more than that. Gradually I also thought: Why not? especially when I saw her genuinely moving towards Islam. I talked to my father about it on the phone, asking him what he thought – my father is a good shock absorber! At that time my mother was actually looking for someone to arrange a marriage for me. She had asked me so many times, 'Do you know anyone you want me to talk to?' I didn't have anyone in mind. None of my friends was Ahmadi and I wasn't prepared to go out of my community, but I wouldn't convert anyone just to get married.

I think that marriage is between two families, not man and wife only. I knew my parents wouldn't disagree unless there was some good, solid reason behind it. Finally my mother was asked about the marriage. She was upset about it, mainly because Naila was Western and white: another culture. The thinking is different. The expectations from each other, from the family, are different. In Britain, marriage is just a relationship between man and wife, no more than that. In our culture, families are central and if that does not go well, the relationship starts getting bad. I did not want to put Naila into a situation where she couldn't cope. I didn't want to put my parents into a situation where they couldn't cope with her either. So not every girl would be suitable to come into our family, and that would be true for her family too.

I didn't want to propose to Naila until I got the OK from everyone else, so I wouldn't have to disappoint her. I knew that if I supported it wholeheartedly and went with reason rather than force, my parents would agree. My reasons were that she respects our ways, is eager to learn rather than having a repulsion for the Asian way of life, she likes the food, the clothes, the culture. And Naila never used to go to parties, pubs, discos, the things that I wouldn't do. So it wouldn't be a matter later on of her forcing me to do these things. She wouldn't try to change me into something else.

Had she been brown, Asian, my parents wouldn't have had any problem. But it was the fact that she's English, she's white, they had a stereotyped attitude to her. But I knew that their thinking was only because they had never seen her – once they had come to know her, they would know that I was right. It was up to me to reassure them that they wouldn't have to try and modify her thinking or change her, she would fit in. It wasn't that I had to mould her into it, these things were already there. It helped that middle- and upper-class families in my culture are quite Westernised.

People at home don't like very forward girls, they like them to be shy, quiet, not pushy, more of a homely type. By then Naila had become an Ahmadi. She saw our Spiritual Leader. He knew my family, and when I talked to him about her he was overjoyed. He thought it would be very good for her to come into my family. So then nobody could really oppose it, my parents were convinced.

Have we compromised? Compromised is the wrong word. We have to be more understanding towards each other. I still think in the Asian way, she thinks in the English way. I have a very measured approach about everything in my life. I realised it was difficult for her to understand the way I thought about things, and marriage in particular. The differences between us are not so big that we want to change anything. They're superficial, our approach is the same. One has to apply Islam according to the different culture you're in. If I make her wear certain clothes at the end of the day she may wear them, but she will feel that I am imposing things on her and I don't want her to feel like that.

We never thought about the kind of problems that a mixed race child would have in this society. I can't see any problems about the baby. When the time comes, we'll think about it. The faith is the overriding priority. And we live mainly within our families. I think Ahmadis are really quite different and more accepting. Once you are Ahmadi, your colour doesn't matter.

We're getting the best of both cultures and backgrounds: the good things about the Asian culture and the good things of the Western culture. We both feel as though we're gaining all the time.

6. To See or Not to See

> **❝** *I took her to college every morning and she came home straight after school. Then this bastard came to the college. A Black boy, you know, no class, like an animal . . . I was going to be so broad-minded with her. I said we will find a husband whom you like. My wife and I married without seeing each other. She was going to have a chance to choose. Of course I loved her, but that love is dead, like she is dead for me.* **❞**

– MR B. SINGH

Val Clark

Val Clark is the mother of Nicola (Naila) who, two years ago, converted to become an Ahmadi Muslim and then married Mabroor, also an Ahmadi Muslim. Val, a hairdresser from Birmingham, has one other child, Martin, and is divorced.

Val

A bit OTT, I think, is the term to describe Naila's conversion. It started three years ago and she became consumed by it as converts do, wanted to understand every bit of it. It was terrible for the rest of the family. First we had the preaching, then came the dress. She stopped eating pork, that caused problems. There were the dietary problems, and then a bottle appeared in the loo for washing – it angered me at the time. She stopped drinking alcohol. She decided she'd go to Soho Road in Birmingham and buy all these shalvar khameez. She'd always had beautiful clothes, hair and make-up and suddenly here she was looking like a 'Paki', which really upset me.

The majority of Asians here are the poorer ones who are viewed in a very bad light – dirty, scruffy, don't want to mix. So the thought that she was deciding to take this way of life really frightened me. Martin was at college with a lot of Asian kids who were loud-mouthed, arrogant and a lot of trouble, and his view of Asians was not good. So she got a lot of flak from both of us. We were trying to make her see common sense, as I thought at the time.

Then she started to talk to me about Islam and I started to listen and what had frightened me to death wasn't half as frightening. It was ignorance. The British talk and don't know what they're talking about, but they think they know it all. You've got the older generation who talk about the British in the days of the Raj and how ignorant the Asians were. I started to realise that these attitudes were so ingrained – a real legacy of colonialism. I'd grown up with them through the indoctrination of my father and I suppose I transmitted them to my children.

My father accepts Mabroor but every other 'Paki' is still a 'Paki', if you know what I mean. He's cordial and warm with him and talks about all his medical problems. This is what makes me so angry – he goes to the hospital and he's treated by Asian doctors, and they're wonderful, and he's nursed by Asian nurses, and they're wonderful, but the Asian guy that wants to move in next door, he's a 'bloody Paki' and he doesn't want him there. This angers me – people are judged by their colour and religion rather than what they are. We've been lucky – through Nicola working at the hospital we've got some fantastic multiracial friends. With me being divorced you lose all your friends and become ostracised. The English say new friends are silver, old friends are gold; I would like to turn that round – the new, non-white, friends accept you as you are and don't judge you. I've learnt a lot in the last five years.

Mabroor has a very persuasive manner. When he talks to you about Islam it makes sense – even to me, and I've never been religious, it falls into place. You feel stupid as a so-called white Christian that what someone else is telling you makes more sense than what you've been taught. At first I found it quite frightening, but now I find it comforting.

Nicola's father didn't meet Mabroor for a long time. His reaction was terrible at first. He was two-faced like most people – he'd go barmy at me on the telephone, then be sweetness and light to Nicola about it. He blamed me for it. I got more flak from my friends, one friend in particular who was a nursing sister. She was horrified. She said if it was her daughter she wouldn't have her in the house – 'I'd kick her out, have nothing to do with her.' She's known Nicola since she was very small. I couldn't understand how she could have this attitude. If you love your children, you have to see their point of view. Just because you're a parent it doesn't mean you're right.

In the first place, I thought Mabroor would take her away from me. We're very close. In fact I told her to go, I couldn't stand the idea of her leaving, I thought she was going to live in Pakistan. I felt that I didn't want to love her any more because it was hurting so much, like living on a knife edge wondering if I was going to lose her. There was this fear that there's this person, he represents something you know nothing about and nothing will ever be the same again. We'd been such a close family, a lot of it was jealousy. Had he been white and English, they would have settled down, perhaps moved a few miles away. In Asian culture, the wife tends to go more with the man's family – I didn't want this other mother taking my daughter away.

I've met Mabroor's mother twice – the first time I was very nervous, frightened to death; she's older than me, much more senior, I felt as if I was relating to my mother's age group. I remember the meeting. I took my elderly aunt with me, and they sat around the room and looked at us. There was his brother, his father, his mother and his older auntie. Auntie Flo and I sat on the settee and made polite conversation and apparently they were waiting for me to approach the subject, and I talked about cabbages and kings and weather, anything but marriage. Afterwards I found out that his parents expected me to say something about them getting married, but I didn't realise that.

What's so nice is the culture exchange which you can give and receive – something we've lost in England. Most people are interested in what Nicola's doing and what's happening with the two of them. I've passed on information about Islam and quite a few of my hairdressing clients don't want to convert, but they want to understand. I didn't want to know until Mabroor came into our lives and I've learnt so much – now I'm passing what little I know on to other people.

Mr and Mrs Singh and Bali

Mr and Mrs Singh live in the Midlands. Mr Singh, who is now retired, was a teacher in the Punjab before he came to Britain. After a few years of low-grade jobs he ran his own business with his sons, which is now very successful. In the 1970s he played some part in helping the Sikh community with immigration problems. Mrs Singh is a housewife and prides herself on the fact that her sons have done so well and still respect her so much. Mr and Mrs Singh have three sons and one daughter, Bali.

Mr Singh

I am talking to you only as a warning for the future of our children – this country has spoilt them. They don't know what respect is. If I had known this thirty years ago, when I came here, I would not have come. What good is this big house if I have lost the respect of my community, the respect of my children? In India our family own land and are very much admired and respected.

When Bali was small, she was the apple of my eye. She was quiet, obedient, home-loving, good at school. She wore shalvar khameez, had her hair long and had no bad fashions and bad habits. I took her to college every morning and she came home straight after school. Then this bastard came to the college. A Black boy, you know, no class, like an animal. I know about them. I was in Kenya for many years. They were our servants.

Bali was seen with this boy a number of times by her brothers, but she said they were classmates. She was nineteen and we were thinking about her future when I saw them, sitting on a bench near the bus stop. I stopped the car and asked her to get in. She started crying. I went home and hit her for the first time in her life, I was shouting and crying too. I broke a chair. I was like a mad lion. That was two years ago. She ran away, and I have not spoken to her again. I wish she was dead. If she died I would feel that is better for us all. I told the police, they could not arrest this boy. My sons tried to follow them once, but I told them she was worthless. She will regret it. She will have no money, she will have no respect. She will be a prostitute. These Blacks are like that. We have not told the family friends. We told them she is in India. If I had more daughters, I would move to India.

I was going to be so broad-minded with her. I said we will find a husband whom you like. My wife and I married without seeing each other. She was going to have a chance to choose. Of course I loved her, but that love is dead, like she is dead for me.

Mrs Singh

Bali is my only daughter. She is my life. My dream was to get her married like all Indian mothers, to have a big wedding, all the relatives from India would come. I dreamt every day about it. Now I have been so sick and I can't stop thinking about her. I know I will die and she will not see me.

She phoned, but her father put the phone down and told her to go away. A mother loves her daughter too much. She is making a mistake, but I know if we gave her a chance she would come back and be good again. We all make mistakes, but my husband is a hard man and will not even let me talk about her.

How can I die without seeing her? Explain to him that we all make mistakes, and she was young. He has even destroyed her pictures. Sometimes he blames me and says that I did not do my job well with my daughter, but we should not have left Punjab if we did not want our children to change. But I wish it was not a Black man. Black men and Muslim men – that is worse than death for us to accept for our daughters. I feel no life in me any more. I am so depressed all the time, so sad. My sons are good to me and maybe when they marry I will get another daughter.

Bali

I ran away after my father beat me with a belt. I thought he would kill me. I went to an English friend whose mother is a probation officer and they helped me to find a place in a hostel. Can you imagine? I had not even been to a cinema on my own and I had to live in a room with all these other people.

I didn't mean to hurt them. I just fell in love with Patrick. He was so gentle, his family were very Christian and he still lives at home. I had never met a man who was so gentle. My father and brothers were very aggressive. I regret hurting them, though, and I miss my mother so much. I heard from a cousin, who is the only one who knows what has happened, that she has been very ill, but I know that if I try to see her, my father will take it out on her; I can't do that to her. I feel so much guilt about hurting her, and also my father. He can't help how he thinks. In Kenya, they thought Africans were nothing. I have finished my training now and am looking for a job.

Things with Patrick are all right but I feel so bad about everything, I think he is fed up with the fact that I am always crying and missing my family. If you are not Asian you can never understand how ashamed and guilty you can feel. All my fun times were with my cousins and aunts, and now I am an outcast. I suppose I should have thought about it all better.

Patrick cannot forgive them for their racist attitudes towards him, and his family is shocked. We are all supposed to be Black and all this hostility that Asians feel about Black people is shocking. I have done nothing wrong, but I am being punished in this way. We are all the children of God. You know I could have been with a Sikh man and he could be beating me, but that would be better than a Black man who treats me so well. That is what I cannot understand. Patrick is so decent. He can't believe that this could have happened – that my father wants me dead just because I was seen with him, holding hands.

Our people are so bad. We complain when white people reject us when we are brown and yet we do the same to Blacks and also to other Asian groups. That is so hypocritical. I have two Pakistani friends, they are Muslim, and I could not take them to my house because they are Muslim, although I went to their house. Their mother is white, converted to Islam, and they too have had rejections from their community, who call them half-castes. They are completely Asian in their outlook and they have Asian names and their mum has done so much to become one of the family who do accept her, but the others treat them so badly. Sometimes I am ashamed to be an Asian.

Will I stay with Patrick? I don't know, I don't think so. There are so many forces against us that I couldn't. I would not be able to live with the entire community seeing us together and saying things. I don't go to Southall with him. My Pakistani friends have not met him, though I have sort of told them. And what would happen to the children? They would be rejected by my people and that would be resented by the Black side. And how could I be happy knowing that my mother nearly died because of my behaviour? Prejudice does have a terrible effect on people like us. You can't fail, you have to make it work – where will I go if it fails? Now I even look at Patrick differently. I see him as a Black man, not the Patrick I once loved. And I am sure if we married, one day I would blame him for losing my family. That would be unfair.

Grace Mackenzie

Grace Mackenzie, now in her nineties, has lived in London all her married life. Her husband worked in the City in the 1920s and it was only recently that she realised he had a Black heritage. (See Chapter 8 for her daughter Annabel's account.)

I had no idea, but I know now that my husband must have been terribly worried about being Black because he worked in the City and at that time they wouldn't have any colour from anywhere at all and he got through. He was the youngest broker in the City and I don't think anyone in the firm ever knew that he was anything but a Canadian. I think if he looked a little un-English they must have thought there was some Red Indian in him or something, because they knew he was from Canada. We met one Christmas and were married in April, so I didn't really have much time to find out who he was or where he was from or anything, and Canada seemed good enough.

I never met his family until I had Annabel and went over to show her to them. Of course I did notice then that they were different, but I didn't pay any serious attention to that at all. I suppose I thought they lived far away and I would probably never see them again, perhaps, so it didn't mean very much to me. I wasn't really shocked or anything. He had told me once that he had been born in Babisse, near Georgetown in Guyana. So I said, 'Where is that?' I didn't even know where British Guiana was. And my husband never talked about it. Never never never. He wanted everyone to think he was Canadian. It was as if he never wanted to talk about that other life. We did know he had a tutor, but I think I learned even that from his sisters, not from my husband. They were that class, you know. And they had had servants and that. I don't know what it must have been like for them. But you know they still want to keep that life away. They were really terrified once, when two people from Guyana came to see them, and they made us promise on pain of death that we would never tell anyone that they were in Montreal.

Most of my husband's sisters and brothers have no children, and there have been some interesting things going on. I suppose we were getting so used to that coffee colour that we didn't think that meant there was anything Black, you know. Though of course Aunt June is very dark. We have no pictures of her and I suppose we used to try to distance ourselves from her because she was so dark.

And for all our lives, we didn't know anyone Black, not even living in London. Did we even know anyone who was coloured? I don't think we did. My daughter did once bring home a girl from Guyana and my husband never really reacted to her. He remained very distant. And when all those riots were happening it didn't affect us because we thought Daddy was white. We didn't think he was coloured at all. And when the girls started going to Guyana and all that, I thought it was rather nice. I would love to go to see my husband's house, but at ninety it might be a bit difficult, I suppose.

Suchdev Singh Chapra

Suchdev Singh was born in a small village in the Punjab where, after his basic education, he went on to teach in primary school. In the evenings he continued his studies and eventually, in 1959, he obtained his BA Honours degree in languages. He taught in high school before coming to Britain in 1959. He worked for many years in hard, low-paid labouring jobs, then moved to Bristol. He is married and has five grown-up children. His wife Karamjit works in a school canteen.

I came first to Gravesend, where there were many Sikhs, and then moved around Kent in various jobs – hard jobs, manual jobs, so different from the dreams we all had before we came. The first thing that hurt me so much was that I had to change my appearance. To get any job, you had to do what they said, they did not like coloured people in those days. They specially did not like Sikhs and they used to say that if you wanted the job you had to take off your turban. Of course they gave showpiece reasons why this was important like for safety and other nonsense, but we knew, and we also knew if we wanted the jobs we had to do it.

I worked in terrible places – in chemical factories, heavy industry. Nobody gave you a chance. I wanted to join training courses for engineering, but it was no use. They were hard days. So then in 1964 I moved to Bristol. I did everything – working in the post office, on the buses . . . I also began to form a small community group so we did not feel so isolated, and that helped a lot. My family joined me in 1965, my wife and my three young daughters. I was so happy, this was the time I was looking ahead to how it was going to be. You know, a good life for them. After that we had two more children, a son and another daughter. And you know we are very different from many other orthodox parents. For us all our children, boys and girls, were a joy. And we tried to be very liberal with them.

As the girls were growing up, we began worrying about their future – what they would grow up to be and, very important, whom they should marry. We were worried that the immigration laws would mean that we could not get fiancés over. But that changed in 1972. That was our custom, you know, and people who always write about how terrible Asian parents are and all that must see that that is our connection with our customs and tradition. It is so important. It is like an artery.

Anyway, as Amrit and Balwant were growing up we arranged their marriages through our families in India, and the ceremonies took place. You see we did not think about what would happen because both girls had grown up here and been through the education system here. They could not accept that tradition easily, though they said nothing then.

Balwant told us she had a boyfriend only after her marriage, a couple of weeks after the registry office wedding. That hurt me a great deal, it upset my wife so much. We were all upset, my parents were upset, it was terrible. She left home *with* her boyfriend – can you imagine? But I did not follow her. Later she did make approaches, but I flatly rejected them. We never saw her for three years and then one day they both arrived at the door. I was not very welcoming, I was still so hurt. He was a Christian, from somewhere I don't know, not English. They asked us to bless their wedding. We accepted their marriage then and there, and gave them our blessings and what we could afford, but I made – very politely – one point: 'We are not coming to the ceremony.' We could not do that, go to the church to watch my child getting married, getting swallowed up by this society. And now they come here, I accept them, and their little girl too, of course I love her – when she was born, we did all the Indian bits we could. So we have had a reconciliation to some certain extent.

Amrit, the other daughter, also could not make the marriage work. He wanted her to live like a typical Indian wife, under his feet, and I told him he was wrong. She was independent, strong, and I could understand why she couldn't do it. But *she* always told me the truth, she never cheated on me, not like Balwant. Anyway, the fellow ran away and they got divorced. I let it go, I supported her in that. And then, after a few years, she married a West Indian from Jamaica. But they had a Sikh ceremony, so at least that was something. She considered our feelings and I think she did not want so much to run away from her traditions. But it was still very difficult.

To be honest with you, I have not been happy for so many years since all this happened. I have been very ill recently and my unhappiness is what has caused it. For sixteen years I could not face the community, I boycotted myself from it. I could not face them – the loss of face, the taunts. I have just started going back, but it is very difficult. You see, *they* are very happy, and I am happy for them. But what do we do? In our lives, marriage is a family affair, and that is missing. Amrit's husband is a very good fellow, and very nice to us. He is educated and of course I like him. Indian boys would be asking us for dowry and all that; at least we have no problems like that.

But the line is broken, and the line, especially for us as immigrants, is very important. That hurts us so deeply. Another daughter has also now messed up her life, with this Black man who was as old as I am, there is a child and now a divorce. These girls or the grandchildren cannot sit with us, with our faith, traditions, values. They do try, and our grandchildren come, and Amrit's husband does not interfere or insist that the child is brought up as a Christian, not like Balwant's husband. But there is always a curtain between us. Please understand I love them very much, but I feel a deep sense of loss. Like you came on a long journey, a hard journey, but when you got there you found you had lost an eye.

I came on this journey to make my family better off, and they have been better off. But this country has disappointed us terribly. Our children were not educated to love their traditions, they took our children away from us; we paid a very high cost for the better standard of living. We lost our children, our grandchildren, our way of life. Whom do I blame? I blame this society. I can't blame the girls. It is not that I feel we are better or that we don't like these men because they are Christian or Black. It is not that. It is just that we have our own ways. My religion is very important to me.

I have a dream that my son will marry an Indian girl, a Sikh. He used to promise that, but now he tells a different story. His mother is so worried it is killing her. We are both living in fear that an atom bomb will fall on us, but we are prepared for the worst. We were hurt so much, we deal with this better and we will recover even if we go through hell if he marries someone else. A son is our future – we say a daughter is someone else's possession, a son is the family possession. We will see. It feels as if I can see the smoke coming out of the ashes again; I can only put on some drops of cold water.

7. 'Can't They See?'

❪ *I've become a white mother in a Black household. As far as you can, while still obviously remaining white, you take on the hurt of racism against your children – initially maybe you take it on more. Because you feel any racist abuse or things . . . that happen to your children as a result of race as keenly as if it was happening to you.* ❫

– KAY REECE

Gill Danesh

Gill Danesh was born in Manchester in 1953, the second child of seven, and was brought up strictly disciplined yet loved and sheltered. Gill's father owned a retail business; the family attended a Church of England church and were conservative in political and social attitudes. In 1974 Gill met Sayeed, who is Iranian, and they became friends but then lost touch. A few years later they met up again, their relationship developed and they were married in April 1980. They have three children: nine-year-old twins Sara and Matthew and a four-year-old son, Ben.

Gill

Living where we do now in a small town is a real contrast to what our lives were like when we met; here it is so narrow and insular. At that time, I had friends from all over the world – Thailand, Iran, South Africa. I was modelling at the time and I spent more time playing than I did working. Then Sayeed and I lost touch. I worked as an air stewardess for a while, then I went back to secretarial work and one day I literally bumped into him in the street and we went for a drink. I remember saying to him – we had quite a bit to drink and I'm a very open person: 'God, your children will be beautiful.' He suddenly said, 'I love you, I've always loved you.' I ran out of the wine bar. Six months later I hadn't seen Sayeed again, but I was seeing someone else whom I didn't particularly want to go out with. We went to a restaurant in Manchester and he said to me, 'If my friend comes along tonight, will you talk to him about why you have problems with me?' The friend was Sayeed and that was it. The other chap was left behind, and three weeks later Sayeed and I got married.

I remember taking him home. My parents had known that I mixed with people from different races but had never said anything. When I took him home to tell them I was going to get married, we'd spent a week in Wales together. My father dragged me into the kitchen and said, 'Have you been with that bugger all week?' When I said we were getting married he changed, just like that. He went in, congratulated Sayeed, got the whisky out and didn't show any animosity to me, didn't try and change my mind, apparently accepted it.

Lots of people – particularly men – tried to warn me that if you marry Iranians, Turks, they take you back and once they're out of the country everything is different, they change once they're married to you. They even brought newspaper cuttings to show me incidents that had happened to girls who'd married those people – and these were good friends. I had no doubts at all when people were saying all these things. When Sayeed asked me to marry him I said yes without hesitation. Before there had been other chaps that I thought I was madly in love with, but when one of them asked me to marry him I just laughed at him.

But with Sayeed there was no hesitation and no doubt. A couple of girlfriends and my sisters were very supportive. My mum was too, because apparently, as soon as she saw him she knew I'd marry him, she had a sixth sense. Once they get over the fact that he is a foreigner, he has olive skin and a slight accent, they like him, he's charming. Once they get to know him, the prejudices everyone has about strangers, which are enhanced when they are of a different race, are overcome. In fact I have friends today who say they forget that he is foreign. He has old-world manners, yet he helps in the house, helps with the children, irons all his own shirts, cooks. Ours is a partnership, probably a much more equal relationship than a lot of the people warning me about him had.

Being married to Sayeed has changed the way I've brought up my children. I really think that – when I look back at the men I nearly married, I would have been an entirely different woman, much less free than I am, more regimented, heavily into the house and housework and socialising. Through marrying him I've been given a wider view of the world and a wider experience and a greater understanding of things.

I find the main prejudice about being married to someone foreign is with men. English men don't like me to be married to a foreigner. We've known people at local functions – where I've known the wives, the wives have tried to introduce their husbands to me and they've literally turned their back on me because I'm married to Sayeed – this has happened on several occasions. What also happened was that Sayeed would be accepted by those men. In one village they had a pantomime and Sayeed was in it. They'd all go to the pub together, then after the premiere night of the panto, all the wives would be invited back to the pub to meet the rest of the cast. This chap had been chatting to Sayeed, who thought he was marvellous, and I said I'd go and introduce myself. This man stood up, looked at me with such disdain and said, 'I don't understand girls who betray their race', then walked away. And this is what I find really hard to take. People think you choose to marry someone of a different race because it's something different to do – it's not for that reason, it's because you love the person, that's why you marry them.

Sayeed has a greater grace than I do – I'm much more angry about it all than he is. If he weren't a handsome man it would be worse. If you're good-looking it compensates in some people's eyes. At work, although he is totally accepted, he does get the occasional challenge from people who want to see how he's going to react to their racist comments. If he laughs it off, they leave him alone the next time. When we first got married and we were struggling, we had more prejudice to put up with than we do now. That is related to the money rather than attitudes changing. A rich Black person is better than a poor one, because they're going to pay their way, not take anything that's 'ours'.

I do have trouble getting accepted. So many people feel I've degraded myself, so I have to prove myself. You get a lot of people being patronising, especially about Sayeed. They are often the nicest people who don't mean to hurt you, but they are so surprised that he is a gentleman. I still get a lot of that, more than I get racist remarks. And terrible unspoken things happen, like with someone who'd been my friend for thirteen years. I noticed that when I went over to see her, her husband was conspicuously absent. Then, when I asked her to sign the document for Sayeed's naturalisation, her husband told her not to see me any more. It was awful, she was so much under his thumb, she just went along with it. Nothing was said, but I know it was because of Sayeed. That's what hurts the most, the unspoken prejudices, the racism that is never aired; you much prefer someone to be openly prejudiced because at least you can deal with that.

That incident was very hurtful. It was a great shock suddenly to start to have to take things like that on board. It made me feel very isolated. I had a very wide social circle, but you suddenly find out who are your friends and who are the acquaintances and hangers-on. And it does hurt. The same thing can happen in other situations – for example, if you have money and then lose it.

I feel terribly angry about it. I'm a very fiery character and most of the time I just bite my tongue and keep the reins on myself. There have been times when I've vented my anger. Then they just give you a sick smile, because they like to see you get upset. It's very hard when people have it so bad, you want to sit and talk it out and make them understand.

At first I was very naive and I had a lot to learn. Like when Sayeed was talking to someone and I didn't feel that he was getting through to that person – I used to try and explain things for him; I was trying to make him more acceptable. But it was me that was the problem, nobody else. I don't know why I felt I had to do that. I think when we first got married, I hadn't experienced any feelings of prejudice, I was just madly interested in people from different cultures, I just found them fascinating, and the more I got to know about different people and cultures, the better. Then when we got married, and particularly when the children came along, we started to experience racist comments. For instance, the twins – the boy is totally white-skinned, the girl is olive-skinned.

The first incident was when I had just had the twins. Somebody came to the hospital who hadn't seen much of me since the marriage. I was surprised to see them and said, 'I haven't seen you for a while.' They said, 'I've only come to see what colour they are.' That was the first time it really hurt. Before you have your children you're still so embroiled in your love affair that you're almost not touched by what happens; with children you become so much more vulnerable.

When the twins were small, Sara would be sitting in the twin buggy – in the sun her skin goes much darker – and people would come up and admire Matthew and totally ignore her, even though she was a beautiful baby. They would say, 'What a beautiful little boy', and then they'd correct themselves and say 'babies', wincing as they said it. Then they would walk a little way down the street and say, 'I don't agree with mixed marriages.' They didn't say it to my face but within earshot, to make sure I heard it. It was terrible. I used to get very angry and shocked.

One time I took the twins out for lunch and my father had one too many drinks and said how upset he was with me and how I had let him down because I had contaminated my Anglo-Saxon blood by marrying an Iranian and having half-breed children. He referred to it as though I were a pedigree bitch who would never be able to go with another pedigree again. It felt as though somebody was cutting into my heart. I thought: My father has played with my children, held them, says he loves them, for eighteen months, and all that time he has been thinking like this. It's just a total disappointment, nobody can disappoint you any more. But then he went on to say how much he liked Sayeed.

I've tried to talk to him about it; he just says, 'I love Sayeed' and dismisses it. He's quite old and one of the true blues, terribly proud of being British, bemoans all the traditions being lost, the country changing and becoming cosmopolitan. I just think he's too old to change. Of course at the same time, he adores the kids. But he'll be at our house for dinner and a Black person will come on the TV and he comments on it. It tears at you.

The pressures on the children worry me constantly. For instance, when the boys turned out to be white-skinned I was relieved for them, because they weren't going to be picked on; I didn't even feel guilty about it. Sara is essentially a beautiful child. It wasn't until she was nine weeks old that her olive skin developed. I found it rather strange having an olive-skinned child at first. You automatically think when you have a child it's going to be a carbon copy of you – if it's not, you don't love the child any the less, but it's a strange experience.

Now I couldn't imagine her any other way. That first

feeling soon passed – like a duck will kick a strange-looking duck egg out of the nest. We're not as sophisticated as we think we are. At the core every single person walking on this earth struggles with one kind of prejudice or another, but most people want to change that and broaden their experience. Not the older generation – they are too full of prejudices and bigotries – my generation. The more educated and travelled a person is, the less full of prejudice and bigotries they are.

Sara gets comments at school, she gets called 'Paki' and also has other children who have been at school with her since the age of four-and-a-half who say, 'I don't believe you're Matthew's sister because he's white and you're brown.' She finds that very hurtful, although it's Matthew that comes and tells me. She deals with them very well – says, 'I tell them, Mummy, that I'm Anglo-Iranian.' She can cope with it. When she was a tiny baby, she wanted to be white. She was in the bath one day, and she looked at the palms of her hands and said, 'Look, Mummy, I'm going white' – she was so delighted.

I told Sara that she could marry a white man and have a baby that looked nothing like her and Matthew could marry a white woman and have a dark-skinned baby – she was amazed. So with us it will perpetuate itself. They like the idea that it might be a surprise.

But children like to be the same as the people they're with. When I came back from holiday I was particularly dark and Sara said, 'Mum, you're brown all over, thank goodness you're like me at last.' When I told her it would disappear in a few weeks, she couldn't understand. She loads sunblock on in the summer, she doesn't want to go darker or be picked out as different because she gets cruel remarks. But the children who know her love her and apparently she's very popular at school, and she's well adjusted.

When we were in the South of France for holidays the French adored her, asked her if she was French or Spanish – they said, 'You're so beautiful you must be French.' She was delighted. When we got home she told me she wanted to go and live in France. She felt totally accepted there because they thought she was beautiful and dark. I never get used to this, I don't just take it as part of life; every time it hurts as much as it did the first time. You know you can cope with it somehow, but you're frightened for them.

I do worry about their future – particularly Sara's. I'm determined that they should have a good education and I want them to be better than other children because I think the better they are, the more they'll be accepted. I know that this is a frailty on my part because it's almost like giving in to the whole thing. They have to go to university, do medicine or something like that. And I'm obsessed about them being well dressed, about Sara wearing funny colours, about looking nice – it's definitely affected me. I want to beat them, beat their prejudices by making my children the best.

I don't talk to the children about it. If they experience prejudice and talk to me, then I will. We've brought them up so that if they do have a problem of any kind, they must come to us and we will talk to them about it. But we've also said to them, 'What's wrong with being called a Paki? You shouldn't say Paki, because it should be Pakistani, but what's wrong with being a Pakistani?' We've discussed those sort of things with the children.

As the children get older we will teach them more about their Iranian background. I want them to be proud of it. It's a fantastic culture, fantastic people. There's so much for them to know. It's difficult to do it sometimes, living here, particularly because Sayeed hasn't been home for so long and I have a large family. It can be quite hard to remember that there is another side to my children's ancestry to give them. It is so easy to say 'We'll learn Farsi tomorrow'. Sayeed is really good and spends a lot of time with the children; he's studied classical Persian and has a very wide knowledge of his country's history.

I've never met Sayeed's family; he became a naturalised Briton a few years ago but he hasn't seen his family since the revolution. His father died three years ago and he's not been back to Iran since we got married. He was told not to go because he would not be able to leave. In the past ten years, there has been a lot of prejudice against Iranians. Again, people are being grouped in batches instead of taken as individuals.

I'd love to see him with his family, although the longer it takes I think the more frightened I'm going to be of meeting my mother-in-law. But I've been told that she's a broad-minded lady. She was a teacher and when she got married she was terribly young and her husband sent her to school and university. She was a career woman. So Sayeed has had a very broad life, not narrow, dominated by religion and tradition.

Are people's attitudes changing? Well, there are more mixed marriages. You always hear of ethnic societies – Pakistanis, Afro-Caribbeans – well, what the hell are our children? We're sort of erased, marginalised out of it. From the school we get these forms saying 'Tell us the ethnic origin of your children'. But they don't fit into any of the boxes, their skin colours don't fit into any of the boxes. You feel like writing 'This is a load of crap.' People should not group people in batches, society should be allowed to broaden to mingle. And until it does, nobody will be accepted.

I remember one incident, when I was carrying Ben, the youngest, which made me very cross. When you sign on at the antenatal clinic, a district midwife is meant to come and see you. No one turned up until after I had the baby. And then when I opened the door, she said, 'Oh, you are Mrs Danesh – if I'd known I'd have come earlier.' The manner of the woman! She'd already set her expression in a stony grimace and when I opened the door, the look of relief that came over her face! They come into your house and if they know you're married to a foreigner they expect you to have funny decorations – like purple gloss paint and orange shag-pile carpet – and they're relieved: 'Oh good, they have taste too.' And sometimes they actually say it – 'Oh, this is a nice house' – with amazement. And food – they all expected my house to stink of curry: 'I bet you have a lot of curries, don't you? Don't you cook them for him?'

When my children were christened, they said in amazement 'He allowed you to christen the children?' I said, 'Well, Sayeed believes in Jesus Christ.' They don't realise that Jesus Christ is one of the prophets, that it's all linked. When Sayeed became angry once, people started saying, 'They do lose their tempers, *these people*, they're very fiery, *these people*, not like us.'

People will always judge you by looking at you, but if they have more overall understanding of the things that frighten them about that person, their religion, their cultural background, then maybe they can learn to accept them. It's taught me so much. I used to hear about other people's prejudice and just say shame and let it pass but never really paid it much attention. But experiencing it yourself, you look at everyone differently, you view the world differently, with a greater understanding. You want to understand more and find out more about the prejudices. And you develop a pioneering spirit, you want to make people acceptors of people, you want a united world.

I have a real dream for the world that everyone accepts everyone for the person they are inside and what they can give. People are always looking for differences – too fat, too thin, too dark – always looking for some reason why they shouldn't accept somebody instead of trying to find the reasons why they should and what they can learn from them.

Sue Norris

(See Chapter 4: Tears and Fears)

Since George left, life has been so difficult. Nobody respects me or understands how people like me feel. There were some skinheads the other day – scum, you know – and one of them kicked my little boy Matthew and when I screamed they just laughed and said, 'Look, one white wog and three bloody Black wogs.' In the park, Esme ran up to this old woman who was feeding ducks and she moved away from her as if she was dirty and said to me quietly, 'You are breeding bloody coons, what do you think you are doing?'

These are my children. How can people see only race and not that? Even my own mother, who didn't get on with me very well but has been trying since George left, won't go down the shops with the children. She is trying, but there is something deep within her that won't let it happen. I catch her looking at the children as if they are another species or something. She has asked them to call her Jenny, I know why: it's because she doesn't want them calling her Granny in public. She buys them things, but she finds it hard to be warm to them. In some ways I understand. Things are so hard where I live – people are poor.

It is terrible to say this, because I am talking about my own children and I love them, but because I am white, if I'm on my own, I can walk anywhere, I feel free, nobody bothers. But when I have my children with me, I am a prisoner to how people feel about me and the children. I can feel their looks and the prejudices, even when my children can't. And you do want to belong. The first day I went to the nursery, all the white mums started getting together and being pals. Then one of them saw this notice about Diwali and started being really rude about Blacks – 'Pakis' – and I just froze. For a second I felt just like my mother and hoped that my daughter wouldn't rush up to me at that point. Once I was walking through a market and I remember thinking 'Thank God it is Terry' – who is light-skinned – 'who is with me and not the other two, who look quite dark.' Another time, I was waiting at the hairdresser's for the children to come and get me, and there were all these women with dyed horribly permed hair, all white, and I remember praying again that Terry and not one of the others would come and get me. I have tried to change myself since then. Afterwards I felt terrible about those feelings. I also realised that I used to tell him, far more than the others, how lovely he was, perhaps because all parents want their children to look like them and when Terry and I were together we didn't look like a mismatch, different-coloured socks that should not be together.

But I have really thought about all this and become better. You do have to fight for your kids. You can't just hide them or be ashamed of them, you have to be proud of them. I try to give them a good feeling about themselves and their dad. They said they wanted their hair straight and white skin, which I felt was really wrong, it was awful that they were thinking like that. I wanted to blame their dad because he should be here more, to do his thing about their Black culture – if you have mixed race children, you do have greater responsibilities. But it is really other people who need to understand how you are made to feel and suffer.

I am trying to protect the children as much as I can and teaching them to defend themselves emotionally, to cope with the racism out there and Black prejudice as well. I just want them to be able to fit in. I teach them the history of slavery – not just to shrug off these hurtful things, but to understand where they are coming from. They know what a racist person is, from what I tell them.

It quite often puts me in a position where I want to burst out crying. I feel as if I've got the guilt for the white lot, and I take it all to heart a lot of the time. But as long as I can convince them that not all white people are the same and that a lot of people are good – the teachers have been great and the caretaker is always telling Terry how lovely his hair is.

But it hurts. It is like that film where you wake up one day and you are Black. You can feel through your children what Black people go through. You get really angry because you know they will need to be twice as good to get what they deserve. I can escape, but they can't. It never stops hurting, but I would never have changed them or given them up for adoption, as my mother suggested, because they were 'half-castes' and would be difficult for me to bring up. Can you imagine? My own mother.

Kay Reece

Kay Reece is a white woman from the North of England. She comes from a working-class family, from a long line of feisty women, including a grandmother who walked forty miles at the age of sixteen when she was pregnant to escape persecution. Kay was a reporter and then a research assistant and now works as an administrator for the Southall Monitoring Group, which campaigns against racial attacks on the Asian community in Southall. Her husband, Winston Reece, is a Black professional and they have two children, Nina and Callum, aged six and two.

Kay

I don't remember as a teenager ever thinking that Black people were different. The first time I realised it I was thirteen. We lived in Maidenhead, which had quite a large Asian population but very few West Indians or Africans. We used to go to the local youth club, and one night a bunch of blokes came from Slough. It was at the time when reggae and music like James Brown's was coming to the fore. Eight of these blokes came, and I was knocked out by the dancing. I remember going home to my parents and saying that these guys came from Slough and took over the dance floor and it was wonderful and that this one guy was really nice. And my mum said to me, 'You know if they have a white girlfriend it's like a feather in their cap. If you start to go out with them people might not like you, your friends might say things, other boys at the youth club might think carefully about you.' I was shocked and offended. I remember thinking: that's so awful, he was really nice.

So it made me think: I'm going to find out more about this, and I started dating one of the boys from the group. I had this boyfriend, Vernon, and I remember thinking I didn't know what all the fuss was about. I think my friends made comments and the rest of the time I'm sure there were things said, but nobody ever said anything to our faces.

When I was younger and had Black boyfriends I was really surprised when someone called me a 'nigger-lover'. I was shocked by this person's animosity and hatred, because it hadn't entered my head that it would be there. That's the only time anybody has ever said anything to me, but that's living in a city and the kind of friends you have – we have friends from all different backgrounds and races.

From quite a young age I felt that I would never marry an Englishman. Most of the ones I met spent a lot of the time down the pub, I thought they were really boring, they didn't like to dance and I always liked to. I never had many English boyfriends, they were often foreigners or different in some way.

I think I went through a sense of guilt for being white as a teenager, when I became aware of what the white race as a whole had done. But no longer. Now I don't feel responsible for what other people have done. I can't as an individual, I think you're responsible for your own individual acts and your own life.

Do I feel resentment from Black women about marrying Winston? Friends and acquaintances will joke, saying, 'Oh yes, the white women always get the nice ones.' Things like that. I don't think you can deny that there is something to do with the daringness or the sexuality, the 'look but don't touch', that works both ways, with Black and white, and might be part of an initial attraction. There is that sexual taboo and attraction. But once you're actually into a relationship, that wanes just as much as any relationship based on those very superficial things, because marriage isn't about that, it's about who did the washing-up and what you talked about after last night's TV programme.

I found Winston physically appealing, but I don't know whether that was because he was Black or not. I couldn't say that had nothing to do with it. There are lots of things within you that you have to give credence to, even though you might not be really conscious of them.

I don't think I am ultra-conscious that I'm white and he's Black, it's just a relationship. I don't consider those elements any more, and I'm sure Winston doesn't either. And even when you stand there rowing – I can't think of any time that race has come into it in a vindictive sense. I'm aware of all the images and stereotypes and hang-ups, but I just think that when it comes right down to it, everyday life isn't about that – an everyday relationship, the things you talk about, argue about, need to co-operate about, aren't about the big things, they're about really small, everyday things. You start to get used to each other and accommodate each other's individual ways.

Winston has always said that from the first time he came to the house as someone I'd been out with only a couple of times, neither of my parents has ever directly shown him any animosity. But I knew some of their views already. They were both uncomfortable with it. My mum was perhaps more open, I knew that my dad might have felt it inside, but was less likely to say anything to me. So when we first decided that we were going to have some kind of permanent relationship, I did sit down with her and say that I couldn't have her saying to me 'Yes, it's all right' to keep me happy and keep me and her friends, but privately saying 'I don't like it, I wish you hadn't done it.' I couldn't put up with that, therefore she had to think deeply and decide that if she wanted us to stay friends she had to support me – not that I wasn't acknowledging that it would be difficult for her at first.

It was a very working-class background: my mother is from a Yorkshire mining village and my dad is from Lancashire, and I think that made a difference to how they felt. Years ago my mum talked about there being great prejudice against Irish people when they first came over and took jobs during the Depression. In lots of ways she has really come on and developed and tried in her own philosophy to be a good person and take people at face value, but it's been hard work to face some of the lies you've been made to believe throughout your life.

But still I've got family . . . when the hurricane hit in Ealing and they showed Ealing on TV, a cousin, in her early sixties, saw the pictures and said to my mum, 'Ealing looks really nice, I always thought Kay lived in a Black ghetto.' I was amazed that she thought that, she's often asked us to come round and she's lovely to the children. It was difficult to judge what Winston's family thought because his parents were in Jamaica and we just went off and got married on our own, we didn't even tell our friends. We just went down the road and got two women from the bus stop with their shopping to be our witnesses. My mother was pleased, my father was furious that I'd deprived him of doing his Spencer Tracy bit. He had the hump for about a week, then he came by with a bottle of champagne. It was probably more of a shock to Winston's parents because we'd been living together and I don't think he told them; they probably would not have approved, in a religious sense. When we phoned and told his mum she burst into tears and handed the phone to his dad. He just said, 'You're old enough to make your own decisions' – that was it, not even congratulations. I kept saying they don't like it because I'm white but in his heart of hearts Winston doesn't believe that. The only thing they asked him afterwards was if my family treated him OK. Both my mum and dad really like him as an individual.

We got married like that because I was pregnant and there was a lot of pressure on us to get married, which we resisted. We didn't want it to be that we got married because they went on at us but because we wanted to, and that was the only way of showing this.

And there were other complications. My parents are divorced, my dad had remarried and my mum had never met my dad's wife. And Winston's elder brother is very prejudiced against white people so it would have meant either him coming and being funny, or refusing to come at all. At the time I don't think Winston was ready to deal with a split, as brothers, over me. Things haven't changed much. Winston doesn't go there any more. His brother is anti-Asian, anti-white, anti-everyone that isn't Black Jamaican.

227

When Winston and I were just going out he told his brother that he was going out with this girl from Maidenhead. His brother said, 'I didn't know many Black people lived out there.' Winston said, 'No, there aren't many.' And his brother said, 'It must be really hard for her and her family, being one of only a couple.' Then Winston told him that it wasn't at all hard, because I was white. Then his brother started saying, 'You can't risk it. It's bad enough if a woman does the dirty on you, but if she does the dirty on you and she's white, that is the ultimate insult.'

I haven't lost friends, but there were people who I thought were quite close who I purposely distanced myself from over probably quite obscure remarks that they have made. I remember having a general discussion about race with a friend and she said something about Indian people that just made me realise she was on a different wavelength.

Some Black people might say it's unfair, but I do feel that I now have a bit more right to part of all the wonderful things that there are about being from the Caribbean or Africa. And I'm glad that my children are open to those cultures, the things to do with the positive side of being African and of African history and culture. I'm glad my children have a right to that. I don't feel I have the same right, but I feel I have a bit of it, I can touch a bit of it although I can't claim it as mine. I feel fortunate about that. I'm glad my children have an English/Irish heritage, which is my background, which has a lot of good things, but that they can also claim as theirs lots of other wonderful things from the world.

Despite all this I don't ever feel that I wish I was Black so my credibility would be there and I wouldn't have to fight for it. That would be denying me, the person I've arrived at now. If you like yourself – and I do quite like myself – you're the product of all your experiences, and if that was the case they would have been totally different. I wouldn't be me.

My children don't have particularly West Indian names. Nina was chosen because of Nina Simone, because we both like her, and Callum was just from the television credits; we couldn't agree on a name and it was just a name we both happened to like.

If you walked into my house you would be able to tell that it's not just a white British house by the books and pictures and the things around. We've got a portrait of a Black man at a piano which dominates the front room, we've got a painting from Egypt, and lots of political things in the kitchen – things from South Africa, for example. We try to have books by writers from Asia and Africa and the Caribbean. I think we actually made a conscious decision to have these things at home, to have positive images to do with art and literature so that there is a lot for them, as they're growing up. You hope to be able to show them different ways. White British influences are all around. If you came and sat with us over dinner, these issues are constantly talked about. We eat lots of different food and have friends from all different backgrounds. I take it for granted, I don't even think about it.

I've become a white mother in a Black household. As far as you can, while still obviously remaining white, you take on the hurt of the racism against your children – initially maybe you take it on more. Because you feel any racist abuse or things at school that happen to your children as a result of race as keenly as if it was happening to you. I know that I feel as strongly as any of the Black mothers I've spoken to about racial stereotyping at school. The only difference is that sometimes, being white, I find it easier to challenge the school about it. Black friends have said, 'You go and talk to them about it, because then they can't say that you've got a chip on your shoulder.'

Things have happened with Nina, it's to do with sexist things too – playing the princess in the school Christmas play, that sort of thing. She's only once told me that someone's called her a name. One day Nina and her friend came out of school and said that this girl had called them 'Black cows'. I said, 'What did you two say?' They both said, 'We just called her a white cow.'

I found out that the little girl who did the name-calling lived really near Nina's friend. My neighbours are really good, but I thought: what if it happens to me? So I spoke to the other little girl's mum about it. She actually pointed some positive things out to me. She said that Nina is more fortunate. She can't hate white people because I'm white and that's luckier, because it's bad for them to have hate. She actually made me feel more positive.

At the moment Nina is striving to be like Snow White and Sleeping Beauty, all these young images. It's a real uphill struggle – even though we constantly try with toys and games and jigsaws and books to have positive images, some of them are still really hard to obtain. Nina was wearing me down for a Barbie doll and I said, 'I can't buy her a Barbie doll.' Then someone said, 'Would a Black one be better?' I thought maybe I could deal with that, so when a friend Jackie, went to America, she brought me back a Black Barbie. It is difficult, but then I don't know how long these things will stay with her.

Things outside do affect me – coverage of South Africa, the Gulf War, sporting events. I refuse to watch certain programmes. I will switch off certain old films. I don't watch such negativeness portrayed. I will make an effort for the children to watch programmes like 'The Cosby Show', which is very twee and sugary, but there is so little else around.

It's often not to do with yourself, it's often to do with challenging things in others. My mum lives in Blackpool, where there are no Black people. We were in a supermarket there and Nina wanted to go to the toilet. So this middle-aged white woman took her to the toilet. When she came back, instead of saying my grandchildren are Black, she said, as lots of people do, 'My granddaughter's got hair just like you.' It's an easier way of saying it. She talked about them for a couple of minutes, obviously with a lot of love, and then said, 'I call them my little chocolate drops.' It was just like – inside you just go *kerchung*. I didn't say anything to her, but I wanted to say, 'I hope my mum never calls my children that.'

I don't know why in that instance I didn't say something,

because there are other times when I have. Not long ago the term 'half-caste' was used by a Black person about my children. At one time I would not have said anything, I think I would have felt intimidated and I wouldn't have challenged it, I would have let it pass. Now, just as an individual and by my rights, I can challenge that – not in an aggressive way, just pointing out that I don't like the term, it's incorrect and it doesn't mean anything. As time has gone by – and it has taken time – I feel a lot surer of myself as a mother and as a mother of Black children. Perhaps when I was younger I was feeling a lot shakier about issues.

We have decided that we couldn't live in some parts of the country. A lot of my family are in the north-west and they've said, 'Why don't you two come up here? You'd be able to buy a bigger house instead of a flat.' But there is no way I would ever ask my children to live in an area that wasn't reasonably cosmopolitan. We wouldn't do it. I've sometimes asked people I know who've been brought up in those areas – sometimes I ask them to make sure I've made the right decision, and each time I ask, I'm sure that I have. Winston would happily go and live somewhere else, but he's an adult and already formed; I wouldn't put that extra pressure on my children. It's hard enough, children are horrible enough to each other in any case and growing up is hard enough, without that. I think they do have to feel that they have some allies.

There haven't been any awful experiences for me, I think they are still to come and I'm sure they are to do with the children and my ability to be able to help them and stay close to them. I'm not frightened for them because I think they will survive, but I'm frightened for our relationship – that there will be very difficult periods for them and very difficult periods for us. I might not always be able to give them the right answers because I haven't experienced the things they are going through. There might be periods when – perhaps during adolescence, when you often do feel distant from your parents for lots of other reasons – there will be an added dimension. And yes, I am frightened for them in that I feel their hurt very keenly, and if it's something that I can do nothing about they're just going to have to learn to survive without me. When you see their tears, you feel for them inside.

A lot of my family make a point of being extra nice to the children. They send birthday cards when I know they don't send other great-nephews and nieces cards, and my mum says that she thinks my children need extra support and love because life is going to be harder for them, they are going to have to be extra sure of the people around them and have to know that there are white people who love them completely.

A relationship like this definitely changes you for the better because it opens you up to different attitudes and ways of life. But I think it's changed my family even more radically than it's changed me, particularly my mother. She now wants to and tries to empathise with the problems that Black people have, which I don't think she would ever have done before. Not even if we hadn't had children, because once the children are born and as a grandparent you give that unconditional love, then you have to take on lots of other things. It's a shame that you can't change the world for everybody, you can't make everyone become a grandparent of Black children.

8. Ways of Looking

> ❛ *I can never remember having a negative image of myself . . . I remember when I was about seventeen, a girl asked me if it wasn't strange that my mother was a different colour – "She must feel like she's not quite your mother." She asked me if I wished I looked like my mother. I laughed, I thought it was so stupid, it had never occurred to me in my life. I said, "No, it's bloody great being brown actually."* ❜

– DAVID UPSHAL

David Upshal

David Upshal was born and grew up in South London. His father is Nigerian, his mother English. He went to Oxford and studied Politics, Philosophy and Economics, worked as a freelance journalist and was on the staff of *The Voice*. He now works for the BBC.

David

My mother's English, from Bournemouth. Her father was from Devon and her mother from Dorset, both from farming families. My grandfather was a shoe-repairer and shoemaker and they moved into Bournemouth – a lower-middle-class family. My father is from Nigeria. He came here to study in the early 1960s. His father was killed in the Second World War in a West African regiment, and then his mother died. He had been at school when his parents died and obviously no more fees were coming in but he managed to string it out with stories about the fees being in the post and never told anybody his parents were dead.

When he was growing up Nigeria was still a colonial country and he'd been taught by white teachers, white missionaries, about England as a land of milk and honey. When he got here, of course, all the qualifications that he got in Nigeria were unrecognised, so he had to go to night school and do O levels and A levels that would be recognised, and sweep floors in the daytime.

He met my mum sometime in 1963 or 1964, in Bournemouth. My knowledge of my father's family is far sparser than my knowledge of my mother's because my parents split up by the time I was eight and I haven't seen my father to speak to since I was ten. There was no more contact between them. I think there was a fear on my mother's part that my father would return to Nigeria at some point and would wish to take me with him. I was her only child so she was more protective, more obstructive than she would have been otherwise in terms of letting him see me.

My grandmother, who was born in 1904, is still alive. She grew up in the days of celebrations of victories in the Boer War and subduing the Zulus and tales of Little Black Sambo and so on, not the most uplifting images of Black people. She was the big matriarchal figure in my family and is the relative I am closest too. The first Black people she ever saw were in the Second World War, when Black GIs arrived. She used to say, 'We didn't like white American soldiers because they were so brash and thought they knew everything, but the Black American soldiers were known for their courtesy and politeness.' Looking back, you can well understand why – back then it was a good way not to get lynched.

The Black GIs were very popular in the community. My grandmother says, 'We used to invite Canadian soldiers and they would come, and we would invite Black American soldiers for tea and they never accepted, they always stayed separate.' Which again you can understand, but I don't think English people quite understood that.

My grandmother describes the day my mother brought my father home, it seemed to me just like *Guess Who's Coming to Dinner?* My grandparents were Labour voters and fairly easygoing people. So here they are, they have a very successful dinner, my grandmother disappears into the kitchen with my mother and my grandfather says to my father, 'Now look, you're a very fine young man, I've nothing against you, but you know the kind of problems you're going to encounter and I'm concerned about what's going to happen to my daughter if she's going out with a Black man. I think for her benefit I should say that I don't want her to suffer those kinds of problems, but I like you very much and I'll be very disappointed if you don't come back to our house. You're always welcome.' And my grandmother ends the story and says, 'Well, you can't say fairer than that.'

I do see things differently because of my background. I'm a lot more tolerant of some kinds of racism than most Black people would be. Not many Black people can say they understand white racism, but I understand it, I got perspectives on racism that nobody brought up in a Black family ever would. Malcolm X talks about this in his autobiography. He was adopted by a white family and went to school with white children and says in later years he understood white racism because he was brought up as part of a white family. A friend's sister came home with a Black guy and his whole family could tell his father was ill at ease. His feelings were transparent to me in a way that they weren't to the rest of his family. He was concerned about his daughter's wellbeing, which isn't incompatible with being non-racist. That man knows what people say, what his workmates say, what his friends say, what's said down the pub, particularly about white women who go out with Black men. He doesn't want his daughter to be subjected to that. The end of the story was that he accepted it and quite missed him when they broke up.

But my parents didn't stop seeing each other, they got married and I materialised. They had to leave Bournemouth. Both of them were abused; my mother lost secretarial jobs in respectable offices because people found out she was married to a Black man. Once she was actually physically attacked by a female colleague because of it. When she complained to the manager about it he said, 'Well, what do you expect?'

There's a perception with white people that you're worse than a Black person if you sleep with a Black person. It's this thing where they can't help being Black but you can certainly help mixing with them. So to be outcast and rejected because of your race is one thing, but to receive that treatment from your own race I'm sure is profoundly upsetting. That stayed with my mother. For the rest of her life she would be anxious about how people feel about the fact that her husband was Black.

I think it's affected my relationship with her. I know a lot of single-parent mothers feel unpleasantly reminded of their husbands, boyfriends, flings, whatever, by sons, who tend to remind them of the father. It's more so in a mixed race relationship. Till I was quite old, when my mother would meet new circles of people she would immediately tell them that she had been married to a Black man even though they had been divorced for ten years. She didn't want even to risk them finding out by accident and changing their attitude.

My parents moved to South London, into lodgings. At one place where they went my mother was six months pregnant with me, the landlord didn't like it and wanted to get them out. He waited until my father went out one day and changed the lock so he couldn't get back in. My mother tried to get down to open the door to him and this bloke attacked her.

That all ended in a court case, he was fined. There were always incidents like that happening.

I know it was very difficult for my father. He had come here with a certain picture of England. All he got was this cold place and these cold people, many of whom would spit at him in the street. He was a well-educated, well-brought-up, well-dressed young man and could only get jobs sweeping floors. That engendered a lot of bitterness in him towards white people.

The treatment they both had was a factor in the relationship splitting up. I think their relationship was doomed because there were so many pressures on them and they weren't wealthy enough to evade them. It just didn't have a chance. My father's response was to become more radicalised. He had started his degree course in Essex, so he was away studying during term time and there was an added financial pressure on my mother to have to work. But he was being exposed to that whole student environment of Black Panthers, civil rights, Martin Luther King, etc.

That was quite separate from what my mother was going through. She didn't understand any of this. I remember one day she saw my father reading *Animal Farm* and said, 'Why is he reading fairy stories about animals that can talk when he's got a kid to feed?' Later on she realised, but there was an intellectual chasm there. I'm sure race was a part of him starting to grow away from her.

My mother had no overt bitterness towards Black people, but I don't think it would have been her first choice to go to the Notting Hill Carnival and be surrounded by them immediately after she split up with my father. She always had Black friends, but there was something else there. She is very conservative with a small c and was one of these unfortunate people who, when the National Front emerged on the scene, believed Asians had come into Britain and taken nice houses and jobs. She had an antipathy towards Asians, maybe because of our experiences when I was little. She was anti-immigration and I'm sure would share Mrs Thatcher's swamping fears. But then I remember where I lived a Black family attempted to go on an NF march because they would have been happy to be repatriated.

As a child I never differentiated along racial grounds between my mother and father, people at school, the neighbours, anybody. And then that was accentuated by the fact that I was closeted in the predominant culture. All the cultural values that were being instilled were English. I loved history at school – for most West Indian kids there would be a real problem with learning about Henry VIII, but I'd see the English as the people my grandmother comes out of. I was brought up as English, not white. I'd make that distinction. I was never steered away from feeling Black or having an identity of being Black, but we were always English through and through. But I would say that by the time I was sixteen, in many ways I was a white boy in a brown skin.

All my first experiences of racism against me were from Black or non-white people. The Kenyan Asians in the post office treated us like scum because we had an African name, Ohwoisi; my mother reverted to her maiden name, Upshal, when she got divorced. I used to think: Why do these Asian people hate us? They would serve everyone else in the queue and call them Madam and Sir and when it got to our turn they would disappear for ten minutes, address us very rudely, never be helpful and always act like they had to know our life story before they could cash a Giro or sell us some stamps.

When I was four we lived below some Jamaican people. They used to give us hell. I was playing in the garden one day and a bone hit me in the back of the neck. When I looked up the Jamaican kids upstairs were throwing everything in the kitchen at me and calling me names – you little African this and that. And their mother was always having rows with my mother, although they never had a go at my dad. Maybe they didn't like this white woman married to a Black man because they were never horrible to my dad, just to us.

And when I went to school, Black kids gave me shit. One kid in my first week said, 'Your mum's white, isn't she?' It astonished me that these kids could tell just by looking at me that one of my parents was white. It was the Black kids who used to beat me up. Then there were very few mixed race kids about, although it's different now.

I don't ever remember, before secondary school, a white kid giving me gip about my colour. My friends at school were white kids. But strange things happened. Once my best friend, who was white, said, 'My mum says you can bring any girl home for me to see, but don't ever bring a Black girl home.' And all the Black kids were saying 'No, that's bad.' And I said, 'I can see his mother's point.' I was Mr Logic: naturally his mother assumes that he will gravitate towards somebody of his own background and culture. And it wasn't taking sides, I didn't think that Black people or white people were any worse than each other, but the incompatibility just hit me, probably because of the experience with my own parents' break-up.

I suppose my first awareness that there was something wrong with colour here was when men, neighbours, would hassle my mum because she had a Black child. Once in a shop she gave her African surname and the salesman said, 'What's a nice girl like you doing married to an African?' And then people would be very overfamiliar. Some Black guys up the road would call after her, and white guys would be really forward.

Gradually I realised that them seeing her with me was a clear symbol that she had slept with a Black man. I can remember all kinds of unpleasant comments as a child – comments about how even prostitutes would never sleep with anybody Black, for instance. I did start to feel a bit conspicuous walking down the street with my mother. People would ask her if I was adopted as a polite way of saying, 'Surely you didn't shag a Black man, surely not?' I remember a neighbour once saying, 'My wife says that he's your boy, but I said he must be adopted. Is he?' Then after she said 'Yes, he's my son', the bloke started coming round in the afternoon for no good reason.

I did go through a period when I was about fourteen when

I avoided going out with my mother or grandmother to any place where I thought people were going to observe us as being relatives.

I did feel that I was a bit of a liability to my mum. I wonder sometimes if she'd have been happier or better off with a white kid. I'm part of a relationship and a situation which is a source of unhappiness and bitterness. We've never talked about that at all. I'm not terribly close to my mum, I don't see her very often. I'm extremely close to my grandmother – I spent long periods with her and I remember her feeding and bathing me more vividly than I can my mother. It's not a question I would have to ask my grandmother. She would just say, 'Don't be stupid.'

When I was little I would get into fights with kids over race things, but I would never tell my mother because I knew that she had enough on her plate. Then a year ago my grandmother broke her hip and was in hospital. All the nurses were Black and my grandmother got on really well with them. One of the nurses told me that my grandmother had described to her these fights I had at school. I had no idea that she had this perception, and this is a woman who is virtually a Victorian. And I'd never told her these things, she'd figured it out for herself. That kind of reflects my upbringing – there was this sensitivity. I have never seen the slightest hint of racism in my grandmother, but to her it is legitimate to say 'nigger brown' or 'work like a Black'. I cringe when she says it, but I don't think that's racism, because I know the way she's brought me up and stuck up for me and I know how she interacts with other Black people.

I can never remember having a negative image of myself. When I was little and they asked me to paint people I'd mix red with white and paint pink people, but I can't ever remember wanting to change the colour of my skin, or wishing that my hair was straight. I remember when I was about seventeen, a girl asked me if it wasn't strange that my mother was a different colour – 'She must feel like she's not quite your mother.' She asked me if I wished I looked like my mother. I laughed, I thought it was so stupid, it had never occurred to me in my life. I said, 'No, it's bloody great being brown actually.'

So there were all these contradictions. I was never steered away from feeling Black, but I was brought up to believe I was British – even my musical tastes were Elvis and white rock. But sixteen was a big turning point. Before that my contact with Black people was limited. I went to school in a place called Downham, on the outskirts of London, and although about a fifth of the kids were Black, most were in the middle band of classes, the average band. I was in the above-average band and no one ever mixed across that intellectual divide, no one.

There were two Black girls in my class, but at that age girls and boys don't mix, so all my friends were white. They would tell some very racist jokes and you'd look at them and they'd say, 'Oh no offence, Dave, but you're not like that, are you? You're one of us.' That always jarred.

The other important fact was that some of the Black kids in my school didn't really trust me because I hung out with the white kids. From white kids it was 'Dave, you're one of them, aren't you?' That's the funniest thing about white racism, it's so irrational. The biggest racists in the world, even Bernard Manning – I would bet my life he would say he's got some Black mate somewhere. They'll tell a Black person their most intimate private business and go round the corner and start talking about 'coons' and 'wogs' and 'niggers', and want to 'chuck 'em all out'.

I can remember getting off with this white girl at a party. My mate really fancied her and within a day, he had been down her house and told her that he didn't approve of 'mixed marriages'. And this was a kid whose head would be the first to turn if we saw a good-looking Black girl.

But as time went on I found myself having a great affinity for Black things and feeling very profoundly about them. By the time I was seventeen I was well into it. That changed my life. Also my first serious girlfriend was Black and that was bizarre, because it was just taken as said in my house that my friends were white, very English background, and although my mother was nice to her, I don't think she ever considered that I'd bring home anything but white girls.

That was probably the first time I had a real relationship with someone who was Black. Talking to her mother about life in Notting Hill in the fifties was great. Her family gave me an insight into West Indian culture at a fairly early age, when I was able to take it all in and embrace it all. This was when I was really hearing Black music for the first time, but I was still with my old friends and still into that white rock music, New Wave stuff. I guess I was just undergoing some changes inside that weren't particularly manifesting themselves outside. My dress and my accent and my general values didn't change appreciably.

I was the only person from my school who went to university, so I had nothing in common with any of them and everybody at college thought I had this quaint down-home London accent. And then I'd go home and everyone would say 'You're talking posh now, in't yer.'

Some people at Oxford made real capital out of being Black or gay. I would walk into a room and people would say, 'Hey, great, Dave's here.' You know, 'He's Black and he's working-class – God, Mum, you won't believe it!' That was all quite funny. Oxford had begun to target state schools and trying to get Black people in. People would listen to you – people wanted to know, if there was a Brixton riot or something, what I had to say about it. I suppose in a way, I was driven more to looking inside myself. Then I met all the Black American students – all the Rhodes scholars that year were Black women from the Southern States – I had a friend from Selma, Alabama, whose parents walked with Dr King; it blew my head open.

So – from being sixteen and knowing very little about Black issues or Black history or Black culture, to being twenty-one and being kind of revered by white liberal students as this kind of icon of Black self-knowledge and awareness, and also this interplay with the American kids, really made me think about things. When I came out of college, I was a righteous Black man!

Since then I've been writing almost exclusively about Black issues and working with Black people. And no one has ever questioned my Blackness or my knowledge or my credentials as a Black person, and I've been mixing with some pretty conscious people! So that was a big transformation, but it was in me, it came out.

It's made me miss my father like hell, I felt there was a hole there. He wasn't around much when I was a kid and when he went away I didn't feel it as a great loss in my life, not overnight anyway. I did miss him between twelve and fourteen, as you do if you are a boy. Later, when I was older, I would miss my father culturally. I just felt a kind of yearning – I knew there was more to my heritage than World War I and Henry VIII, and I wasn't getting it. I wasn't angry with my father for going away; the only thing I was angry about was that he didn't teach me a word of his language – that was absurd, he spoke Yoruba and there are many dialects, I don't know which one. I've never been to Nigeria – one day I'll track the dude down, do an Alex Haley.

And it's made me look back on things and appreciate experiences, the kinds of things that when I was a kid I wouldn't have registered as being particularly Black and white things. Attitudes more than words. I never remember undergoing any kind of transformation except when I read the autobiography of Malcolm X. I felt as if someone had taken the top off my head and emptied a box called knowledge in there and banged the top back on. Wow! That changed a lot of my thoughts on things. Moving away from home moved me away from my mother profoundly so I can't really pin any of that on race at all, it wouldn't be fair to, but certainly it changed my perception of things.

What I'd say is strangest about being mixed race is to have been brought up so white and feel so Black. I pin that entirely on the way white society treats non-white people. I don't believe you have a choice. I am half Black and half white, my upbringing was all white. Now if I go into a room full of white people and say, 'Hi everyone, I'm white', they'll piss themselves laughing. If I go into a room full of Black people and say, 'Hi everybody, I'm Black', they'll say 'Come on in' and 'Yes, of course you are.' I find that absolutely peculiar.

Inside, I'm English and I'm also Black, there's no incompatibility, I can't see any. There are white people living in Johannesburg who are Africans, call themselves Africans, even the ANC would accept as being African. I don't see anything incompatible about being Black and English and I refuse to let anyone take that heritage away from me.

I'm too young and idealistic to be bitter, but I'm thoroughly mad about a number of things. I truly, deeply, profoundly hate what I see to be the prevalent intolerance of white society towards anything non-white, non-anglicised. This attitude that even if you're Black you can just make it on certain terms, if you're good. If you'll talk like this, be like this, laugh at this and not say anything. Also the attitude towards white people who marry or live with Black people. I find that abhorrent.

I feel enriched by my knowlege of the Black half of my culture, but it's still half. What do I feel about the white side? I feel it's very sad that the predominant view in white society is that someone like me doesn't belong, but I think it's too bad – they're stuck with me and people like me, I'm not going anywhere and there's more of me every day.

Things are different now to when my parents were starting out. There's not an acceptance, but it would be hard to imagine my parents, for example, being run out of Bournemouth now in the same way that they were in the sixties. We take these tiny strides: two steps forward and one step back, or sometimes one forward and two back. I'm not saying that everybody has suddenly become more enlightened, but they've got to get used to it. When there's only one mixed race couple down the road, and you all want to turn out and throw things and shout abuse at them, then they're pretty stuck with it; but when there are ten or twenty in the area it gets a bit more difficult – you can't bar them all from the pub because you'll lose your business.

I don't reject white people, I feel comfortable with white people, I give people the benefit of the doubt – nobody's

racist until they prove themselves to be. But it's very important to me to know where I'm coming from in terms of culture
and to know them both. I'm as proud of Oliver Cromwell
being in my heritage as I am of Malcolm X or Shaka the Zulu
or whatever. They're of equal importance, so that's where
the balance lies for me. I've never disliked or hated what I
am. That's just the way I look at things.

Denise Seneviratne

Denise Seneviratne was born in London in 1963 of a Sri
Lankan father and a French mother and lived in Manchester
for ten years, although most of her life, before she left home,
was spent in Leamington Spa. She did a degree course in
History of Art and Design and went on to do a postgraduate
course. She then worked in an art gallery in Liverpool and is
now an assistant producer in the Asian Programmes Unit at
the BBC.

Denise

My mother is French, from Lyon; her father is Jewish, and
there is some Spanish blood in the family. When she was
twenty she went to Egypt, where my father was posted,
working for the British army out there. He was an officer in
charge of white soldiers in the desert. They got married while
they were there and all three of my brothers were born out
in Egypt.

Then, after twenty years' service in the British army, the
family came back to Britain and went to live in the Midlands,
in Leamington. Two of my brothers were very affected by
the move – in fact they still are – and must have had a terrible
time adjusting to the complete change in their lives. It must
have been so hard for them – there was the insecurity of
moving across very different kinds of lives at a vulnerable
age and then having to learn to cope with racism and things

like that. My younger brother and I assimilated best, although as you can imagine we had a lot of flak too. We always supported each other and would take some of these things as a joke, or pretend they didn't hurt.

. What was most difficult was the fact that my father refused to acknowledge that it was happening. He was so proud of his British passport and that he fought for the British that he would shut his mind when we said we had been called 'wogs'. I remember he used to turn it round and say, 'But that means a Western oriental gentleman.' He has always refused to believe that colour could be a hindrance in this country, or that racism exists. He really doesn't understand.

He was born a Buddhist and then converted to Catholicism. I used to hate going to Mass with my dad. He stood out, he was the only Black person there, and I would be cringing. I think he had a lot of problems, and that's where it has all come from. When his parents died, his sister wanted to come over here and my father couldn't afford it, he really couldn't. So his family sort of excommunicated him and he lost all contact with his people and his culture. So none of it was ever given to us. He never tried to go into his religious or cultural origins again. He was very Westernised, so proud of the Empire. He wanted to be British and that meant white British, proper British. So we always lived in very white areas, in a white environment. If Asians came into the area in any numbers, we would move.

My mother was also affected by some of these attitudes. She had lived abroad for so many years and depended on my father to some extent throughout her life. In many ways, my father is a very Asian husband. He never encouraged her to do anything with her life, and believed that women should not have big mouths, almost wait to be spoken to. He was very angry once when he saw me shouting at my first boyfriend – he thought as a girl I should treat him with more respect. He didn't want me to carry on with my education, and my mother never rebelled against this. I resent her for that. I remember twice a week she had to cook curry, as my dad's mother had taught her, and my brother and I would refuse to eat it. We would ask for beefburgers. I remember thinking all the neighbours could smell the garlic. But on the other hand, because she was white she was accepted. I remember her telling me never, ever to say that I had Jewish blood. You know I have Jewish relatives, people I didn't discover until I was sixteen. It was easier to be cute and French, I suppose. Last year when her sister came over I found out more about all this.

My father's family accepted her more readily than hers did him. I think she has always felt guilty that she married my father instead of a white man.

When I was child I had a diary and I wrote in it: 'I wish I was white' again and again. I remember thinking that if I wished hard enough I would wake up white one day. I think at the time there was a gang of kids who were giving me real trouble, throwing stones and that, and I was feeling very insecure.

I think the problem was worse because I looked Asian and really wasn't. So it was not just having the dark skin. I felt white with a brown skin, and when we went swimming Asian kids used to walk up to me and try to speak to me in one of the languages. I would be so embarrassed and humiliated because I couldn't communicate with them and wasn't part of them. I didn't feel a part of them and didn't want to feel a part of them.

I used to love it when people thought I was Italian or Spanish, or that I had a really nice tan. So I was happy to have this slightly exotic colour. I had mainly white friends because I went to clubs, places with punk bands and that kind of thing – very few Asians went to these places. Blacks and whites did and Asians do now, but then I was about the only one. These days there are more Asians, but their attitudes are worrying. It is still mainly men, who leave their wives at home and think they are being really cool. A couple of Asian men have called me a prostitute – that kind of thing just makes you sick. These sorts of moral dictators who assimilate and do the right thing, but are such hypocrites. They will do drugs, and have women, but if they see an independent Asian woman it makes their blood boil. It really scares me that the young have these attitudes too, and that they are busy importing all the enmities from Pakistan and the Punjab.

I went to Sri Lanka for the first time recently and although I didn't have massive expectations, I did feel differently about that from going anywhere else. And it did have an effect on me. I was different, but all these men I saw around looked like my father, so it felt strange. In a way, of course, I felt a bond. I put an advert in the papers to see if any of my father's relatives would come forward but no one did.

The more I think about it, the more I believe it is very important to be proud of where you come from. But it is equally important to be honest. I feel a part of this country. I feel British, I don't feel Sri Lankan – perhaps because that side was not nurtured. Children should know, and I was not brought up as a Black child, so I don't know.

It *has* affected my life. I found it difficult not to be able to talk about it to my parents because of the denial that came from them. I don't blame them. They didn't know any better, they thought it was the best thing. They wanted to start a new life with as few problems as possible and they thought the way they chose was the best. I think they were scared that we would not be accepted. They should have given us a sense of our background – especially my father, who gave us his colour, but I think he didn't want racial attitudes to build up against us. He is a very hard man, my father, an ex-army man, he does not express his feelings. And my parents have a very traditional relationship. My mother is the softer one, but even she has never really accepted some things. I remember her telling my father not to wear a trilby because West Indians wore them and people might think he was one of them. I was really shocked when she said that. It was really racist.

But it didn't matter what my parents thought or what they did, I was always Black in the eyes of other people. I always had racist abuse thrown at me. Or if I didn't get it it would be, 'You are all right, but the others . . .' and you were identified on the side of people who despised other Blacks and Asians. I have had to confront this in a very direct way at the BBC Asian Programmes Unit, East, where I work. And here there were other things to confront too. I didn't have any of this Asian culture, whatever that is, and I was really made to feel it. There can be this extreme sense of identity, language, culture, and it leads to a shocking amount of self-righteousness. You need a kind of brown ticket of how Asian you are. How Asian is it all right to be, then? Who decides who is more Asian than anyone else? That has been very difficult, and I have felt very angry about that kind of thing. They are so condescending and treat you as if you don't have a real grasp.

I find that Asians think they are superior to Blacks and whites. Who do we think we are? This talk about our 'rich' culture – no culture is static, or the best, in any sense. Everybody just idealises it all the time instead of looking at it honestly. I feel confident now that I do have the right to point this out, that I am not an outsider because I am mixed race. I hope this doesn't mean I have become more racist, I don't think I have.

And that has also made me think about the positive side of how I was brought up – the good side of a British upbringing, especially as a woman. I have no regrets about the way I lived. I could not have survived for one minute in one of those Asian households where you are not allowed to go out, where I would have been pushed into a particular religion and not allowed to have relationships with men, or would have had to keep it secret or hidden.

As I have grown up I have realised the advantages of being the colour that I am. So many men have this fantasy, you know – dark skin, dark eyes, mysterious, unattainable, the forbidden fruit. All that does go on for white men, and I know it. And temperamentally, there is much about me that is from my two parents. I am very un-English in the way I am physical, in my temper, the way I say or shout what I feel. I do think brown skin is more attractive than white skin and I love it when my skin is darker after I have been in the sun, but I wouldn't want to go out with a traditional Asian guy, however good-looking. I am so independent, he wouldn't have the same values as me. Materialism, which is so deep in Asians, is not my scene; marriage is not my scene.

There are many young Asians who think as I do. Our 'culture' is just as valid, and neither whites nor Asians have the right to reject people like me or reject my experiences and views. What is happening now is inevitable – so there will be the children not just of mixed marriages, but of mixed cultures. And a good thing too. We are perhaps the children of the future – not having any strong addiction to any one culture, but being a mixture. Being a different colour but being at least partly very English. I see myself as a Black woman now, but I don't fit into any traditional cultural categories and I don't crave that. I am learning aspects of Asian culture, almost as a subject, and it is fascinating, but I don't want to own it, be owned by it, or be trapped by it. This is my country and really, is it worth looking back?

Annabel Mackenzie

Annabel Mackenzie was born in London, where she has lived all her life except when she was travelling around the world, one of her many obsessions. Her father, who died many years ago, was pale-skinned Guyanese, and her mother was English. She has a brother, Gordon, to whom she is very close. Annabel is a painter. (See Chapter 6 for her mother Grace's account.)

Annabel

My father was born in 1896, a second son. My grandfather had African blood in him because he came down from a line where there had been a liaison between a slave and a white man, which was very common in these slave colonies. What would happen down the generations was that people would

try and marry, if not white then light, and they couldn't
inherit anything because the white side of the family didn't
want anything to get into the hands of what are called half-
caste children. But these children could become managers on
the plantations, though never inherit anything. The manager
would marry a half-caste girl, and they would go on like that.

My grandfather knew this so I think that is why he
decided, in 1910, to move out. He first went to San Francisco
and then tried New York, where I seem to remember either
there were racist remarks or a fight in a bar. He decided New
York wasn't a very good idea, and went to Montreal.

I wouldn't be surprised if they weren't one of the first
'coloured' families in the area, and I think this is why they
became an entity in themselves. They ended up a large
family – there were ten children, so they could play with one
another and protect themselves from the standard racist
remarks. They looked different – they didn't look African,
but you could see that there was coloured blood there. That
was one reason why they never talked about their background. I used to ask my father to talk about Guyana and he
never did. And you know once they arrived in Canada, not
one of them ever went back to Guyana. Isn't that incredible?
There was a trunk with photographs which remained in the
cellar, and that was their life in British Guyana. They never
spoke about it either.

My father stayed in Canada until 1922, then he came here
and worked in the City. Now can you imagine? In the City
in the twenties and thirties you were basically from Oxford
or Cambridge. You weren't even accepted if you were Jewish.
My father would never have dared to mention the word
Guyanese there. As far as everybody was concerned, he was
Canadian. As far as we were concerned as his children, he
was Canadian. His whole other side was absolutely blotted
out. I think it stemmed from childhood memories and a
feeling children have of not wanting to be different from
everyone else. It went right through. They all felt that way.
When my brother and I said to the aunts in Montreal, literally
like fifteen years ago, that we were going to go to Guyana,

they said, 'Don't tell anyone there that we are here, will you?' There was real fear. Apparently one relative had knocked on the door in Montreal, a Black relative, and the shame of it was terrible.

I think it has taken its toll, especially as all this had obviously come out of deep pressures. One of my aunts had a spectacular West Indian nervous breakdown at some point and was taken to a psychiatric hospital and talked about the old days in Guyana. Instead of psychologists there were sociologists around her bed taking it all down. But you know, funnily, as she got better, down came the barrier again. I think the reason for leaving Guyana was purely economic. I don't think there was any other reason, it was worry about their economic security in the future.

When we went back to find out about our father, there were many branches of the family who came from these offshoots and it was muddling to piece things together. My grandmother, like many Guyanese women then, obeyed her husband. They had quite a lot of money, maids – my grandmother had never even boiled an egg in her life – so it wasn't poverty but insecurity that made my grandfather decide to leave that heritage behind and head for the New World, which it was then. And to leave it all behind, they had to keep it hidden from the rest of the family. They must have felt as my father did, desperate to keep it hidden.

I was really upset when I went back to Guyana and I looked around and I realised that everyone there was my father – the way he spoke, the way he looked, the way he moved. I almost burst into tears because there he was and yet all that time, all those years, I hadn't seen it. I had seen a white person. I remember once we were waiting in my primary school, which was all-white, and we were looking out of the window, it was a parents' day or something. One of the girls said, 'Who is that funny-looking man?' I turned to look, and it was my father. All of a sudden I remember looking at him not through my eyes but through the eyes of someone else, and seeing a funny-looking man. There was that second when I didn't want to acknowledge him and to agree and say 'Yes, isn't he?' I was that awful age, you know, and I didn't want to be different.

I remember when I came back from Guyana and the BBC wanted me to do a programme about my father, through my new perceptions, and I quite casually told my mother – who had only recently discovered this about my father herself – that I was going to do this, she was so upset. She said, 'You can't do it. There are people alive, colleagues in the City and that, who he'd never want to know about this. You have to respect his wishes.' I didn't do it in the end, not for her but for his memory.

You have to understand that as far as my mother was concerned, she had married a white man. And it wasn't as if my father denied that British Guyana existed and that is where he came from, but that was all it was allowed to be. And after he died and all this began to change, it really came to me as a revelation that yes, I am half Guyanese. This was twenty-two years ago now, when I was obviously already an adult. And of course even if we had asked our father, there were years of reticence there – maybe things had gone so far he just couldn't have told us. I think in some ways I feel a bit cheated by it.

But it isn't too late, is it? New chapters begin. When I first went there a Guyanese friend said to me, 'Be careful when you shake your family tree in Guyana, a lot of dark fruit may fall out.' But the problem turned out to be the white fruit that started appearing for the relatives in Guyana. This shocked, provoked and embarrassed them at first, but there were contradictions in those attitudes too. One of them said to me, 'You have come here to look for Black relatives? How strange – we are usually going over to England in search of white relatives.'

Someone else said, 'You are Comrade Mackenzie's relatives? Jesus, he will never live this one down!' This was all made more conspicuous by the fact that some of my ancestors had been involved in an attempted revolution and there are 'Wanted' posters for them in some parts of the country. The anti-white feelings were quite shocking and ironic, I suppose, after all my father and his family tried to do, keeping their Black relatives away. People would cross themselves, stare, spit and things like that. One person actually recoiled and said, 'Jesus, they are back!'

But there are deep links which cross these things. You know how I love wearing all the bright colours under the sun all the time, and when I was there Gordon, my brother, said, 'I really understand where this is coming from. You really fit in here.' And it's true. Now, when I am with Guyanese people, I really fit in and I can go to an English party and stand in the corner the entire time. But there is a part of me that is really out there. I really believe there is something inherent in me. I want to wear green skirts and yellow shoes and I think I am much more that way inclined than I have ever been in England. I think it was in subtle ways that I sensed I was different. I was terribly restless as I was growing up. I had to travel to become something, and going to Guyana was a very central part of this process.

I would think very, very seriously about going to South America – not to work, because I can't see how I could work there. Last year I went to Guyana, Surinam and other places. When I am there I feel: I am not quite here as a tourist, because I am introduced as 'Annabel Mackenzie, she is Guyanese'. It is a warming feeling, though it wasn't like that at the beginning. The other thing many of them ask is why I haven't got a Guyanese passport, and I have thought I must get one. I am part Guyanese, a part I have found late in life and a part that is quite important to me.

There is a difference between the way my brother and I have reacted. I went the first time, came back, thought about it, and then got on with my life, changed but not transformed. Gordon, I think, was taken over by it. Most of his friends are now West Indian; I haven't changed in that way. I haven't got that many West Indian friends, but it's been important to me and in many ways it is becoming more and more important. I am very close to a Guyanese woman there and I know I will keep going back. Gordon's change has been more political. In his case there is very much a before and after. Suddenly his reading changed and he started to focus on everything to do with South America. I have seen that change. With hindsight, maybe I feel we both felt there was something there to find, although I cannot truly say that I felt at the time that something was missing or lacking in my life.

But looking back, there are things that strike me now. I made one Guyanese friend in Canada and she turned up once. Even then, I realise now, my father didn't ask her anything about the country. My parents never talked about the fact that we might or might not have relationships with Black people. At that time there were no Black people around really, it was before the great influx. I suspect he envisaged we would settle with someone white and respectable. He would, I suspect, have been quite disconcerted if one of us had turned up with someone Black. When all those race riots happened in the cities, he basically took a very English law-and-order stand. There was no point of identification at all between him and the Black people out there. Never ever did anybody West Indian come home. And when I went to Canada and saw his family they all looked, like I said, sort of Mediterranean. They didn't look English, but not African either – except for Aunt June, who did look very Black and of whom I was ashamed because she was different. And I remember when she came over and I felt awful because I really didn't want to be identified with her, and I think that is the only time in my life that I have had really racist feelings about anybody.

The original Mackenzie was Scottish and went off to Guyana, presumably with enough money to buy a plot of land, and the place was simply carved up between him and two other white families. And then when you went to visit another plantation, the best slave was in your bed, just like a hot-water bottle. One of these owners, according to one book, had sixty-four children by these slaves. Up until the twenties, if you were a mulatto, you married white or light if you possibly could, or half-caste, and you got lighter and lighter. Now, of course, there is pride in being Black, but not then. There are other problems now. There is no love lost between the Afro-Guyanese and the Indo-Guyanese. You hear them calling each other 'nigger' and 'coon' – it is awful.

Identity is a funny thing. When I am out there I can get very, very brown and look as if I belong there somehow. And I have brown eyes and when I was young I had tight, tight curls and yes, then I can see that I am half Guyanese. But if you are not aware of it and you are not looking for it, it is very, very difficult to tell. My average English friends would say, 'What are you talking about?' My brother has deep-blue eyes and is deeply envious of my brown eyes, yet I think he sounds less English, maybe more Caribbean.

And my father's family – they have spent almost all their lives in Canada and would never accept that they were Black in any way at all, which is rather sad, but even in their eighties there *is* something about them which is Black. I remember being there a couple of years ago and I had to take one of my aunts to hospital. The other aunt came with us and they were standing close to each other, talking. I was talking to the psychiatrist and as I looked towards them and the psychiatrist and others did too, they seemed to be getting darker by the minute. And I could see from the way he was looking at them that he was waiting to dismiss them because they didn't belong, talking and gesticulating in that very conspicuous way. They didn't fit in with all the other people around them. So these two, in effect, Black women who refused to see themselves as Black, were being summed up in terms that would have shocked them. Their origins defined them – there was no question about it. Fifty years in Canada, and trying so hard to disappear and to be accepted and yet if anything, they were more conspicuous as Black people. Yet they had really tried. All their lives they had tried to win accolades. And you know it is sad, because so much of the pain and resentment about their lives is now coming out – not directly, but leaking out in bits. Deep, deep resentment – about the fact that they were coloured and people looked down on them. And to think it all happened in Canada, the great New World.

They really tried. They were incredibly competitive. One of my aunts was a top tennis player; they felt they had to prove themselves. I try and imagine what it must have been like for them all those years ago – even physically, after Guyana – to go to somewhere like Montreal, with the harsh climate and endless winters. And of course for my mother, who thought all her life that she was married to a white Canadian, it has all been a revelation too.

My mother gets on incredibly well with anybody – Black, brown or white. She has a lovely nature and no feelings of prejudice. But the twenties and thirties were very different times in this country and I think then, as for other women, her husband laid down the law and decided what was what, and that was simply the way it was.

Rosalind Scarce

Rosalind Scarce is twenty-five and has three brothers and two sisters, all older. Her mother was born in Guyana of Asian parents; her father is Black Guyanese. She left college in 1987 with two A levels in dance and communications and after that 'I bummed around doing a bit of everything' – pirate radio, DJ-ing, music journalism and choreography, all at once! She has now been with the BBC for two years, working as a researcher and presenter.

Rosalind

At the time my parents married, in the early fifties, there were great cultural problems between the Asians and Blacks in Guyana. It was definitely not the done thing for Asians and Blacks to marry.

So my mother shamed her Asian family by being with my father. She came from a very middle-class family – my grandfather was an MP. When she was very young she agreed – because of family pressures – to an arranged marriage to a 'suitable' man – a very well-to-do Asian professional, a doctor. She had one child, my brother. My father was her childhood sweetheart, but of course because he had black skin he was seen as unsuitable, as 'lower class'.

But my mother loved my father and didn't love the man she was married to and she did an unthinkable thing for an Asian married woman with a child from this respectable family: she eloped with my father to Surinam to stay with a Black woman, a friend of my father's family, who owned a poultry farm. They thought that once they were there they would be left alone, but even the woman who owned the poultry farm thought my mother was too good for my father and telegraphed my grandfather to tell him where they were. He came and brought her back, locked her up, kept her there against her will – she was fed under the door. I don't know what she must have gone through. Then they discovered she was pregnant with my sister. Her marriage to the doctor was dissolved.

Because she had brought such shame on the family and was still determined to be with my father, they banished her to England. She was sent away because they couldn't bear the shame of her being in Guyana and everybody knowing.

After three or four years, when my parents had bought a house, the rest of the family decided to come over here and live with them. My mother loved them very much and really internalised this idea that she had disgraced her family; she was always trying to do anything that would win their approval. So she allowed them to come and live with her, and use her, after all that they had done to her. And eventually they accepted the inevitability of what had happened.

The Asian side of the family always rejected us and looked down on us, from the start. One of my earliest memories is of my grandmother. Because both my parents were doing shiftwork we used to be dropped off at her house during the day – this was before I was even five. I have a vivid memory of looking out of the back of our beat-up Vauxhall and knowing, when we turned a certain corner, that we were going to my grandmother's and having hysterics once I realised that this was happening. As well as looking after me and my brother, who is five years older, my grandmother also looked after my other cousins, who were Anglo-Asian, who always got treated better. It was small things – for example, I remember if she had an old packet of cornflakes and a new one, my brother and I would always be given the old stale ones and the new ones would be saved for my cousins. I remember being made to lie head to toe with my brother on the sofa and being told not to move an inch, while my cousins were allowed to play.

One of the most blatant examples was just ten years ago. In 1980 my mother had a stroke – she died two years later after another stroke. I remember being at the hospital, calling up my aunts and uncles to get them to come round. They were weeping and wailing as my mother was lying there. Then the nurse asked me if I could tell them to go because my mother needed to rest. When I suggested this to them they turned on me and said that my brother and I had driven her to an early grave because of our Black associations – because we both went around with Black people. Even at that stage they had not forgotten or forgiven what my mother did.

Pre-puberty, I looked very Asian. I grew up in a part of North London where there are a lot of Afro-Caribbeans, particularly Jamaicans, so from an early age those were the people who became my friends. I remember that every Asian man was like my uncle and every Asian woman was like my auntie – they would look disapprovingly at me if I walked into a shop, for example, with a Black person. Those who detected that I had some Black blood in me treated me like total scum. It used to make me really angry.

I realise now that it might not have happened to the extent that I thought it did – perhaps it was partly the result of my internalising the aggression from my own family. But still I was in this very weird situation where at school I was called 'Paki' and all I got from my own, Asian part of the family was shit.

As a result of all this I moved completely away from Asian culture. I was rejected by my Asian relatives, and so were the rest of my family. To the end, when my mother died, my father was just tolerated, although my aunties and uncles have mellowed a lot – perhaps because they're older, because there's now second-generation mixing and because they have had to accept it. But it is still there, not very far underneath the surface. I still get certain reactions from them. For example, snide remarks when I got the job at the BBC – they said, 'How did that happen?' They just assumed that it would be the kind of thing their kids, with such a good education, would be capable of, but not me.

Inevitably we all turned towards Black history and culture. At this time my brothers and sisters who were older were getting into sound systems, my sister got really interested in the Black rights movements in the USA and in what Angela Davis was doing, so it was very natural for me to align myself with West Indian culture. So from a young age I learned the cultural codes and identified very strongly with West Indians. You learn how to handle yourself, and I embraced and adopted West Indian culture.

When I was older, things got more complicated. When I began to recognise my own sexuality I realised that the Asian part of me made others regard me as slightly more attractive. Funnily, then, I came up against some jealousy and hostility from West Indian women. Probably because of all this, I was always very aware of race, politics and discrimination. From a very early age, because of the way my family behaved, I grew up knowing that for some reason I was different and treated differently.

My mother was the greatest influence on my life. She went through an enormous amount of suffering and turmoil because of what happened, and she never let go of her kindness and essential belief in humanity. We never got to the stage where we could talk about what happened, because she died when I was fifteen. I wish so much that we could have had that opportunity. There is so much I want to know, and you know these things go on and on. Our house was like a refuge for everyone who had the kinds of problems my mother had had. I remember when I was ten my fifteen-year-old cousin, who was half Chinese and half Guyanese, started dating an African – she's still with him today. She wasn't allowed to see him at her house, they didn't approve of him, so she came to our house. So there were all these things going on, and as time went by I took it further and started to ask why.

In the last year I've had more of a reassessment of who I am. It seemed natural to apply to Black programming rather than the Asian unit because I see myself as a Black person. But having made friends with people from the Asian unit, for the first time in my life I started to realise the richness of my Asian heritage and that it's not something to reject and be ashamed of. I suppose I didn't reject it, it was taken away from me at an early age by my family. It's become important to question myself as to why for many years I had the Asian side of me denied. I didn't like being called 'Paki' at school and I suppose I took on the stereotypes of my English and West Indian friends at school. It seemed OK; I didn't feel firmly Asian because I'd been so rejected. I have never been turned on by Asian men – so far, at any rate – maybe because I grew up with these stereotypes of Asians as passive. I would go out with an Asian guy; now I've released all these stereotypes. There are probably practical reasons why I don't, I just don't meet any.

Now I realise that there's a whole heritage there, it enhances my being and I'm more and more intrigued by it. I've become more and more interested in the dynamics of the subcontinent, although I still haven't found out where my family come from originally. It is a strange feeling. I've always felt like an honorary Asian, I don't know the cultural codes, and I still feel like a bit of an outsider. I feel embarrassed sometimes now because I don't know very much.

My father really internalised his own oppression and never really thought he was good enough for my mother. He has a lot more respect for white people than for his own kind – I wonder if he has ever looked in the mirror. It showed in his attitudes to my boyfriends. He used to ask me why I didn't marry someone white and escape from being Black. Several times I brought Black male friends or Black boyfriends home; he would barely grunt and look up from his newspaper. But I remember when I brought this white guy Dave home, he really brought out the Sunday best – I found it sickening. I was about seventeen and it was a real turning point in my life.

We knew Dave's family because he was a cousin of my brother's wife, who was white. We started dating, but when I went to his house I had to pretend that we were just friends. It really made me mad that while my father was so over-whelmed and so obsequious to Dave because he was white, Dave's family really loved me only so long as I was just a friend; as soon as they knew we were dating, they rejected me. It was so hypocritical. Something like that must throw up so many questions.

I have never been out with a white man since, although I couldn't say that I definitely wouldn't ever. But yes, it was a conscious decision. It was a political decision for me. My personal view is that I can't divorce my political life from my personal life, they are intrinsically linked. I don't think a white person can share the same politics or experiences as me. There are many white people whom I love, but I don't have the same cultural codes and eventually there is a gap. I don't feel there is the same common ground in terms of having a relationship. I mean physically, yes, I think Don Johnson is gorgeous, and physically I could be attracted to white men, and have been, but culturally we are worlds apart.

I feel that any white man who is attracted to me regards me as a piece of 'exotica'. I would always suspect this. I remember I went out with a white guy and he said to me, 'You're really lovely, you know. I mean I've never been out with a Black girl before. For me to go out with a Black girl, you must know you're beautiful.'

I couldn't sleep with a white man – I feel that there would be a throwback memory. I've read too much about slave-owners pressing themselves on my sisters and raping them, I'd feel very violated by it – even the thought of lying with a white man makes me feel that very strongly. I couldn't give a white man the privilege of being in that position.

There is a problem in terms of white people's self-awareness and awareness of other people too. When I walk round the place where I work and have conversations with white men, I feel as if they are all missionaries. They all want to discover what it's like to be Black and oppressed. Well, I'm not a museum piece, I don't feel like talking to anyone about being Black, they don't have to define their whiteness; if they want to find out about it, they should go and read a book.

I consider myself a very powerful Black woman in terms of my knowledge of self and identity, and now I know that is something that cannot be shaken.

Yvette Alexander

Yvette Alexander is training to be a youth and community worker and is also running a special support group at a Women's Centre in Coventry for mothers of mixed race children. She herself has a white mother and a West Indian father. She has been with her partner, who is Asian, for five years.

Yvette

From as early as I can remember, I was aware that my parents were different in colour from each other, and that I seemed to be a mixture of both of them. I was darker than my mother and lighter than my father, although at this stage, when I was about three or four, I wasn't aware that this meant being treated any differently to anybody else I knew.

I didn't become aware of it until I went to primary school at the age of five. I went to a predominantly white school, where perhaps 2 per cent of the children were Black. I remember one boy in particular took great delight in making me cry when he called me 'Blackie' and 'nig nog'. This really hurt, but my teacher just treated it as a childish tease and did nothing except tell the boy that he shouldn't do it and tell me that it was nothing to cry about. All this made me think that it was really unjust that I was Black, more like my dad than my mum. And because instances of racism were so frequent then – they were constant in the early years – I felt it a lot. Being called names, having so-called friends turning their backs on me if I didn't toe the line.

When I went home very upset and told my parents why I felt that way, my father was adamant that we were Black and that we would have to work twice as hard as anyone else at school to get as far as them. That was his way of explaining why it was happening. But all it did was to make me hate the fact that my father spoke like this, when all I really wanted was to be accepted. On the other hand my mother, the white part of the partnership, would tell us that we weren't Black, we were brown, usually behind my father's back.

By the time I was ten, I had learnt many lessons in my life – perhaps most of all that being Black was not just a skin colour, it meant getting certain treatment. I was internalising everything, as if it was all my fault. Everything about my world seemed to say that Black was bad, dirty or wrong, and there was no getting away from that. So it took me a long time to accept that I was Black and to feel that I could call myself Black because of all of the associations and also because there weren't any positive Black images when I was young.

So most of my experiences as a child were negative – they made me wish constantly that I wasn't me – and part of the reason was that the messages coming from my parents were incompatible. My father's message was essentially that society was at fault. But I couldn't take that on board, because it was only his word against everything that I was being socialised into. The television showed things like 'Love Thy Neighbour' or 'Mixed Blessings', where calling Black people racist names was justified. 'Mixed Blessings', about a mixed marriage, made me think that everything about my life was wrong. How awful it was that this Black woman and white man had come together! There was no positive reinforcement. There were no Black teachers in my school.

It wasn't until I was eight that I stopped thinking that my father came from a place where he wore a loincloth and swung through trees and had only really become civilised as a result of coming to Britain. But culturally, we had a rich life at home. We had all sorts of food and my dad would tell us lots of stories and show us pictures of his country.

I really started to think things through when I left school and went to college at the age of eighteen. Until then I was blaming myself for my situation, which many Black and mixed race people tend to do. So I stopped internalising the experiences of racism that I was receiving. That was quite difficult; I could justify it only because that internalisation made me feel really awful. But when I actually started to think about the societal effects of racism, the political and economic and social forces that went into play when racism was happening, I started to realise that I had been wrong to internalise it because it hadn't been anything to do with me at all – it was more an institutional thing and something that happened because of the power and prejudice of others.

When I left college I started to do some voluntary work in a young women's group and again, one of the workers there really valued me as a Black woman, and my skills, and gave me the space to grow in my own right. So then I could start to relate to myself as a Black person, but I was still aware that I was mixed race. I came to the conclusion that I was lucky in lots of ways, that I've got two sets of culture – my father gave us his from the Caribbean and my mother hers from this country. But at the end of the day I was a Black person, that's how I would be treated in society and that's how I'm happy seeing myself, but I've got lots of experience of other things. I'm at my best when people actually value that in me. I no longer – as I did when I was a child – just grasp for friends; I look for people who I know will understand where I'm coming from.

My father was very much against his daughters being in relationships with men who were either white European or Asian, it was a case of 'Don't bring anybody like that home here or you're going to be in real trouble.' We were very frightened of our father in lots of ways because he was very strict with us, very restrictive about how much we could go out. Because for him, to get on in this country you needed a good education; perhaps what he didn't tell us or hadn't realised was that the education system is actually something that's put together by predominantly white middle-class people and it isn't necessarily about getting yourself a good education, it actually depends on the way you're treated because of what you are in the education system. That aside, I was quite afraid actually to bring anybody home until I was about nineteen. That restricted me an awful lot. I've never been immature, but in terms of personal relationships it was kind of causing me to be a little bit immature because I knew I couldn't do the things my friends did – have an open relationship with people my father would respect.

My partner at the moment is Asian – that's a bit of a turn-round. I was going out with him before my father died and even though he must have got to the stage where he respected the fact that I was going out with him, I think in his heart of hearts he didn't like it. But again I'm not sure how much of that is a kind of bigotry or how much is just being afraid of what the consequences of a mixed relationship would be, having been in one himself.

I made the decision to do the things I'm doing now quite a long time ago. My second-year placement at college at the Women's Health and Information Centre in Coventry seemed the perfect place to put into operation the things I had been thinking about. So I've organised a group for women – predominantly white women but with one mixed race woman – who have mixed race children. They meet on a weekly basis, and we look at things like a child's self-identity, hair and skin care, prejudice from other Black people in terms of you not being pure – and the prejudice that white women face from Black people. The most important thing – and I think it's something I didn't really have – was for parents or guardians of mixed race children to be honest with them and explore with them what they are going through. I was told I was Black, from my father, and that's what I was and there was no getting away from it. On the other hand, I was brown as far as my mother was concerned, but it didn't matter anyway because 'everybody loves you and you're OK'. That doesn't help at all. In retrospect, it would have been more valuable for me if someone had sat down and said, 'How do you feel about what you are? What do you think you are?' instead of just telling me what I was supposed to be.

Many of the problems I had were in terms of the negative experiences as a young Black person. Like going into shops with my mother and people not realising we were with her and saying 'What do you want?' in a very stern way because we were Black children and they were probably afraid we were going to steal something. My mum would say, 'They're with me, it's OK', and then not talk about it afterwards, as though it was a really awful thing that had happened. And I thought it was my fault, because if I hadn't been there it wouldn't have happened. Sometimes it isn't appropriate to deal with something out in the street or in the middle of town, but there must be a time when it *is* appropriate and then it *must* be dealt with or it becomes a sort of taboo, and I don't think that's healthy.

I'm not into making sure mixed race children are Black, full stop. I'm more into making sure they get a good balance in their life, that no side of their culture is ignored and that they don't feel restricted or pushed into being one thing or another. They can actually feel like very special people who have more than most people. That's really what our project is about, and I hope in the future we'll look at ways of drawing more women in.

In terms of the future, I think that mixed race young people are a growing force and quite possibly one of the most rapidly growing groups of children around. With that in mind, the whole issue needs to be addressed – of what mixed race people are called and the kind of difficulties they sometimes grow up with in terms of their identity and the messages that go on around them. When I was young and read things to do with Black people – issues around the way they are treated in this society and the racism that's prevalent – I thought: There's more than that for me, there are other things which don't seem to be touched on here in terms of the self-identity thing. In the past mixed race people have tended to get lumped in with the issues around Black people – we were all getting lumped into one, and we're not. It's great if mixed race people can identify themselves as Black because in society's terms that's the way they will be treated and it makes it easier to fight racism in this country, or individual experiences of racism. The last thing I would want is to start splitting people up, that doesn't help in the struggle against racism. But my aim is that people should explore where a person's at and the experiences they are having. So then if we talk about that subject, it doesn't become a thing that someone feels but something that's quite clearly an issue in this society – something that people are talking about and addressing, something that is no longer isolated.

Coming back to the group: quite often when people decide they are going to have children, they don't think of any issues around them apart from the fact that they want a child in terms of their own fulfilment as a couple. But whether you like it or not, that child will probably receive treatment in society that can be quite damaging to its own personal development. And the more aware parents are of that, I think, the easier it will be for young people as they are growing up.

Vicky Philipps

Vicky Philipps was born in London in 1956 of a half Sierra Leonean, half English mother and an English father. When she was nine her parents divorced, and one year later she and her two brothers and sisters moved with their mother to Sierra Leone. She lived there until she was twenty and then came back to Britain. She now lives in London and works as a designer.

Vicky

When we were kids we were aware of racist things happening; we would walk down the road and someone would shout 'Shit Legs' to Mary, my sister, and we would burst out laughing, we just found it funny. This was when we were in England, when I was about eight. I never really 'knew' that my mother was Black, although she had Black brothers and sisters and I knew *they* were Black. But I never thought about it, it just didn't connect.

The first time I realised my mother was Black was when we went to Sierra Leone when I was ten and I saw her sister, who looks just like her. But because she wasn't my mother, I could see she was Black. That was my first actual consciousness that my mother was Black, but then I was in Sierra Leone and everyone was Black, so it didn't really make any difference. If it had been here it might have been different. We were fair-skinned but because we were my mother's children, it didn't really make any difference to the way we were treated by family. But ironically, strangers always treated us as though we were white. So there was this situation where Mary was Black here and white there. That's the stupid thing about it.

People thought we were odd when we were at school in England, but I always thought I was white in spite of the things that happened to us. I remember exchanging racist abuse with Jews in the area – we called them yids, they called us niggers. We just accepted the racist abuse as correct; we *were* niggers as far as they were concerned. On one level it didn't seem odd that they were calling us niggers – in fact my father used to call us niggers when he was angry, and he used to call my mother a Black bitch. In the divorce there was a lot of racist abuse from him to her. We were aware of all this, but it didn't really mean anything to us.

So you see, even though we were Black or niggers to other people, I never thought of myself as anything other than white, not consciously. At school I didn't think about the abuse but all my friends were either Greek or Pakistani, so I was obviously seen as 'other' by other children. I do notice now that children whom you might class as 'other' tend to stick together. My mother doesn't have a consciousness as such of being Black but Matt, my brother, was already conscious, having had to deal with much more racist abuse because he was much darker.

I remember once when my mum had hit my father because he'd done something, he contacted the police and they came to pick her up for assault. They came expecting to find an aggressive Black woman who would have her Black lover hanging around the house and her five Black offspring all in rags and tatters. My mother's a very middle-class, respectable woman and we were always dressed impeccably, even when we were in the house. They arrived and both the girls were in matching floral dresses and red shoes and all the boys in grey shorts, white shirts and ties, playing happily in the garden. They were completely flummoxed by this.

My father abandoned us when we were little. As a child I stopped seeing him when I was about eight. My sister was his favourite, although she's Black. It was my mother who I was close to. I grew up without him and then when I came back here, I saw him once in a while; it became clear that he didn't want much to do with us for his own reasons. I doubt if his wife knows we are mixed race. I've never met her, my sister is the only one who has, and she's the fairest.

My grandparents weren't that keen on us, because we were mixed race. I think my father didn't tell them about us for that very reason, because for a long time they didn't know we existed. His sister found us or my mother found his sister, and just before we left for Sierra Leone we met them. They knew that my father had children but I don't think they knew my mother was Black. I think they were very patronising. It was like a rerun. My mother's father, who was white, came back to England and sent money to Sierra Leone, but although he loved my grandmother he didn't bring her back here, and when his children came over here he never saw them in his home. My father was working-class and he was well-educated and clever, but they always thought he was getting above his station.

Now we have an affectionate but rather detached relationship. He rings me up, he's terribly concerned about me and I see him maybe once a year. I don't think he's any more racist than any other English person is, culturally. He fancies Black women and makes suggestive remarks about Black news presenters. I think it's a power thing; it usually is. Because he is of working-class origin, he would never have been comfortable marrying a middle-class white woman, so he married a middle-class Black woman.

But racism is always made more complicated by other kinds of hang-ups. When we were children it was Mary who was his favourite, and she is the blackest. My mum is not a racist because she's Black, but she's a terrible racial bigot; somehow she's allowed her bigotry because she's Black.

In our family we range in colour from completely black to apparently completely white, and there are attitudes within the family. There are my mum and her sisters. One married a Black guy, so her children are three-quarters Sierra Leonean; another married a mixed race guy, so her children are half Black; and my mother married a white guy, so her children are three-quarters white. It's complicated, but there's a kind of status thing within the family and a difference between the Black and the mixed race people. Even within the mixed race people there's a kind of consciousness, depending on how dark you are. There's a sensitivity to it. I think these dynamics, whether they are about race or something else, occur within every family.

It was when my mother, after getting custody of the children, took us to Sierra Leone that everything began to click into place. Being there made it much easier to realise I was Black, because everyone was Black there and I had the security of the family and did not have to deal with it in a hostile environment. It was completely normal and natural.

So now if I meet another Sierra Leonean I feel completely relaxed and at ease. I feel there's a lot of subliminal communication going on. The thing is that it doesn't always work both ways because they don't see me like that, maybe because I don't look obviously Black, so it can be a one-sided thing. It does bother me now because you feel like an alien to virtually everyone you meet. And I think that's why my family see each other so much, all mixed brothers and sisters and cousins. We seem not to fit in anywhere.

And it was only when I came back here when I was twenty that I suddenly began to perceive racial conflicts which obviously applied to me in some way, but it took me a long time. I found that nothing was what it seemed; I behaved in a certain way, would say something I meant, and realised I was dealing with a race of people who didn't mean what they said. I found that really difficult to come to terms with. English people are not direct. I found that I was constantly being called aggressive – a label which, I subsequently realised, is often attributed to Black women. There are lots of reasons why people are perceived as aggressive – different body language, different ways of reading people. We all have ways of scanning other people for subtle, familiar clues, and maybe if you don't find them you operate in a way that is based much more on fear.

When I first came here I didn't look as though I belonged, I was very tanned, I probably looked like a white South African. And I had an accent, so people kept asking me where I was from. So I was aware that I was different, but I was quite naive. I remember I couldn't get a grant to do my postgraduate work and I thought at first it was because I wasn't English and white, but then I remember thinking: they think I'm Black, that's why I can't get one; maybe if I go down there in person to get a grant and show the colour of my skin. Now that is the reaction of a racially unaware person.

I was very conscious of my class background, too. I think

I've always been much more aware of it, although my mother was middle-class in Sierra Leone. Here anyone who comes from a country like that automatically operates in a working-class way because they don't have access to the system.

My self-perception changed in different ways. When I went to university I was in an all-white environment, not aware of being in a racially conscious environment. My first embarrassment was when I started going out with Peter. I'd never thought to pretend I was anything different to what I was. I remember making a joke about my great-grandfather being a witch doctor – he was a medicine man (my mother calls him a pharmacist), he probably didn't wear a grass skirt, but he probably didn't wear a white coat either – and Peter's jaw dropped. He said, 'Do you mean he was Black?' and I was overcome with embarrassment, which might have been tinged with shame, but it wasn't because I was ashamed, it was because of the tone of his voice – horror, almost. I was completely taken aback by it – it was the first time I'd ever been embarrassed about my racial origins.

When we moved to London Peter was hostile to my family, partly because they infringed on my time, and partly because I think he found it too much – that was a cultural difference between us. But fashions change. As he became more politicised, he began to regard my racial origins as something of an asset, it appealed to his sense of libertarian socialism that he was associating freely and in a friendly way with Black people. I never really thought about it as far as he was concerned, but I do remember that I was very much aware that his family thought I was a white African and I never contradicted it because I was too embarrassed to do so. He never contradicted it either. I liked his parents. Years later, after they met my mother, they realised.

Then I came to London, which is a much more racially conscious place, and started working in the voluntary sector. That was when I began to perceive and identify myself as a mixed race person. But that took years. The consciousness was slow to develop because it's very easy to go around being forgiving and tolerant of the day-to-day abuse that you get and not recognise it as a pattern. It's particularly important for me to do that; it would be a real cop-out for me to decide it's a non-issue because I don't get racial abuse directly. But I feel it all around me every time I step out of the house, if I walk into a shop with a relative or a Black friend.

I think that the experience of being culturally Black but perceived as white gives you a very interesting, slightly objective view of what it is to be white and what it is to be Black. I've gone through a lot of intellectualising about it and I do think that there isn't a predominance of well-developed arguments or rationalisations from the Black perspective about the Black experience – Black people should not be concerned with trying to win on white people's terms. And white people shouldn't be trying to look at making things better for Black people, they should be looking at their own imperatives. Then, perhaps, they can redress the balance. I'd be interested to know what white people think about the need for the white man to go and dominate other countries, the deep-seated psychological urges of white people to dominate the world. Because on the whole it's been white people who've done that – and not because they have been more advanced than other very civilised societies.

What I have realised is that being Black isn't just about a political awareness or choice, it is about being culturally and socially a Black African. There are things about me which I've inherited from generations back, attitudes and habits which the culture has bred. Because a lot of my time in this country has been in London, the equivalent white development and white cultural awareness haven't come to the surface as much as the Sierra Leonean side has.

I do have a lot of Caribbean friends, which is strange because Africans and Caribbeans don't tend to mix, but I think it's because, like me, they are seen as 'other'. What I have realised, though, is that even after I became intimate with them, there was a point at which they rejected me because I was white. At that time they obviously didn't place any validation on my experience as a Black person, simply because my skin was white. I remember one misunderstanding when I referred to a Sierra Leonean as a 'bush boy', which is a colloquial term, and they were offended by my language. I told them I don't have to justify myself to anyone, it's my language. They found it offensive because they did not accept my cultural experience, they perceived me as white. Another term which is not accepted here by Caribbeans but is in common use at home is 'half-caste'.

Another time, I went somewhere with a Caribbean friend and she introduced me as a Sierra Leonean to a Caribbean guy, who was doing a study on ethnicity. He basically told me that as a white Sierra Leonean I didn't exist. He was using the white racist definition of colour to determine something which was actually very complex. He left in anger. But that experience brought home to me that as far as people like him were concerned, there was no point at which my experiences were valid. On the other hand, when I got involved in race questions in white groups they thought I had no right to be critical of well-meaning white women for being racist, and when I wrote a letter complaining they rejected it, saying: 'Who is this white woman to tell us these things?' If a Black person had written, they would have beaten their breasts.

I never had the sense of disadvantage before I came here – you don't when you live in an all-Black country. In Sierra Leone I was treated as white to some extent (by strangers), though if I went to an all-Black party, I remember wondering whether some people wondered what I was doing there. Of course it is possible that other people have that sense of disadvantage when they're talking to me because I look white and sound middle-class.

Black people have to get into the issue of racism from a deeply psychological and sophisticated intellectual perspective in order to understand some of the mechanisms that are at work, because it is an extremely complicated thing.

The most valuable realisation after all this was that because of the way I was brought up I was Black, and that I was also part white, not because of my experience but because of my colour. So it is very complex. When I look at myself I expect people to see me as white, though I am Black through my experiences, my cultural background and my value system, and the way I function. White people see me as hostile, aggressive, all the kinds of things they accuse Black women of being. But when you separate out the actual colour element – the seeing bit, not the understanding, feeling, experiential bit – there is a split.

I think other friends have had the same split perspective on me as I have had on myself. For example, I felt that one close friend who is Black actually related to me as another Black woman. But I realised that there was also a split in her perception – she had done what I do, seen that split between the self and the body.

I would be much more comfortable if I was seen as Black, because then I would be seen for what I am and there wouldn't be a split between what I am and how I feel in terms of expectations of me and what they actually get. There is a split in my persona, like I'm carrying with me two things which aren't connected. I don't see the white thing as negative, but I do see it as – alien is too strong a word – but I don't have a lot of experience of being white. My father was white but I was brought up by my Black mother in an African country, so my appearance is something which is rather separate from myself.

At one stage I decided I would get my hair seriously permed, to look more like a Black woman, but my family and friends whom I told laughed at me – they said I'd just look like a white person with permed hair. So I abandoned it. I just wanted to see what I felt like.

I've looked at white people looking at Black people. They seem to blank off; once they see a Black person they fail to make any other kind of recognition or connection. When you meet someone, a whole lot of filing and processing goes on, but when a white person meets a Black person, they stop looking because they don't recognise anything. And it affects you in many different ways. I would like to be thinner than I am, but I am aware that culturally, socially, and visually a biggish Black person seems to look better than a biggish white woman. So I think if I was black-skinned I would have no complaints about my size at all.

I know my experiences would have been different if I had black skin. Half our family have enough colour to get racial abuse when they walk down the street – the others don't. But interestingly, those who have colour are different – they dress up as Black. I dress like a white woman – mind you, one of my brothers dresses like a Black man and he's blond.

My mother never taught us her language – she is a Black woman, but she doesn't really accept it in the most welcoming way. Maybe it's because she's from a different generation and has had different experiences. The one practical thing I wish she had done is taught us her language, because not teaching us our own mother tongue gives us a real disconnection. She said it never occurred to her. And if there's one thing I could have changed in the whole of my experience, it would have been that my mother had a Black consciousness so that I could have understood these things much earlier and have been equipped to deal with it instead of having to deal with it entirely on my own.

Saying all this makes me wonder why Black people have to spend so much time and effort thinking about it and sorting it all out – white people don't have to, they just take it all for granted. Maybe that's the problem.

9. An Eye to the Future

> ❝ *I think this racial purity thing is stupid. We are talking like the Ku Klux Klan. We are talking like Nazis. This is the new world.* ❞

– TINA, BLACK AFRO-CARIBBEAN WOMAN

> ❝ *I am Black. I am Rasta. I do not want to pollute my race. I don't want to see my sister pollute our race. There is nothing else to say.* ❞

– ZED, BLACK RASTA

> ❝ *It is all crap, this Black and white thing. If I desire someone, why can I not have a Black or Asian or Chinese woman? They are all prettier than those English women who have lost their femininity.* ❞

– MARK, WHITE ENGLISH MAN

> ❝ *White and Black women are fun to go to clubs with, to take around, to speed around with, to go to bed with. They are out when it comes to marriage. Then I marry a nice Indian virgin and show her all that I have learnt.* ❞

– RAJOO, ASIAN MAN

David Upshal

(See Chapter 8: Ways of Looking)

Malcolm X, towards the end of his life, said mixed marriage was a matter of conscience for the individual. But to stay sane in any society, regardless of your colour, you need a pretty strong notion of self, a strong self-image, so you need to have people around who reinforce that. Most white English people have it, it's on the TV every day, every day is a celebration of Waterloo, Agincourt, Trafalgar. To have a self-image if you're Black, you need to love your Black self. I'm talking about looking in a mirror and being happy with what you see. A lot of Black people, for example, are in a white office where everyone's putting them down – from calling them names to tiny things, being dismissive of Black culture, the Black perspective. If that's the case it may very well be necessary for them, when they come home, to be able to wrap themselves up in – recharge themselves in – a Black family atmosphere. I think that's very necessary for a lot of people; it's what most people take for granted.

I feel no one's got any business to tell anyone else who they should go out with, live with, sleep with; it's purely a matter for the individual. And I would far rather my daughter went out with someone of a different culture to her own and was happy, than went out with someone of a similar culture, and was unhappy. It's that simple. But it would seem that not too many mixed race relationships work out. There are enough pressures anyway, and the racial pressure makes things intolerable.

You do get this situation of Black people who'll go out only with white people and white people who'll go out only with Black people. I'm certainly wary of being somebody's fetish. For example, when I was at school there were always white women who were termed 'Black men's meat' because they went out only with Black boys. Equally, I've known Black people who go out only with white people. There are many reasons – Black people who are high achievers career-wise feel that there aren't other Black people in their job market and they just don't meet other suitable Black people. There's a great Public Enemy record, 'Dollyana Craka', about that. This guy's saying: 'I need a woman who can understand me, talk my language, Black women just want my money.' A lot of Black women feel that if they've had a bad experience with a Black man, white men treat them better. Eldridge Cleaver, in *Soul on Ice*, puts it so well when he writes that every image he's seen since he was a little boy is about white women being objects of beauty – whether it's in a fairy story, Snow White, Cinderella, white, white, white – and at the same time he's told: 'That is not for you, boy'. So he wants that more than anything in the whole world. I think this kind of 'you must not have' thing is a bad kick, that's what I mean by fetish, I don't think it's a substance for a lasting, thriving relationship.

Anybody who enters into a mixed relationship has to have their eyes open, has to be aware, has to be accommodating, I think it's very easy in a predominantly white society for a Black person to back down on their culture – not just individually but to the culture which is bound to predominate. I've certainly seen that happen. I was doing some filming last year with a guy who's married to a girl I know really well. The girl's Black, he's white; she's just had his third child. So this is not a person I would single out as being racist. He got a bit drunk one night with two other white people and they're saying, 'Oh, do you remember nig nog Charlie?' and all this stuff. It all came out – 'spade', 'coon', 'wog', everything. Now when he goes out drinking with his mates, that's what's coming out and he's got a Black wife and mixed race kids at home. I remember his wedding – half the people there were white and half were Black and this guy's sister was crying because she thought Black people were taking over. I remember his mates complaining that too much Black music was being played. I'm not doing them down, if their marriage works for them that's fine, but personally I don't think it's too healthy that someone's got to bring up their Black children with a partner who talks like that about Black people. How are the children going to be brought up? What's their image of themselves going to be? How are they going to see other Black people?

A lot of Black people distrust mixed race people because they have had experience of mixed race people not considering themselves Black but considering themselves white and saying, 'I don't want to have anything to do with you.' I can see why it happens – you're brought up in this predominantly white society where the pressure's on you to be as white as possible and you're told: 'You can be one of us if you just fit in, stop doing that, you've got a chip on your shoulder.' And it's very alluring to say, 'Yes, I want to be that, I reject this.' And that's what I'd be wary of. But at the end of the day people are people, and if I meet somebody great who I get on wonderfully with and I love and can talk to I'm not going to say, 'Sorry, love, I'm afraid you're white.' I'm not going to reject anyone who's going to be good for me because of their colour. It just happens to be much more probable that a Black woman will understand my cultural needs and aspirations than a white one.

Conversations with young people and students at colleges, parties and clubs

Brian (white English man)

I recently had a relationship with an Asian girl and – well, for us, the different cultural aspects didn't come into it at all. I must admit I had never even thought about the different cultures and problems and that. We were just a boy and a girl going out.

But we did have some problems. It was horrible walking down the street and getting all the 'Paki-lover' shit. And the relationship had to be a secret because basically her family wouldn't allow it; she came from a fairly orthodox religious family. It was a shame because in the end it all fell apart because of that. I couldn't really phone her, although she could phone me, there was no problem on that side, but we couldn't have a normal life. Her parents wanted her to marry some rich person from the same religion. My brother is going out with a Black girl and she is going to have his child. And as I said, the culture thing doesn't come into it. It very much is a boy–girl thing.

My family are from Sussex and they have had no problems with this at all. There is no racial prejudice in the family. When my girlfriend's parents behaved in this way, I did feel resentful. I am a human being, though I could understand why they wanted to keep to their traditions. What I really resented most is that I didn't even get a chance to meet them. I feel if they had met me, I might have convinced them that their daughter would be OK with me. They should have judged me for what I was, not for culture and creed.

My brother's girlfriend has had a lot of problems, especially from other Black men who say to her, 'What do you think you are doing?' These things are funny. My Asian girlfriend was Sikh and for her to go out with a Muslim would have been a thousand times worse than going out with me. She would have had her feet cut off for going out with a white guy, but she would have her head cut off for going out with a Muslim.

Andy (white English man)

I went out with an Asian girl for a year. Her parents were OK about it, I used to go round to the house. My dad was not too keen on it, but that is typical British – you know, 'Don't go out with an Asian girl, she is different from you.' Eventually for one reason or another we drifted apart, but it was sad to have those reactions.

Terese (Black Afro-Caribbean woman)

I can't imagine myself with a white or Asian for the rest of my life, because in this society today there is so much conflict that it just wouldn't work. It is also true that it is easier for a Black guy to go out with a white girl than it is for a Black girl to go out with a white guy. If I did that I would get grief from my parents and from those outside. My father would say, 'What has a white guy got that a Black guy doesn't have?' I don't know about my mum so much, but I think she would like me to marry a Black man. In some ways I think that too. You have a better understanding of cultures and it isn't that difficult. Otherwise you would have to find out how different their culture is and what their expectations are. It is hard enough – why make it harder for yourself? Maybe you can say it is an easy option. I was born here, but I would never ever say I am British. If someone asks me, I always say I am from the West Indies. The majority of Black people don't say that they are British. It is not that they are ashamed, it just doesn't feel right.

When I was younger I didn't think there was that much difference, but when I got older it all changed. Before I thought that underneath the skin we were all alike. When I went to high school it came as a shock that people didn't see me the same as everyone else. They saw me as Black and that meant not as good as them. And I realised I didn't know what my identity was. In school they taught me the history of Hitler, and nothing else. Yet when I go to Jamaica, I don't belong there either. I am a tourist. People see me as a tourist, they treat me as a tourist, not as one of their people. So I started to go to Black awareness classes to find out where I am from, and now I wouldn't go with a white or an Asian. It's not that we Black youngsters hate white people, or Asians, it's just that we want to have something to belong to, we want to know where we came from. I want to be able to say, positively, 'That is my group, that is where I come from.'

I am not racist, but it is difficult. I used to go out with this guy who was an Asian from the West Indies and whenever we were out, these Black guys used to say things and tap me on the shoulder and ask what I was doing with another race. I know if I went out with a white guy, a lot of my friends would never see me again. They talk about you behind your back and that kind of thing, you know, so it is hard.

The reason all this is happening is that we expected to belong, we expected to be treated like all of you and instead we got nothing, so we feel alienated from your society and that is why we are feeling like this.

Hardip (Asian man)

I was born and raised here, and it was only when I was in high school that I thought, 'I am British and proud of it.' Right now I am very proud of it, but the first twelve years of my life were years of 'fucking Paki', 'Paki cunt', and that kind of stuff. And then it is pretty hard to accept yourself as a British person. Even if you were born and raised here and you have a British passport, they treat you like an outsider. Then one day I realised, 'Yes, I am British and nobody should take that away from me', and right now I am very proud of that.

I know my parents are from India, but I can't say that I feel the way they do. Especially those double standards in our community – I don't believe in them. If I saw my sister walking down the road with a Black man it would not bother me at all. It would probably bother my dad. In his background everything was so classified, he can't help it. His mind has been shaped into that strict mould. Whereas my mum is very different. She doesn't want me to fool around, but she doesn't mind who I go out with.

All this saddens me because Asians and Blacks have never met on this neutral ground. We have similar experiences, we have grown up here, and yet even here at the college or in the Students' Union, we all keep in our own separate groups of white, Black and brown. I live in Acton in a very mixed area and you would have thought that Blacks and Asians would have so much in common. But no, in fact the tension between them is getting greater than between white and either group. That saddens me. It's the same in the canteen, like South Africa.

Sandra (Black Afro-Caribbean woman)

Today we are all deep into our cultures, particularly Black people. We are all into Africa and are descendants of Africans and all that. Maybe it is a craze, but I think it is more. You wear African garb and learn about the history because it is like our heritage. It is like in the sixties in America, like Black being beautiful and people being proud.

My gran is one hundred per cent Indian, a Muslim from Trinidad, and we have a lot of Indian in my family, but when she married my grandfather it was not seen as right. But although she is Indian she still expects her grandchildren to marry Black people. I have a little boy and he is not half-caste or anything, he is Black. If I look at a child and think 'She is nice', she is always, like, Black. It is not conscious. And the same with guys. It must be because you know that if you like a white guy a lot of people will come to grief so you censor yourself, you stop yourself before you start. You don't want to be disowned. But you know there is a lot of racism among Asians against us. A white guy is all right, and a white girl. But Black? No way.

And I am scared of my Black friends. They would give me such a hard time, so even if I did fall in love, it can be impossible. I am scared of these reactions.

Famida (Asian woman)

I think the same hypocrisies happen in our societies. Asian men think they have more rights than Asian girls do. When it comes to marriage they tend to go to the traditional Asian girls but when it comes to having a good time, it is white girls. You still don't see many of them with Black girls, though.

Ashad (Asian man)

If you go to parties and things with white girls, then it is silly if you suddenly decide to be a good little Asian boy and marry your own to please your parents and community. You can't be both. You have to decide to move with the times.

I must confess I think like that, but I also know that we all have to change because it is so two-faced. It is so difficult. We have been brought up not to hurt our parents, but if we want to change these things we should take them with us. If it isn't colour, it is religion or class, you know. It is so complex. I am Sikh and I went out with a Muslim and got a lot of grief from my relatives. It is all right to go out with a Black or a white, but not a Muslim girl.

Matthew (white English man)

I think it is a shame when people here talk like this about keeping their identity, because in many respects these are the old ways and we should be trying to break away from them. I can understand why it is happening. I can understand, if people are being racist towards you, why you need to find another identity and another home. I am not blaming you, but it is a shame that we can't all say 'away with all this'. I'm saying this to my creed as much as I am to all of you. But you are helping to carry it on by wearing this kind of 'uniform' which says this is your culture.

Tahera (Asian Muslim woman)

I just couldn't do it. I wouldn't be allowed by my family to marry someone outside the community. I couldn't fall in love with anybody. The family comes first, you see. I could never be happy if I hurt them. In our family, religion takes a more important place than culture or colour. And if I married an African Muslim, that would be accepted a thousand times more easily than if I married an Asian Hindu. And the same for a white man. The best choice for them would be a Muslim Pakistani, preferably a cousin. The males in the family would disown me otherwise. So in spite of a ten-year relationship with a Hindu guy, I have decided to break it off because I don't want to lose my family. I would be more unhappy if I broke out of that and broke the family rules. I think in this racist society it is frightening out there. I need the protection of my family. And I have to protect them. They have been so hurt by their lives here. If they lose us too, they feel it was all worthless.

My mother would accept my brother marrying anyone, but my sisters and I would have to marry Muslims. Ninety per cent of these decisions in our lives are made on how the family feels and not on personal choice, so it is a very different way of thinking. You can't let it happen. You know you can't allow it to happen so it doesn't, it is as simple as that.

Javed (Asian Muslim man)

I used to think I was white and I was so cool, but the way I have been treated, the way my father was treated – he was beaten senseless by thugs, they wouldn't give me a place in the college that I wanted to go to, and it was because it was a white place. I now hate them. I cancel them out of my life and I would kill any sister of mine who wanted to go out with a white guy. My older brother is married to this snotty woman who is white and lives in Surrey and he thinks he is a white man. He hardly phones my mother. She adored him as her eldest son. Now he has called his children English names, and celebrates Christmas, and he had no pride in his life. He broke my mother's heart.

Meena (Asian woman)

I think all this is rubbish. I am going out with Cal, who is white, and after a few months my parents accepted that this is what I want and need to make me happy. Now they adore him. My mother also says that at least she knows he is not marrying me for a dowry, he is marrying me for what I am. We are getting married after I finish college and it will be a really happy occasion. In our culture my parents, because they are the girl's parents, would be expected to treat an Asian man, even an educated one, like a god and be grateful to him all their lives for being so kind as to marry their daughter, who would otherwise have ended up on the shelf, the biggest shame for the family. It is all crap. With Cal, *he* is so grateful because of the warmth my family show him. My father is so pleased too. He says that with Cal he can be open and himself because there are no silly traditions. Cal treats me like a queen. I have seen the way my own brothers treat their wives and although they are very nice to them, you know who the boss is.

Tina (Black Afro-Caribbean woman)

I feel like Meena. I think this racial purity thing is stupid. We are talking like the Ku Klux Klan. We are talking like Nazis. This is the new world. I have had Black boyfriends and white boyfriends, but I must say, as a professional Black woman, the freedom and support I got from both my white boyfriends, including the solicitor I am with now, has been unbelievable.

Zed (Black Rasta)

I am Black. I am Rasta. I do not want to pollute my race. I don't want to see my sister pollute our race. There is nothing else to say.

Steve (Black Afro-Caribbean man)

Too many Black men are going with white women as status. We are really letting our women down, you know. We never see beautiful Black women in magazines and films – except as a prostitute or a fat mama – and we think our Black women are worthless. My father was a preacher and he used to say it was because we felt guilty that our women had to go through hell with slavery and even now, we feel ashamed of going with Black women. I think they are lovely – look at the women in 'The Cosby Show', they have class and style. Have you ever seen a young Black woman who didn't know how to dress or move? They have such sexual heat and we just put them down. All my girlfriends are Black and if my friends go out with white women, I just cancel them out.

I think the Black men who hate white men are often the ones who have white women. It is the only area they can have power in this society, over their women. And all whites think we have big dicks and we can make love fifty times a minute. Others are so pleased to go to those boring cocktail parties with their white women. And white women do put up with a lot more shit than Black women. Some even do stupid things like turning Black – having beads in their hair and, like, owning our music.

You know I can't just be a stud. They expect more. And it can never work. These friends who really seem to have made it, it is only on the surface. One day I was watching South Africa news and they just blew up and soon she is saying racist things and he is calling her white shit and that. But what I hate most of all is white guys with our sisters. They are really coming in and taking the women out. And all those stuck-up women are going because the guy is white, probably has a nice car and house. I hate it when I see them cuddling our women. I once tripped one up in the street, a yuppie, and he couldn't say anything because a gang of us were there and he was scared. We should stick to our own race, otherwise there will be nothing left. It is all wrong. It comes from Black women being used as slaves by white bwanas and white women forcing their servants to fuck them. That is the honest truth.

Sylvina (Black Afro-Caribbean woman)

How can people understand how it feels? You grow up believing that things have changed because we all now listen to rap and reggae – but it's crap. When Timothy and I were together I don't remember a single moment when I felt easy, even when we were making love. I felt I was letting the Black side down and that I was cheap, a whore. His mother hardly looked at me and fumbled in her cupboards to look busy. They all won and we lost.

I really loved the guy. He was a lawyer and he treated me so special. He taught me about opera and the theatre. It was a new world for me as a working-class Black girl. In spite of my guilt, sex was great with him, though I think he expected me to be like a high-class hooker every time, but I soon cured him of that. And we did have a good time, but underneath I knew it would not be allowed to work. I hid him from my friends, family, clubs, I didn't want them to think I was being uppity. And I hate the attitudes of Black men – they think you are a traitor and a prostitute or something. It is OK for them to have white girls, but not the other way. But in the end the forces against you are too much. I couldn't forget the racism and all that guilt and anger. He didn't deserve the way I treated him, but I had to send him away. And I am alone now, there are no new Black men out there.

Lorraine (Black Afro-Caribbean woman), Sylvina's friend

I don't know why she did it. It is like sleeping with your enemy. It doesn't work. You live in between everything. You are nothing, both of you. You are let down by whities all your life, they spit on you, don't give you jobs, and yet when the time comes, let him into your body? No way. I have seen these Black girls trying to be madams to please their white men. Pretending to be white. Being ashamed of their hair and bodies and lips. One of my friends, she couldn't wear tight clothes because her white man thought her bum was too black! And you know you can never share the deep culture that you can with your own. Being with Black people if you are Black you feel at ease, comfortable, not ashamed to be Black and to be you. It is the difference between coming home, kicking off your heels, getting into your tracksuit and enjoying being you and getting all dressed up to impress someone important. With a white guy that is what I would feel like – that I have to perform all the time. We must be proud of our Blackness. They have told us we are nothing for centuries. If you go with them, you are agreeing with that.

Mark (white English man)

It is all crap, this Black and white thing. If I desire someone, why can I not have a Black or Asian or Chinese woman? They are all prettier than those English women who have lost their femininity. I love these women, I have fantasies about them, I treat them like queens. It is all going to be mixed in the future anyway. I wouldn't worry about taking them home. My mother loves Indian cooking and all that. They are real women, not bloody feminists burning their bras and all that. Rani is soft to touch and soft as a person. I know she will be faithful to me and not run around. She will have a lovely meal ready when I come home, and sexually too she doesn't try and make me feel inadequate, or compete with me. She appreciates me. I love her wearing her sari and all that – those feelings you get when you see a beautiful Indian woman in her sensual sari, it's unbelievable. And you know we British have such hang-ups about sexuality, these other nationalities have a much better sex life.

Ran (Asian woman, Mark's girlfriend)

I lived with a white guy for years – my parents didn't know. And then, I suppose I was attracted to the weddings in the Indian families and I thought I would come back home and get married to someone who was Asian. I met this guy at a family party and it wasn't exactly a love marriage, but it was a dynamic attraction. We went out. The family were delighted. He seemed really modern, the best of both worlds, and I was over the moon. He looked like Omar Sharif and he couldn't keep his hands off me. In fact we had to get married in a hurry because we would have got into trouble and I knew one never goes to bed with an Asian man if you want to marry him. He knew I had seen the world, but he was so proud that I was worldly and pretty and that. The biggest shock began with our wedding night. I mean a lot is made of it and families drop you off and the next day they come and get you, so it isn't easy at the best of times. But he turned into a very shy, introverted person. He had no idea of how a woman's body is. He made love quickly and wanted just to get it done so he could sing songs to me again. He didn't treat me badly, but he really didn't know about sexual pleasure. I tried after a few months to become more active, and that put him off even more. Indian women have to have no sexuality, you see. You suffer sex in silence, and that makes you a good woman. Anyway, it became intolerable and he reverted to the old Asian male stereotypes, asserting his masculinity over me in that way: by expecting me to be passive. I left after three years and moved away from Birmingham to save my parents the shame.

I am back with a white guy, Mark, and he knows what makes me tick – how to treat a woman, especially someone like me who has a strong personality. A lot of our feminist women are doing this, going off with white men, and our men then have to go and get pliant women from the villages. In the end they have been brought up to believe that is the way it should be. Their mothers are to blame. They like to remain the centre of their sons' lives and a sexual wife is a threat to them too. After marriage, I am supposed to turn into a goddess. Give me a white guy any time. He respects my individuality, my freedom, he doesn't think I am there as a possession for his family. He doesn't expect me to be good.

Rajoo (Asian man)

White and Black women are fun to go to clubs with, to take around, to speed around with, to go to bed with. They are out when it comes to marriage. Then I marry a nice Indian virgin and show her all that I have learnt! Maybe I am being hard on Asian women, maybe they would be fantastic lovers – *Kama Sutra* and all. But I have never even kissed one, I couldn't.

I couldn't marry these women I run around with because marriage is something which is not just for me, it is for the family, and I couldn't marry someone who was that free and easy with herself. How could she be the mother of my children? Maybe I would miss the sexual excitement, though I could still sneak out, I guess.

I think we should all marry our own; it is important not to let it all disappear. I would expect that with my own daughters. There is a difference between men and women. I know my sister has a white boyfriend and I don't talk to her. My parents have thrown her out, and if she fails now it is her own problem. She can't come home. I know my mother is on her side and wants them to marry, but she can't do anything. She is quite jealous of my sister's life and she jokes that at least she won't need a dowry. I told my sister she is an outcast. She has to stay there now. I respect our women, I just don't respect these white and Black women. Shirley, the girl I am seeing at the moment, is mad about me and thinks I am some prince or something, you know, so stupid these people are.

Tony (white English man)

I would never marry anyone who wasn't from my class or race. I wouldn't contaminate my genes in that way, downgrade them. They are all promiscuous and dirty, and even physically I would be revolted by it. I have friends who are Black but no physical contact, no way. These mongrel children you see around you these days, it is disgusting. I think people who do it are doing it because it is forbidden and they get their kicks out of that.

Mandy (mixed race woman)

My parents had a mixed race marriage – that is, my father and my stepmother, who has been a wonderful mother to me and my brother. She is white and my father is Black. My own mother left us when we were young and I have never seen her. I wouldn't want to. But Christine, my stepmother, has been there for us all these years, even more than my father. She agreed not to have children of her own – can you imagine? And my father has not been an easy man to live with. He was often out of work and used to come home and talk about whites being pigs and that in front of her. She was always so understanding and patient with him. And they used to get such abuse when they were out together. We live in a white suburb, and people would refuse to serve them in restaurants and twice they were beaten up by gangs; once my father's back was agonising for weeks. They called Christine a slut, threatened to rape her, and it was terrible. A burning rag was put through the letterbox, but it went out as it fell. After all that, how could I even think of having a white man? I would never do it. It is too painful, too soon maybe.

SELECTED BIBLIOGRAPHY

Benson, Susan, *Ambiguous Ethnicity: Interracial Families in London*, Cambridge University Press, Cambridge, 1981

Day, Beth, *Sexual Life Between Blacks and Whites*, Collins, London, 1974

Fanon, Frantz, *Black Skin, White Masks*, Pluto, London, 1986

Henriques, Fernando, *Children of Conflict: A Study of Interracial Sex and Marriage*, Dutton, New York, 1975

Rich, Paul B., *Race and Empire in British Politics*, Cambridge University Press, Cambridge, 1986

Visram, Rozina, *Ayahs, Lascars and Princes: Indians in Britain 1700–1947*, Pluto, London, 1986

Williamson, Joel, *New People: Miscegenation and Mulattoes in the United States*, Free Press, New York, 1980

Wilson, Anne, *Mixed Race Children: A Study of Identity*, Allen & Unwin, London, 1987